Race Brokers

Race Brokers

Housing Markets and Segregation in 21st-Century Urban America

ELIZABETH KORVER-GLENN

OXFORD
UNIVERSITY PRESS

OXFORD
UNIVERSITY PRESS

Oxford University Press is a department of the University of Oxford. It furthers
the University's objective of excellence in research, scholarship, and education
by publishing worldwide. Oxford is a registered trade mark of Oxford University
Press in the UK and certain other countries.

Published in the United States of America by Oxford University Press
198 Madison Avenue, New York, NY 10016, United States of America.

Library of Congress Cataloging-in-Publication Data
Names: Korver-Glenn, Elizabeth, author.
Title: Race brokers : housing markets and racial segregation in 21st century urban America /
Elizabeth Korver-Glenn, University of New Mexico.
Description: New York, NY : Oxford University Press, [2022] |
Includes bibliographical references and index.
Identifiers: LCCN 2020046521 (print) | LCCN 2020046522 (ebook) |
ISBN 9780190063870 (paperback) | ISBN 9780190063863 (hardback) |
ISBN 9780190063894 (epub) | ISBN 9780190063887 | ISBN 9780190063900
Subjects: LCSH: Discrimination in housing—Texas—Houston—History—21st century. |
Housing policy—Texas—Houston—History—21st century. |
African Americans—Housing—Texas—Houston—History—21st century. |
Houston (Tex.)—Race relations—History—21st century.
Classification: LCC HD7288.76.U52 H68 2022 (print) | LCC HD7288.76.U52 (ebook) |
DDC 333.33/80899607307641411—dc23
LC record available at https://lccn.loc.gov/2020046521
LC ebook record available at https://lccn.loc.gov/2020046522

DOI: 10.1093/oso/9780190063863.001.0001

1 3 5 7 9 8 6 4 2

Paperback printed by LSC Communications, United States of America
Hardback printed by Bridgeport National Bindery, Inc., United States of America

For Randall, Jude, and Emma
With deepest love

For Rice Sociology
With deepest gratitude

Contents

Acknowledgments

One of the deep joys of pursuing an academic career has been sharing life and research with a supportive, generous, critical, and brilliant community made up of academic colleagues, acquaintances, friends, and family. While any errors in this work are my responsibility alone, *Race Brokers* would not exist without the web of intellectual, emotional, and practical supports my community has provided along the way.

Rice University's Sociology Department started a new PhD program, and as part of their initial graduate student recruiting, the faculty took a chance (from my perspective) and accepted me into the program. Because I had no research background, they basically had to start from scratch when I matriculated. They expended countless hours advising and training me as well as equipping me with practical resources to progress through and excel in graduate school. Jim Elliott: Thank you. I will never forget your eagerness to join me in a day of fieldwork as I drove you around Houston and explained what I was doing. Your keen questions and insight, constructive criticism and encouragement, and general good humor motivated me and made me a stronger and better person and scholar. You made all the difference. Michael Emerson: Thank you. You believed in this project from the beginning and have cheered me on ever since. I hope you know that you and your work have long been one of my main sources of inspiration. Thank you also for providing feedback and encouragement on this book at various stages. You helped me cross the finish line. Jenifer Bratter, Sergio Chávez, Elaine Howard Ecklund, and Ruth López Turley: Thank you. You all trained and mentored me through multiple important milestones and served key roles as members of my master's thesis, comprehensive exam, and/or doctoral dissertation committees. You also helped immensely with my professionalization into academia; I learned and continue to learn so much from each of you from afar. Other Rice Sociology faculty provided many other kinds of valuable support, including Rachel Kimbro, who helped me transition to the world of being both a graduate student and a mother.

Being a member of the Rice Sociology community also meant joining an incredible group of graduate students and post-docs, many of whom remain close colleagues and friends. Junia Howell: I cannot believe the good fortune I have had to know, work with, and love you. Thank you for your honesty, encouragement, and support. From helping me understand contemporary theory during the first semester of graduate school to caring for my children, picking me up from airports, cooking for me, co-authoring with me, and reading and providing critical feedback on multiple iterations of this book—thank you. Sandra Alvear, Kevin Smiley, and Ellen Whitehead: I'm so grateful to each of you for the constructive and generous ways you live and work. Each of you has shaped me in profound ways. Thanks, friends.

While at Rice, I also had the amazing privilege of learning with and from brilliant and generous faculty, staff, and students in other departments. In the history department, Alex Byrd and David Ponton III deeply influenced this particular project as well as my long-term research trajectory. Dr. Byrd: Thank you for supporting this project and pushing me to read and think critically about race, racism, and cities. Your comments during my dissertation defense remain with me to this day. David: Thank you. I continue to learn from your brilliance and thank my lucky stars that you and I were in that same graduate seminar that first semester. I cherish our friendship. Thanks also for reading and providing helpful feedback on various book chapter iterations. Other faculty and staff at Rice, including Jean Aroom at the GIS/Data Center and Libby Vann and Alan Steinberg at the Center for Civic Leadership, shaped not only this project but also who I am as an academic and how I approach my work. And, undergraduate students at Rice breathed life into my tired bones. Working with you all in teaching and research roles and advising you in community-based participatory research confirmed that I did really want to pursue this academic life. I also thank the Social Sciences Research Institute at Rice, which provided grant support for professional transcription of the in-depth interviews I conducted. Speaking of in-depth interviews, I am grateful for the many dozens of people who participated in this study as interviewees and informants—I learned much because you generously shared your time and professional expertise.

I am also deeply grateful for the many scholars I now have the pleasure of knowing as departmental and professional colleagues and friends. Many colleagues at or previously at the University of New Mexico (UNM) have helped me with the book-writing process. Sharon Erickson Nepstad and Owen Whooley both provided valuable feedback on my book prospectus and advised me through the book contract process. Lisa Broidy, Felipe Gonzales, Sofia Locklear, Nancy López, Wayne Santoro, María Vélez, Owen

Whooley, Jon Williams, and Eli Wilson all provided valuable feedback on previous iterations of book chapters. To my students at UNM: thank you for your sharp questions and critical insights. You inspire me every day. In fact, I had you in mind as I wrote each chapter of this book. Outside of UNM, Clayton Childress, Nicole Gonzalez Van Cleve, Neda Maghbouleh, Amaka Okechukwu, Ranita Ray, and Chris Smith all helped me through the book prospectus writing, feedback-getting, and submission process in various ways. Thank you all. Thanks also to Dan Hirschman, Whitney Pirtle, Victor Ray, Jake Rugh, Louise Seamster, and Haj Yazdiha, all of whom read portions of this book in its previous iterations and provided incisive, encouraging feedback. Special thanks to Haj, who has been an extraordinary book buddy, friend, and fellow academic mama. Thanks also to Max Besbris, who provided critical, generative comments on my writing and helpful advice on the book publishing process. I also thank Cristina Mora, Mary Pattillo, and Robert Vargas, each of whom asked important questions and gave valuable comments at various stages of the analysis process. Thanks to Jeff Guhin and Tony Lin, who co-hosted an early morning Zoom writing group during the COVID-19 crisis that gave me the structure I needed to complete final book revisions. I also thank Michael Allen, Diane Houk, and Morgan Williams, all of whom generously shared their fair housing legal expertise with me. Prentiss Dantzler read through and provided detailed, extremely helpful feedback on the penultimate draft of this book—thank you, dear friend. I'm so grateful to share the journey with you! Audra Wolfe (The Outside Reader): Thank you for helping me strengthen this manuscript through critical, constructive editorial assistance. Thank you to James Cook and Emily Mackenzie at Oxford University Press and to the reviewers who helped make this book stronger. Each of you has shaped my thinking and writing in profound ways. Thank you all.

Other key organizations and people made this work possible by providing fellowship and childcare support. The Institute for Analytic Sociology at Linköping University in Sweden awarded me a Robert K. Merton Visiting Research Fellowship, which supported me as I made book revisions. Thanks especially to Peter Hedström, Karl Wennberg, Sarah Valdez, Ben Jarvis, Åsa Arnoldson, and Madelene Töpfer, who all welcomed me and facilitated a productive stay at the Institute. While in Sweden, my dear friends Alex and Nate Messarra, sister Allegra, mom Marcia, and dad Bill provided childcare, and Alex also provided feedback on book chapters. Thank you to you all. My deepest thanks also to St. Matthew's, especially Lisa, who cared for Jude and made me think that everything would be okay during the data collection for this project. Thanks also to Wesley Kids, especially Alex, Angelica, Christina, Lori, Jackie, Roberta, Terri, and Vanessa who cared for Jude and Emma while I completed this book. All of you have loved my children so well—thank you from the bottom of my heart.

Others have provided the intellectual, emotional, and motivational support to bring this project to fruition. Gloria Kenyon, Lenora McNamara, Cynthia Muccio, and Lesley Vanaman: We must be the only "us" in the world, right? Grateful for 20+ years with you all; thankful, too, for the general and specific comments and questions you offered about this project that helped strengthen it. Lynne Graham: You taught me how to read and write and, when I was around you, never once did I feel weird or uncool (as I did most of the time in high school). Thank you. Jennifer Aycock: Miracles happen when kindred spirits come together. Running the race with you is my soul's deep delight. Je t'aime. Emily Zimbrick-Rogers: you have inspired me for ten years! I can't wait until we actually meet in person one day. Karla and Rob Woodruff: Your friendship has saved me over the past few years. Thank you for sharing your lives and joy.

Finally, my family. Mom and dad, thank you for loving me unconditionally, for teaching me grace, and for cultivating a thirst for knowledge and justice. I love you. Jared and Allegra: You have shown me, in word and deed, how to be whole and at peace. I wouldn't trade growing up and old with you for the world. Each of you write in ways that motivate me to keep growing past the limitations of my own writing: Thank you. Amy: What a joy it has been to share life with you over the past decade. Your strength, courage, and independence inspire me daily. Resa and Dell: Thank you for welcoming me as your own and always finding ways to encourage me. Jude: I was terrified of you at first, mainly because I had no idea what I was doing. But you, my firstborn, are a force of nature. You single-handedly transformed my fear into purpose and you are the joy of my life. Emma: My firecracker, my comedienne, my independent, fierce second-born. You make me a stronger woman every day; you are the light of my life. Randall: You have supported me in every possible way; with you, I flourish. Thank you for journeying with me through it all with humor, patience, hope, and steadfast love.

Introduction

Racial segregation is so prevalent in American cities that it can seem normal, even natural. Many Americans, including government officials and everyday housing consumers, view segregation in this way.[1] Housing market professionals, or those who professionally assist consumers with home buying or selling, are no exception. For example, in April 2015, Jay, a White middle-aged real estate agent, invited me to his real estate brokerage in Houston's Montrose neighborhood. He wanted to show me a contract he had drawn up for a house he had listed for sale in Near Northside, a Latinx[2] neighborhood just north of downtown. After inviting me into the conference room near the front of the brokerage office space, Jay explained the terms of the contract. As he did so, he described who the buyers and sellers were and also provided running commentary on Near Northside and its surrounding areas, including several White neighborhoods west of Near Northside. "In the last six months," he said, "I've had lots of young hipsters calling. People are being pushed out of the Heights, Norhill, and Brooke Smith. That's the natural progression, to come to Near Northside. The tide of hipsters is coming." Jay did not think that Near Northside would stay a Latinx neighborhood for long.

Two months after I observed Jay at his brokerage, I met and interviewed Diego, a Mexican American appraiser, at a diner in southeast Houston. Diego explained that he tries not to allow "ethnicity" to come into his appraising. But he went on to say that he thinks racial segregation exists because Black, Latinx, and White individuals want to live near "someone who is your equal." For this reason, he explained, Black individuals wanted to live in the Black Third Ward neighborhood "amongst their peers—not *my* natural peers—but young Black urban professionals that are buying in that area." From Diego's perspective, it seemed "natural" that Black professionals wanted to live near Black peers and that he and other Latinx individuals—such as his sister, who had purchased a home in a Latinx neighborhood—wanted to live near Latinx peers.

Race Brokers. Elizabeth Korver-Glenn, Oxford University Press (2021). © Oxford University Press.
DOI: 10.1093/oso/9780190063863.003.0001

Then, in July 2015—a month after I interviewed Diego—I met Lauren, a White real estate agent, at her brokerage on the west side of Houston. She led me into a large multipurpose room that had several long tables and dozens of chairs set up in anticipation of a continuing education class. We sat together at one of these tables for our interview. Lauren told me that her White clients make housing decisions based on neighborhood racial composition:

> But, you know, I definitely see in clients when I'm showing them proper-
> ties in some areas that they think, "Oh, you know, we love the look of this
> neighborhood, we love the location. You know we love the price." And I'll
> go and show them and they'll make comments like, "Nobody here looks
> like me." And, you know, I think that's natural. I don't think that's neces-
> sarily a racist thing.

Less than a month after I interviewed Lauren, I interviewed Howie, a White mortgage banker. Like Jay, Howie referred to the Heights and Brooke Smith neighborhoods when he discussed differences in home values across neighborhoods. Inhabited by White residents as the neighborhoods were developed from the late nineteenth through the mid-twentieth centuries, these areas became predominantly Latinx after several decades of White flight that began in the 1960s. More recently, White residents have returned to these areas. By the time I conducted my research, these areas were once again predominantly White, and property values were higher than before. Echoing Jay's comments, Howie explained that he thought these changes in both neighborhood race and home values were a "natural progression."

These housing market professionals recognized that Houston and other American cities are racially segregated. In fact, Jay, Diego, Lauren, Howie, and many other housing market professionals I studied viewed racial segregation as so ever-present as to seem "natural." These professionals were correct in their assessment that racial segregation is the way things are in the United States. Most White Americans live in White neighborhoods and most Asian, Black, and Latinx Americans live in neighborhoods of color. In fact, although segregation appears to be slowly fading in some cities, it is remaining stagnant or intensifying in other cities. This is especially true in cities with large populations of residents of color, such as Atlanta, Houston, and Miami (Frey 2010a, 2010b; Krysan and Crowder 2017).

Even as real estate professionals describe this situation as "natural," it is anything but, particularly given recent legal and social trends. Beginning in

1968, the U.S. Congress began to pass a series of laws that prohibited explicit racial discrimination in the sale or rental of a home. Defendants of color won numerous lawsuits against real estate agents, mortgage lenders, appraisers, and other housing market professionals who had discriminated against them. At approximately the same time these legal changes occurred, America's social landscape began to shift dramatically. The proportion of Americans who identified as White declined as White families began to have fewer children. During the same period, millions of African, Asian, and Latin American individuals—most of whom moved directly to American cities rather than rural areas—immigrated to the United States, dramatically increasing urban ethnoracial diversity. White Americans began to report more favorable and less explicitly racist attitudes toward groups of color on surveys. Individuals of color were increasingly able to purchase homes, and they more frequently expressed a desire to live in racially diverse neighborhoods than their White counterparts.

In other words, multiple conditions that could have contributed to more rapid or steep declines in racial segregation did not do so and at times actually coincided with increases in racial segregation. This is because these social and legal changes occurred even as racism, or the ideas and practices that justify and maintain racial inequality and White dominance (Bonilla-Silva 2006; Fields and Fields 2014; Lewis and Diamond 2015), has persisted in every major sphere of contemporary American life (Seamster and Ray 2018), including the housing market (Howell and Korver-Glenn 2018; Korver-Glenn 2018a, 2018b).[3] Indeed, racism, like racial segregation, has become naturalized—so pervasive that it seems natural (Jung 2015). Thus, when considering the housing market and the role real estate professionals play in shaping housing opportunities and urban residential landscapes, the key question is not *whether* racial segregation is an inevitable, or natural, outcome of market exchanges or *whether* racism contributes to racial segregation (see also Taylor 2019). Rather, it is *how* racism in real estate contributes to racial segregation in twenty-first-century urban America.

The question is pressing. Racial segregation poses serious problems for American society more broadly. Among many other problems, it is tied to ongoing wealth, educational, and health inequalities; intensified and more violent policing of Black and Latinx people; social isolation and lack of interracial contact; and sociopolitical conflict. In other words, racial segregation is one of the key mechanisms at the core of systemic American racial inequality (Reskin 2012).

This book examines how racism enables racial segregation to persist in order to denaturalize and chip away at this inequality. To do so, it examines real estate professionals, a group of individuals at the heart of the housing market. Many of these professionals, including housing developers, real estate agents, mortgage bankers, and appraisers, often portray their work and its relationship to racial segregation as a passive—and not necessarily color-blind—response to market dynamics or the purportedly "natural" way people prefer to live. But as I studied these individuals and learned about their work from their perspectives, I came to the opposite conclusion. Racial segregation is not a natural feature of the American urban landscape, a surface contour that market professionals trace as they find it. Instead, housing market professionals—especially those who are White—actively create racially unequal housing markets and urban landscapes. They do so by using racist ideas to inform how they implement professional norms and policies and how they distribute their professional resources, including authority, knowledge, and capital. These housing market professionals are race and racism brokers: They make a hierarchy of racial categories socially and materially real by ensuring that people who fall into what they perceive as different categories receive unequal housing opportunities. Despite their insistence otherwise, housing market professionals are the visible hands of the housing market, and they often use racism to re-create and exacerbate racial segregation in their everyday work.

Among the housing market professionals I studied, one small group—almost all individuals of color—were a sharp foil for how their White counterparts and, at times, counterparts of color actively contribute to the process of segregation. They drew on equitable, people-affirming ideas[4] that emphasized the worth and deservingness of people of color and used their experiences and observations of racial discrimination to generate alternate professional strategies that better served communities of color. Importantly, at the same time they subverted real estate business as usual, these professionals built economically profitable businesses. These professionals also brokered race. But they did so through reference to racial equity, thus undermining racism and mitigating, rather than exacerbating, racial inequality in the housing exchange process.

Real estate professionals are the gatekeepers of the housing market. As such, the choices they make influence who has access to homes, under what conditions that access is granted, and where such access is granted. In the next section, I discuss the relationship between housing market professionals, racism, and racial segregation by drawing attention to their interactions with housing consumers and other professionals as well as their professional and organizational routines. Housing market professionals interpret their interactions and routines through the lens of racist or equitable, people-affirming ideas and make decisions about allocating housing resources based on their interpretations. In doing so, these race brokers recycle or challenge housing market racism.

Racism, Racial Segregation, and Housing Market Professionals

Through the early and mid-twentieth century, the U.S. federal government, state and municipal governments, professional real estate organizations, and individual White real estate professionals actively implemented policies and practices that explicitly aimed to segregate American neighborhoods (Connolly 2014; Gotham 2014; Jackson 1985; Rothstein 2017). Such practices included cities' use of racial zoning ordinances, which forbade Americans of color—especially Black Americans—from purchasing homes in White neighborhoods and vice versa (Rothstein 2017);[5] the National Association of Real Estate Boards' harsh penalization of real estate agents who violated its explicit goal of maintaining racial segregation (Taylor 2019); and White real estate agents' refusal to show or sell homes in White neighborhoods to Asian, Black, Indigenous, or Latinx home buyers (e.g., Helper 1969). These practices effectively cemented racially segregated urban landscapes. By the 1960s, many American cities were extremely segregated by race and class (Massey and Denton 1993). Since then, in terms of overall national patterns, segregation between Black and White Americans has declined slightly, slowly, and unevenly. Segregation between Asian and White Americans and Latinx and White Americans has remained virtually unchanged. But, in many urban areas with large or growing populations of residents of color, racial segregation between White residents and residents of color appears to be on the rise (Frey 2010a, 2010b; Krysan and Crowder 2017).

The system of racial segregation continues to influence how everyday Americans experience their lives, with dire consequences for communities of color. Alongside other forms of inequality, racial segregation is at the heart of unequal educational opportunities, wealth accumulation, and criminal justice system encounters. For example, relative to their peers in otherwise equal Black and Latinx neighborhoods, children in White neighborhoods are disproportionately likely to access higher quality educational opportunities and achieve higher educational attainment. This is in part because local public schools are funded by property taxes based on local home values, and home values are systematically higher in White neighborhoods net of home and other neighborhood characteristics (Howell and Korver-Glenn 2018; Lareau and Goyette 2014). These differences in home values across White neighborhoods and neighborhoods of color also mean that homeowners in White neighborhoods are disproportionately likely to gain more wealth from the sale of their homes than their counterparts in neighborhoods of color (Flippen 2004; Howell and Korver-Glenn 2018, forthcoming; Thomas et al. 2018). Moreover, residents in neighborhoods of color are far more likely to encounter police and experience violence at the hands of police than residents in White neighborhoods (Bell 2020a; Terrill and Reisig 2003). Policing in neighborhoods of color, especially poor neighborhoods of color, "exacerbates disadvantage by cycling people through unending rounds of arrest, misdemeanor prosecution, and various modalities of supervision" (Bell 2020a:690). And, when people of color enter or exist in White areas, they are likely to "seem particularly out of place, and thus police are more likely to intervene" (Bell 2020a:697; see also Anderson 2015).

However, racial segregation in and of itself does not cause these and other inequalities. Rather, *people*, including politicians, educators, police officers, residential appraisers, business owners, health care providers, and many others, use racial segregation as a tool for making decisions about where and how to allocate resources. As sociologist and legal scholar Monica Bell (2020a) argues, segregation first means separation and confinement, or cutting off people and those who represent them from each other. In a system of segregation, White people are rarely exposed to individuals or neighborhoods of color and individuals of color, regardless of their class status, are less likely to be exposed to White neighborhoods than poor White individuals (Wang et al. 2018). Segregation then becomes a means for White people—who control a disproportionate share of American resources—to subordinate and dominate communities of color (Bell 2020a). They do so by keeping their resources in White areas and excluding individuals of color from entering these neighborhoods or policing them if they do.

Likewise, it is *people* who maintain contemporary racial segregation at above-expected levels given decades of legal and social transformation. American housing consumers and housing market professionals play key roles in these processes. American home buyers, for example, purchase millions of homes each year. These home buyers frequently have existing knowledge about local communities and preferences about where to live. Moreover, White home buyers and home buyers of color have very different knowledge and preferences. Home buyers of color tend to know more about neighborhoods of color and prefer to live in more racially diverse areas (Howell and Emerson 2018; Krysan and Crowder 2017). By contrast, White home buyers know the most about White communities and have the strongest preferences to live near other White neighbors and avoid neighbors of color. To the extent that they act on their community knowledge and residential preferences, White home buyers help sustain racially segregated neighborhoods.

Housing market professionals also shape the process of racial segregation by influencing home buyers' and sellers' knowledge, preferences, prejudices, and opportunities. Especially when purchasing or selling a home, housing consumers rely extensively on housing market professionals to facilitate the process by providing access to information, social connections, and other resources (Besbris 2016, 2020; Shi and Tapia 2016). Although professionals' behaviors appear to be less racially discriminatory now than they were fifty years ago (Turner et al. 2013), real estate agents and mortgage lenders (among others) still treat buyers and sellers of different races in systematically different ways. For example, a 2012 national audit study of real estate agents revealed that agents told prospective White home buyers about 17 percent more homes and showed them 17.7 percent more homes than equally qualified prospective Black home buyers. Similarly, agents told prospective White home buyers about 15.5 percent more homes and showed them 18.8 percent more homes than equally qualified prospective Asian buyers (Turner et al. 2013). Moreover, mortgage lenders targeted Black and Latinx mortgage borrowers with predatory lending schemes in the lead-up to the housing crash. Such predatory lending meant that Black and Latinx mortgage borrowers were disproportionately likely to experience foreclosure and wealth loss during and after the housing crash (Rugh et al. 2015).

Because housing market professionals often interact with each other and make decisions in background, or behind-the-scenes, settings, home buyers and sellers may not be aware that professionals are treating them differently or that they have different housing opportunities than their counterparts. Among other professionals, real estate agents often interact with one another when home buyers and sellers are not present. Such contact takes place at real estate brokerage offices, broker open houses, continuing education classes, and other professional events. Housing market professionals' interactions with one another can shape how they perceive buyers and sellers as well as the opportunities they extend to these consumers. For example, in their mixed-methods study of real estate agents in New York, Besbris and Faber (2017:866) found that a real estate broker influenced a relatively junior real estate agent's business strategy:

REA [real estate agent]: My boss talks about race all the time but never actually says it. But I know what he's referring to. He'll say [of clients], "Are they good people?" Are they good people? And for the first few months my response to that is, "What do you mean?" I would get angry about that. But then he just kept asking and other people I worked with kind of clued me in about what that means. I have unfortunately had to let that cloud my judgments a little bit.

INTERVIEWER: In what way?

REA: Disclosure, fair housing, honestly these things don't help me right now . . . race definitely plays a part in how we show homes.

Although it took some time and the assistance of coworkers, this real estate agent eventually understood that his boss's "backstage," or behind-the-scenes, reference to "good" clients meant "White" clients (see also Picca and Feagin 2007). The agent then altered his business strategies based on his boss's continual questions and even began to view disclosure and fair housing as an unwelcome interference in his work.

Such behind-the-scenes interactions between professionals can influence consumers' opportunities and, ultimately, can contribute in subtle and not-so-subtle ways to racial segregation. For instance, in addition to networking with current or prospective clients, housing market professionals regularly network with one another. This networking happens in racially determined ways. Such networking occurs when they meet at industry luncheons, attend open houses to make introductions, or invite each other to lunch. Yet consumers may not be aware that professionals' networking strategies can affect the range of opportunities consumers perceive as available or desirable. In asking a real estate agent for recommendations regarding a mortgage banker or home inspector (among other professionals), a home buyer may assume that whomever the agent recommends is the "best" option because of the agent's expert status. But agents' recommendations may not be based on these professionals' demonstrated capabilities or experience. Instead, it is entirely possible that agents' recommendations are rooted in their racialized networking strategies, or whom they happen to meet along the way who fits their racial criteria. Such *segregated interindustry networking* has the capacity to funnel consumers to distinct sets of resources and opportunities, and consumers may have no knowledge of them. In addition, such strategies function to segregate real estate professionals' opportunities, which is particularly harmful for professionals of color (Korver-Glenn 2018a).

Housing market professionals also affect how racial segregation persists by acting out professional and organizational routines, or status quo ways of perceiving and behaving in real estate (for a discussion of racialized organizational routines, see Ray 2019). Routines can be informal and optional. For example, it was not Wells Fargo's official policy to target mortgage borrowers of color with predatory mortgage loans, but it also did not immediately sanction employees who did so. As increasingly more Wells Fargo employees throughout the nation chose to stereotype Black and Latinx borrowers and target them with high-risk loan products without immediate consequence, such behavior became routine (Massey et al. 2016; Steil et al. 2018). Ultimately, Black and Latinx borrowers paid millions of dollars in excess costs for high-risk loans and lost millions of dollars during the resultant foreclosures because of this racist routine.[6] Routines can also be formally stated and required. In mortgage lending, for example, lenders whose loans are purchased or guaranteed by the U.S. federal government (e.g., Fannie Mae or Freddie Mac) must comply with these institutions' underwriting guidelines (Stuart 2003). Among other ramifications, this means that, in practice, most lenders require single-family home mortgage borrowers to complete the standardized Fannie Mae Uniform Residential Loan Application (Form 1003). This form directs mortgage loan officers or originators to fill in borrower race, ethnicity, and sex if the borrower completed the form in person and did not do so themselves. These checkboxes nominally exist for statistical purposes but have the effect of priming lending professionals to interpret mortgage applicant race or ethnicity (Korver-Glenn 2018b).

Housing market professionals tend to stick to the routines they learn from their respective professional and organizational contexts, even those that are optional. But these individuals can also depart from or bend routines, including those that are formally stated and required (Feldman and Pentland 2003; Ray 2019). Scholars who study routine-based processes find the presence of individuals who depart from those routines illuminating for several reasons, two of which I highlight here. First, it can be difficult for those embedded in a routine to describe or even acknowledge its shape or contours, but those who choose a separate option, or an alternate route, help identify and describe the routine. (A current can be difficult to identify when swimming with it but unmistakable when swimming against it.) Second, the existence of people who choose alternate options demonstrates that conforming to routines is a passive choice, or a choice of least resistance, rather than an automatic or natural outcome. In doing so, these individuals can denaturalize routines and open up new pathways for action and understanding—in this case, ways of doing real estate work.

Whether they are acting in accord with or departure from routines or are interacting with others, housing market professionals are interpreting their professional worlds. In my study, they did this interpretive work through housing market-specific racial frames, or sets of guiding ideas about race used to evaluate people and neighborhoods and make housing decisions. The dominant frame, what I call the *racist market rubric*, applied and adapted multiple elements from the long-established White racial frame—the White worldview that interprets others through the lens of racist ideas and induces them to treat others according to these ideas (Feagin 2013)[7]—to the housing market context. Housing market professionals who used the racist market rubric in their everyday work perceived White individuals and neighborhoods as the best, most desirable, most valuable, most educated, least dangerous, and most lucrative for the least amount of work (Table I.1).[8] Simultaneously, they perceived individuals and neighborhoods of color as the least desirable, low income, least educated, dangerous, culturally or morally deficient, and a lot of unwanted work. Almost all White housing market professionals in my study relied on aspects of the racist market rubric[9] when they interpreted people (consumers and each other); properties; and their professional norms, policies, and practices.

Rarely, professionals of color also interpreted people and professional routines using elements of the racist market rubric. Unlike their White counterparts, however, these professionals of color often expressed an awareness of ongoing discrimination or housing exclusion, thus tempering their views.

In contrast to professionals using the racist market rubric, most professionals of color in my study used elements of a housing market context-specific counterframe, or a set of ideas that resisted White racism in housing market spaces by affirming racial equality (Clergé 2019; Feagin 2013; Lipsitz

Table I.1 The Racist Market Rubric

Asian	Black	Latinx	White
Affluent Difficult to work with Loyal to co-ethnics Smart/value education	Unsafe or dangerous Undesirable as neighbors Working class or low income Occupationally inferior to Whites Financially unstable and not knowledgeable about U.S. financial system	Spanish-speaking or speaking English with an "accent" "Ethnic" names Undocumented/ immigrant Working class or low income Occupationally inferior to Whites Financially *stable* but not knowledgeable or trusting of U.S. financial system Financially *unstable* and not knowledgeable or trusting of U.S. financial system	Hip lifestyle Lacking culture Affluent or middle class Occupationally and educationally superior to Blacks and Latinxs More financially savvy and knowledgeable about U.S. financial system than other groups

Note: Professionals who used the racist market rubric did not use all of the rubric's elements at all times. Rather, they selectively chose from these racist ideas depending on the context. I have deliberately not grouped or arranged these ideas into "economic," "cultural," or other stereotype categories because the professionals in my study did not separate these categories. Racist-economic ideas merged with racist-cultural ideas, which merged with racist-linguistic ideas, and so on. Finally, professionals in my study almost never mentioned Indigenous people, paralleling their erasure in broader American culture.

2011). When they drew on what I call the *people-oriented market rubric*,[10] real estate professionals perceived neighborhoods and individuals of color as valuable, deserving, historic, hardworking, family oriented, or beautiful, and they worked in ways that reinforced these perceptions (Table I.2).[11] Although these professionals perceived White individuals and neighborhoods as economically advantaged, they also expressed and acted on favorable perceptions of individuals and neighborhoods of color, prioritizing them when allocating time and other resources (see Dantzler and Reynolds (2020) on redistributive housing).

As housing market professionals in my study used one of these two rubrics to interpret people and organizational routines, they became what I call *race brokers*. This concept does not just refer to real estate brokers, or real estate agents with additional specialized training, credentials, and professional authority. Instead, race brokers are gatekeeping individuals in any social sphere who are more influential than most other people in shaping what race means

Table I.2 The People-Oriented Market Rubric

Asian	Black	Latinx	White
Affluent	Beautiful	Family centered	Distinct architectural
Loyal to	Strong/resilient	Hardworking and	preferences
co-ethnics	Family centered	entrepreneurial	Affluent or
Smart/value	Rich history	Financially stable	middle class
education	Long track	and upwardly	Occupational and
	record of being	mobile	educational
	discriminated		achievement
	against and		
	overcoming		
	discrimination		

Note: Professionals who used the people-oriented market rubric did not use all of the rubric's elements at all times. Rather, they selectively chose from these ideas depending on the context.

and whether and how ideas about race are connected to resources (Blumer 1958). Race brokers are influential because of what they do and how they do it. First, race brokers express views about race (whether in explicit or coded ways) and act on their views. Because race brokers are the experts, the authority figures, the official representatives, or the elites in their respective spheres, their views about race and the ways they act on these views can also seem expert or authoritative to those around them (Blumer 1958; Flores 2018). Second, race brokers make connections or avoid making connections between individuals and institutional resources in ways that reinforce racial inequality or racial equity.[12] Because they are positioned between everyday individuals (e.g., home buyers and sellers) and institutions (e.g., governments and industries), they shape how systemic racial inequalities—in this case, racial segregation—are reproduced or challenged. In my study, for example, housing developers shaped home buyers' access to neighborhoods, land, and homes. Real estate agents influenced buyers' and sellers' access to other housing consumers and mortgage bankers, among other financial representatives. Mortgage bankers shaped home buyers' access to capital and representation to the federal government. And, appraisers affected home buyers' access to mortgage loan capital and home sellers' access to wealth.

When the race brokers I studied recycled ideas from the racist market rubric in their everyday work, they made a hierarchy of racial differences seem natural and real. Indeed, in doing so, they upheld racist discourse and racist interpretations of routines that perpetuated racial inequality in housing opportunities and outcomes. This was most obviously the case when housing

market professionals expressed explicitly racist views, whether stated in biological or color-blind terms, taken directly from the racist market rubric
playbook (see Feagin 2013; Lewis 2003). But these individuals also made
racist discourse and routines seem acceptable when they enabled others
to perpetuate such racist views and routines through *complicit racism*,[13] or
expressing shock and dismay at others' racism while hiding their own cooperation with racial prejudice, discrimination, and structural inequality.
In my study, professionals cooperated with racism by expressing helpless-
ness to change the interpersonal, organizational, or institutional status quo;
using organizational or institutional norms to justify silence or inaction in
the context of racial inequality; giving second, third, and fourth chances
to social relations who engaged in explicit or color-blind racism; and providing insider information to help others avoid the consequences of explicit
racism. Complicit racism masqueraded as racial pathos, or awareness and
distaste of racial inequality, while in reality enabling color-blind or explicit
racist ideas and behaviors to flourish (see also Mayorga-Gallo 2019). These
professionals' racist discourse and routines also shaped the connections they
made between individuals and resources, sustaining the process of racial segregation. They were thus brokers of both race and racism.

By contrast, when the race brokers I studied adopted ideas from the
people-oriented market rubric, they countered such racist discourse and
routines. Instead of allowing racist ideas to flourish, they saw "other possibilities for organizing the world" (Itzigsohn and Brown 2015:240). Such
race brokers circulated discourse and established routines that emphasized
the worth and inherent equality of individuals and neighborhoods of color.
Then, they made connections between individuals and resources through
these perceptions, undermining the racist market logic of their White
counterparts as well as aspects of racial segregation. They were thus brokers
of race—in alternate, counter- and people-affirming forms—and *breakers* of
racism.

Although racial segregation remains entrenched through the interlocked
racist ideas, actions, and policies of multiple sets of professionals and government and private agencies (including those described previously), the racism
breakers I studied in the real estate sector demonstrated that it is possible to
foster a more equitable housing market and intervene in America's racially
segregated landscape. Whereas their racism brokering counterparts, especially White housing market professionals, routinely perceived and assumed
the inferiority of individuals and neighborhoods of color and then acted on

such racist assumptions, racism breakers shared a commitment to themselves and their communities of color as worthy and wonderful. Their commitment highlighted and denaturalized the racism in which their colleagues participated. Moreover, racism breakers' alternate strategies pointed toward other ways of doing real estate. If routinized, such alternate strategies (e.g., flat-fee real estate brokerage) could make it more difficult for other professionals to use the racist market rubric and broker racism in their work. The real estate professionals of color I studied—their experiences, perceptions, and strategies—are thus the foundation for the policy recommendations I suggest at the end of the book.

Understanding Housing Market Professionals

To examine housing market professionals and their relationships to racism and racial segregation, I conducted an ethnographic and in-depth interview study of housing developers, real estate agents, mortgage bankers, and appraisers in Houston, Texas. Dubbed one of America's "next great" and truly "cosmopolitan" cities (Perrottet 2013), Houston is both extremely racially diverse and highly segregated. Moreover, according to some metrics, it is the most active housing market in the United States. In Chapter 1, I describe the Houston context, providing a historical overview of the city's rapid urbanization and diversification; its persistent and, in some cases, growing racial segregation; and its housing market. I also introduce six Houston neighborhoods to anchor the city to local areas that served as the reference points for the professionals in my study. Chapter 1 shows that although Houston is unique, it also has much to teach us about how an ostensibly free market approach to housing and development obscures the very active role market professionals play in shaping unequal urban landscapes.

Once I chose my research site, I decided to follow the housing market professionals whom previous research suggested would play key roles in shaping the housing exchange process—that is, the process through which homes are built, bought, and sold.[14] I began where new homes begin—with housing developers—and then proceeded to study real estate agents, mortgage bankers, and appraisers. I repeatedly observed six housing developers between February 2015 and February 2016. Of these six developers, one was Black, four were Latinx, and one was White. Among other activities throughout the year, I followed these individuals as they hosted open houses for both the public and real estate brokers; prospected for land; networked with other professionals; waited for city inspectors and visited the city's planning department; met and networked with investors, consultants, contractors, and architects; attended home-sale closings; and examined current and prospective home construction sites. I took detailed field notes by hand in a small notebook each time I followed these professionals and then typed these notes up on my computer as soon after the interaction as I could. As I learned from these individuals and from the in-depth interviews I was conducting (discussed later), I adjusted my approach, sometimes asking more pointed questions during my field observations to gain more insight into informants' perceptions and strategies (see Kusenbach 2003). Concurrently, I also conducted in-depth interviews with eight housing developers; five of these developers were White and three were developers of color.[15] I had developed an interview guide for professionals, including developers, that consisted of two main sections. The first was a section that asked respondents general questions about their history in real estate, their perceptions of the market, and their approach to doing real estate work. The second section consisted of questions that asked respondents about their perceptions of race and racial segregation, among other topics. Often, developers brought race up in the first battery of questions, indicating its salience to their work.

Chapter 2 discusses how these housing developers used the rubrics described previously to interpret their mental maps of Houston and made choices about where to develop land for residential use. (In reporting these and all empirical results, I have used pseudonyms and occasionally changed other potentially identifying details to protect the confidentiality of these and all other study participants.) Developers first thought about development at the local neighborhood level, reading neighborhoods through the racist or people-oriented market rubric to make choices about where to build and where not to build. When they considered specific plots of land to purchase, they engaged in *reverse blockbusting*. Several housing developers targeted homeowners of color and others they perceived as gullible or more likely to sell for cheap. They did so in order to purchase land at bargain prices and then increase their profit margins when selling the new homes they constructed on this land.[16]

Once a home is built, it can be bought and sold multiple times throughout its life. To sell a home, homeowners frequently engage the services of a listing real estate agent, or listing agent, who assists with preparing and marketing the home for sale. One important step listing agents usually take in marketing a home is to add it to the local Multiple Listing Service (MLS), a public repository of information about for-sale homes. Meanwhile, prospective home buyers typically work with a real estate agent, or buyer's agent, who will facilitate the home search and purchase process; this agent is often someone they know or to whom they were referred. Buyer's agents use the MLS and other insider knowledge to provide detailed information about for-sale homes and the neighborhoods in which they are located. Buyer's agents schedule showings for for-sale homes and often drive their customers to these showings. In addition to providing access to for-sale homes, real estate agents can provide buyers with contacts to mortgage bankers and offer advice on how to get prequalified for a mortgage loan.

Given how central real estate agents are to the housing exchange process (e.g., they are the professionals who have the most contact with home buyers and sellers), I followed seven Houston real estate agents for a year beginning in February 2015. These agents, like the housing developers I studied, were all active in urban Houston's housing market. Some were also active in suburban areas; they could spend hours driving around the metropolitan area within a single day to accommodate different clients' needs. Two of these agents were Black, one was Latinx, and four were White.[17] Among other activities throughout the year, I followed these individuals as they went to listing appointments with current and prospective home sellers, showed homes to home buyers, hosted public and broker open houses, taught continuing education classes, networked with other professionals, networked with current and prospective clients, and attended home-sale closings. As for my observations of housing developers, I took detailed field notes by hand in a small notebook each time I followed these professionals and then typed these notes up on my computer as soon after the interaction as I could. As with the developers, I also began to ask them more questions over time as I learned more about their practices from other real estate agents. I interviewed thirty-one real estate agents during that year. I also interviewed seven real estate agents who occupied other professional roles (e.g., developer, mortgage banker, or escrow/title officer). Of all thirty-eight real estate agents, one was Asian, six were Black, eleven were Latinx, two were multiracial, and eighteen were White.

Chapter 3 uses the data I collected from these observations of and interviews with real estate agents to examine how real estate brokerage routines pressured agents to use the racist market rubric in their work and how brokerages' silence about unofficial yet discriminatory routines served as a form of approval for agents adopting these routines. When agents interpreted established brokerage routines through the racist market rubric, they cultivated relationships with White individuals and excluded Asian, Black, and Latinx individuals. At times, brokerage routines—such as the automated use of the local real estate board's market area map—required agents to advertise homes according to a racial–spatial hierarchy. I also found that brokerages remained silent when White agents pursued alternate routines outside the bounds of brokerage organizations, such as when they took on *pocket listings*—that is, homes not advertised publicly on the MLS. Given the racial patterns of real estate networking in Houston, White home buyers had disproportionate access to pocket listings, yet White agents faced no verbal, professional, or legal sanctions for adopting this behavior.

Once a home buyer places an offer to purchase a home and the seller accepts, other stages of the housing exchange process are set in motion. One very important stage involves the mortgage loan application and its evaluation. Most single-family homes are purchased via mortgage loans, and most buyers who purchase a single-family home with such loans must complete the Uniform Residential Loan Application (Form 1003). On this form, buyers must provide extremely detailed information on their income, expenses, and employment. They also give the mortgage lender—the financial institution staffed by mortgage bankers and other professionals—permission to check their credit score, which goes into the loan application file. If these professionals assess the buyer or the for-sale property as too risky, the lender will not loan the money to purchase the home or it will alter the conditions of the loan such that it takes on less risk.

Mortgage bankers thus play another key role in shaping the housing exchange process. To examine how their perceptions and professional routines are related to race and segregation, I relied on ethnographic observations conducted with developers and real estate agents as well as in-depth interviews with mortgage bankers. The fieldwork I did with the thirteen housing developers and real estate agents brought me into contact with hundreds of other housing market professionals and consumers, including seven unique mortgage bankers. I encountered and interacted with some of these bankers multiple times throughout the year of ethnographic research. I was not able to ascertain the racial identity of some of these individuals by asking them directly. But, using my field notes as a guide, I estimate that four were

Black, one was Latinx, and two were White. I also interviewed an additional ten mortgage bankers. Of these ten, one was Black and nine were White.[18]

Chapter 4 describes how the White mortgage bankers I observed and interviewed relied on segregated interindustry networking with real estate agents to shore up their lending portfolios. In doing so, they helped sustain racially segregated buyer–agent–banker networks and loan opportunities. I also show how White real estate agents undertook such networking and, in some cases, used the racist market rubric to interpret mortgage bankers of color, whom they excluded from their professional circles. Chapter 4 also describes how mortgage bankers depended on the routine of *racialized discretion* when they interpreted mortgage borrower and property risk. They gave White borrowers and homes in White neighborhoods the benefit of the doubt, assuming they were the least risky and most valuable. By contrast, they cast shadows of doubt on borrowers of color and homes in neighborhoods of color, interpreting these individuals and areas through the racist market rubric. Racialized discretion has consequences for whether and under what conditions mortgage loans are approved.

While mortgage loan applications are under initial review by the lending agency, mortgage lenders contact appraisal management companies or other third-party appraisal entities, which then assign individual appraisers to assess the value of the property being considered for the loan. Lenders use the home's value and other specifics appraisers include in their assessment reports to evaluate property risk. Once assigned to a property by the appraisal management company, appraisers make an appointment to visit the for-sale home in person. When they arrive, they gather in-depth data on the home (e.g., its physical condition, size, and features) and take photos to include in their reports. Then, once back at the office, appraisers select comparable sales, or "comps," of previously sold homes in the vicinity of the for-sale home. Consisting of home sale price, physical condition, size, and features, among other data, comps are the main data appraisers use to assess the for-sale home's value in conjunction with its physical characteristics. If the appraisal meets or exceeds the contract price and the buyer's mortgage loan application is approved by the underwriter(s), then the sale can move forward to closing.

Appraisers thus play a crucial role in determining property value and, from the lending perspective, risk. Because their assessments affect whether and under what conditions mortgage loans are approved as well as how much wealth home sellers can accumulate, and because they enter the housing exchange process at a late and near-final stage, I examined appraisers as the last key group of housing market professionals. I encountered and observed two appraisers during my fieldwork; one was Latinx and the other was White. I also conducted in-depth interviews with seven appraisers, three of whom owned appraisal management companies and oversaw hundreds of appraisers. Of the seven, two were Latinx and five were White.[19]

Chapter 5 thus analyzes how appraisers assess home value. It shows that despite surface changes to appraisal requirements and training nominally designed to render the process color-blind, the logic and methods guiding contemporary appraisers' work reflected the explicitly racist appraisal logic and methods instituted by the U.S. federal government and the appraisal industry in the early and mid-twentieth century. When using such logic, appraisers assumed that racially uniform, White neighborhoods (neighborhoods that were racially homogeneous and White) were the most valuable. They also assumed that White home buyers were the reference point for neighborhood desirability and value. This logic guided their methods, such that they typically chose comps from within singular neighborhoods. If forced to cross neighborhood boundaries, they chose comps from racially similar (and not necessarily geographically close or socioeconomically similar) areas. Using a large body of quantitative data, I demonstrate that the appraisers in my sample were not outliers. Rather, homes in White Houston neighborhoods were systematically appraised at two times the value of homes in otherwise similar Black and Latinx Houston neighborhoods in 2015 (Howell and Korver-Glenn 2018). Further quantitative analyses demonstrate that such appraisal inequality is not merely an artifact of explicitly racist historical appraisals; rather, it is actively produced by contemporary appraisers (Howell and Korver-Glenn, forthcoming).

Once an appraisal comes in at or above the contract price and the mortgage borrowers' application is deemed to be sufficiently low risk, the title company—a third party that scours the property deed for liens or other issues and facilitates the exchange of funds—steps in to finalize the sale.[20] When the sale is complete or closed, the buyer's mortgage lender disburses funds to the title company, which pays the balance of the seller's mortgage to their lender (if any) and the remaining funds to the seller. At the same time, the title company takes the previously agreed upon amount of real estate commission out of the seller's funds and sends it to the appropriate brokerage(s). Then, after both home sellers and home buyers have signed the closing documents, home buyers receive the keys to their new home. The housing exchange process has come to a close.

After collecting these data and analyzing how housing market professionals understand race as well as how they affect the process of racial segregation, I identified potential policy interventions that could interrupt professionals' contributions to these racist processes. Chapter 6 describes these policy recommendations, which are directed toward governmental entities as well as real estate and fair housing organizations rather than toward individual professionals. Broadly, I recommend focusing on how to monitor housing market professionals (particularly housing developers and appraisers), prosecute violations of fair housing law, and directly intervene in organizational routines that implicitly or explicitly enable racist interpretations of individuals and neighborhoods. These recommendations return to the fundamental point of this book: Racial segregation is not a natural or neutral feature of urban landscapes. *Race Brokers* shows how housing market professionals are at the center of actively constructing racial segregation with racist tools. In so doing, it points to ways this process can be interrupted with the aim of fostering equitable opportunities for all Americans.

1

H-Town

Houston is a quintessentially Texan city. It is larger than life, fiercely opposed to (or at least suspicious of) governments that intervene or regulate "planning" and development, and dependent on oil to power its economic engine. It bucks many of the social trends that have long characterized the intensely studied cities of the Northeast and Midwest United States. One of its major cultural events is the Houston Livestock Show and Rodeo, which drew more than 2.5 million people in 2019. As of this writing, Houston is the most rapidly growing city in the United States and is second only to the Dallas/Fort Worth, Texas, area in new home construction. This building boom is sending the ripples of urban, suburban, and exurban sprawl ever further into the rural Texas landscape. Compared to other major cities, Houston's housing stock is relatively affordable and more accessible to wider swaths of its increasingly diverse population. And, last but hardly least, Houston has long clung to its claim of being the only major city in the United States without a master zoning plan.

Houston is also a quintessentially American city. It is teeming with people who have come from all over the world in search of freedom and opportunity. It is now the most ethnically diverse city in the United States. Its residents prize single-family homeownership and, in particular, the claim to a piece of land that they can call their own. Despite the cultural pride attached to the claim of no master zoning, Houstonians rely heavily on deed restrictions, or hyper-local restrictions on land use. Moreover, despite the city's much-touted disdain for government interference, it has been increasingly dependent on the federal government to subsidize its highways and other transportation systems and its recovery from increasingly common, disastrous flooding. As in other American cities, income inequality has been increasing, with more wealth concentrated among the ranks of a select few and more poverty concentrated among a growing group at the bottom of the economic ladder. And, like most other American cities, Houston is characterized by relatively stagnant or increasing levels of ethnoracial segregation.

Race Brokers. Elizabeth Korver-Glenn, Oxford University Press (2021). © Oxford University Press.
DOI: 10.1093/oso/9780190063863.003.0002

The Houston real estate professionals I studied were embedded in this paradoxical context. They worked in a city of massive growth, ethnoracial diversity, and economic opportunity simultaneously characterized by stagnant or increasing ethnoracial segregation and income inequality. These professionals worked on the basis of their local knowledge of the city and specific neighborhoods within it. Yet how they understood neighborhoods— particularly with regard to the racial identity of neighborhood residents— echoed how powerful individuals in other sectors, such as employers in the labor market, judges and lawyers in the criminal justice system, and landlords in rental markets, have interpreted individuals and places in many cities throughout the United States.[1] Understanding the Houston context is thus vital to making sense of professionals' perceptions of local people and places, their actions, and how their work may be indicative of housing markets and real estate professionals in other U.S. cities.

Houston: A Brief Historical Overview of Racial Change

Houston was originally the territory of the Indigenous Akokisa tribe.[2] In the eighteenth and early nineteenth centuries, however, White settlers decimated the Akokisa population through violence and disease. Once the remaining Akokisa had fled the area, Augustus and John Allen ("the Allen brothers") laid claim to what is now known as Buffalo Bayou, establishing Houston at a bayou landing in 1836. They aimed to establish Houston as a formidable trade center and the capital of Texas. The latter aim was short-lived; the former set in motion a century and a half of cultivating the city's economic prowess (Emerson and Smiley 2018).

By the mid-nineteenth century, White landowners and slaveholders were drawn to Houston by opportunities for agriculturally driven profit. They also wished to escape the turmoil of the Civil War in other areas of the South. These White Texans brought enslaved Black individuals to Houston—the far western front of the Confederate states—to try to replicate their pre-Civil War life (Steptoe 2016).[3] After the Civil War, Houston's Black population grew rapidly, as newly emancipated migrants made their way to the city to pursue employment opportunities. Pockets of Black, formerly enslaved people from rural areas grew in number in multiple Houston wards, or small political districts, including the Third, Fourth, and Fifth Wards. At the same time, Jim Crow became increasingly entrenched in Houston as White

residents sought to protect their status and economic advantages and maintain the racial hierarchy that Reconstruction appeared to threaten (Ponton
2017; Steptoe 2016; Woodward 2002 [1955]).

As Houston's population and housing needs grew in the twentieth century, the city remained committed to a low-regulation, high-sprawl approach
to development (Feagin 1988). Although Houston's pro-growth orientation supported more affordable housing options relative to its major-city
counterparts (Emerson and Smiley 2018; Vojnovic 2003), it placed little emphasis on historic preservation and demonstrated no overarching, sustained
commitment to municipal services (Feagin 1988). Indeed, city growth, combined with a laissez-faire ethos and lack of sustained political commitment to
master plans, meant that wealthy White landowners and developers directly
shaped Houston's growth processes according to their own private interests
(Fisher 1989; Lin 1995; Qian 2010). The City of Houston, run by White elites,
thus engaged in a bifurcated approach to infrastructural support. It funded
and developed extensive utility and transportation projects for White areas.
And, it neglected Black areas, providing low levels of infrastructural support
and burdening these areas by disproportionately locating hazardous waste
sites in them (Bullard 1987; Feagin 1988).

Houston's local racially restrictive covenants paralleled the city's bifurcated approach to urbanization (Feagin 1988). White Houstonians formal-
ized racially restrictive covenants, for example, through deed restrictions.
Still in use today, deed restrictions are mutually agreed-upon rules that current residents of a neighborhood must follow. Whereas contemporary deed
restrictions often focus on architectural and other aesthetic guidelines, in
the past, deed restrictions often included racist directives alongside architectural guidelines. These directives often prohibited White homeowners
from selling their home to Black buyers or other buyers of color or stipu-
lated that only Whites could own homes in the neighborhood. In Houston,
deed restrictions were the only legal means for excluding Black residents
from White neighborhoods prior to 1948 (Ponton 2017; Rothstein 2017).
Figure 1.1 illustrates one such racially exclusionary deed restriction attached to a property in the Heights neighborhood. In 1948, however,
the U.S. Supreme Court majority decision in *Shelley v. Kraemer* dictated
that racially exclusionary residential covenants were unconstitutional. In
Houston, this meant that the only legal means of racial exclusion had been
stripped from White homeowners.[4]

    (g) Until July 1, 1981, this property shall not be
conveyed to, owned, used or occupied by any person other
than of the White or Caucasian race, except that owner's
servant or servants other than of the White or Caucasian
race may occupy servant houses, garage or outhouses, when
residence is occupied by owner.

Figure 1.1 Excerpt of a racially exclusionary residential deed restriction from
the Heights neighborhood, Houston.
Source: Screenshot of a publicly available title deed provided to the author by an escrow officer.

At approximately the same time, Houston began to experience further
demographic change as more immigrants from Mexico and other areas of
Latin America began to arrive. Although ethnic Mexicans had lived in the
area for generations (indeed, since before Texas entered the United States),[5]
Mexican-origin and Central American populations grew dramatically after
World War II when Houston experienced a technological and economic
boom (Esparza 2011; Steptoe 2016). During this period, Latinx Houstonians
largely continued to settle in already established Latinx neighborhoods in
Houston's urban core, including El Crisol, El Segundo, Northside, and
Magnolia Park (Korver-Glenn 2014; San Miguel 2001). Similar to their Black
counterparts, native- and foreign-born Latinx Houstonians often lived in
neighborhoods that the city neglected and experienced exclusion parallel to
their Black counterparts through Juan Crow customs and restrictions. Many
of these areas had little or no infrastructural development, low levels of municipal servicing, and few amenities (Feagin 1988; San Miguel 2001).

In the latter half of the twentieth century and into the early twenty-first
century, Black and Latinx Houstonians began to move outside the boundaries of these established urban neighborhoods and into Houston's sprawling
suburban landscape (Bader and Warkentien 2016; Korver-Glenn and Elliott
2016). Although some of this movement occurred in southwest Houston—in
Fort Bend County, for example—much of it occurred along Houston's north,
northeast, east, and southeastern transportation and industrial corridors
(Korver-Glenn and Elliott 2016). Meanwhile, Houston's White population
grew between 1960 and 1990, but it declined in both relative and absolute
numbers between 1990 and 2010.

At the end of the twentieth century, an increasing number of Asian
immigrants also began to arrive in Houston, yet again altering the city's
ethnoracial landscape (Feagin 1988). Relative to their Black, Latinx, and

White counterparts, Asian Houstonians have comprised a much smaller proportion of the Houston-area population and have tended to live in a smaller number of predominantly Asian neighborhoods, several of which are located southwest of Houston's urban core. Nevertheless, Asian Houstonians are growing in number across Houston, particularly in suburban and exurban areas. Table 1.1 reports Houston's racial demographics for 1990, 2000, 2010, and 2017.

Houston's rapid ethnoracial change coincided with its emergence as the fourth-largest city in the United States, behind New York City, Los Angeles, and Chicago. These cities, too, saw dramatic increases in ethnic and racial diversity during the same period. But unlike these cities, housing in Houston remained far more affordable for its residents. Between 2000 and 2017, for example, the median value of an owner-occupied home in Houston rose from $121,132 to $154,100—a 27 percent increase. During the same period, median home values of owner-occupied homes in Chicago, Los Angeles, and Manhattan rose by 2 percent, 71 percent, and 76 percent, respectively (adjusting for inflation to 2017 dollars).[6] Figure 1.2 shows home value changes for these areas during this period.

Table 1.1 Harris County (Houston), Texas, Racial Demographics: 1990–2017

	Number (Percentage of Total Population)			
	1990	2000	2010	2017
American Indian/Alaska Native	6,143 (0.2)	7,103 (0.2)	6,780 (0.2)	8,078 (0.2)
Asian	106,327 (3.8)	170,080 (5.0)	240,381 (6.1)	307,109 (6.8)
Black	527,964 (18.7)	618,551 (18.2)	739,423 (18.7)	838,285 (18.5)
Hispanic/Latino	644,935 (22.9)	1,120,625 (33.0)	1,563,194 (39.6)	1,910,535 (42.2)
White	1,528,113 (54.2)	1,429,684 (42.0)	1,356,404 (34.3)	1,386,576 (30.6)
Total	2,818,199	3,400,578	3,950,999	4,525,519

Notes: For 1990, the Asian category includes Asian or Pacific Islander Harris County residents. For 2000, 2010, and 2017, the Asian category does not include Native Hawaiian or Pacific Islander residents. For all decades, American Indian/Alaska Native, Asian, Black, and White refer to non-Hispanic American Indian/Alaska Native, Asian, Black, and White populations; for 2000, 2010, and 2017, these categories refer to non-Hispanic American Indian/Alaska Native, Asian, Black, and White-alone populations. The data describe Harris County, Texas, which is largely coterminous with the City of Houston.

Sources: Social Explorer (n.d.), U.S. Census Long Form (1990 and 2000), and 2010 and 2017 American Community Survey five-year estimates.

These differences in home values do not simply reflect differences in the cost of living. In 2017, the median household income in Houston was $57,791. For the same year, the median household income was $59,426 in Chicago, $61,015 in Los Angeles, and $79,781 in Manhattan (American Community Survey 2017). In Houston, the 2017 ratio of median owner-occupied home values to median household income was 2.7:1, compared to 3.8:1, 8.1:1, and 11.5:1 in Chicago, Los Angeles, and Manhattan, respectively. In other words, an average-income household in Houston would only need to spend 2.7 times its income to purchase a house of average value in Houston. But average-income households in the country's other largest cities would need to spend much, much more to do likewise. Compared to these three other major areas—especially Los Angeles and Manhattan—homes in Houston are more affordable, even when considering local differences in income.

Because housing affordability is a major factor driving home buyers' purchase decisions, more affordable housing opens the possibility of homeownership to a larger number of people and, theoretically, widens the available

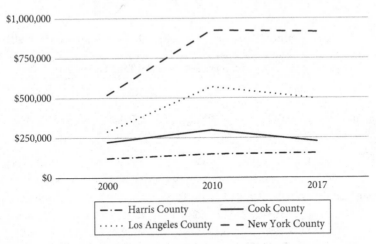

Figure 1.2 Median home values for owner-occupied housing units, 2000–2017. Harris County and Cook County are the central counties for Houston and Chicago, respectively. New York County is coterminous with Manhattan. All values are adjusted for inflation to 2017 dollars. Values are median values for owner-occupied homes as reported by Social Explorer (using U.S. Census Decennial (2000) and American Community Survey (2006–2010 and 2013–2017 five-year estimates) data).

pool of homes from which buyers can choose. In turn, this expansion can reduce housing inequality and segregation (see, for example, Foster and Kleit 2015; Sahasranaman and Jensen 2016). Indeed, Houston's relatively affordable housing has meant that homeownership has been within reach of a larger proportion of Houston residents—including individuals of color, whose incomes reflect ongoing discrimination and inequality in education and employment. For example, in 2017, approximately 61 percent of Asian-headed households, 37 percent of Black-headed households, 49 percent of Latinx-headed households, and 68 percent of White-headed households lived in owner-occupied homes in Houston. By contrast, in Los Angeles, only approximately 53 percent, 34 percent, 38 percent, and 55 percent of Asian, Black, Latinx, and White-headed households, respectively, lived in owner-occupied housing (American Community Survey 2017).

Despite these favorable conditions—the end of legal means to enforce racially restrictive covenants, the passage of fair housing laws and other civil rights legislation, dramatic upticks in the city's racial diversity, and affordable housing relative to other major cities—Houston remains deeply divided by race.

Trends in Racial Segregation and Houston's Housing Market

The overall portrait of racial segregation in Houston has been, and remains, bleak. White and Latinx Houstonians are more segregated from each other now than they were thirty years ago. And although White and Black Houstonians became slightly less segregated from each other during the same period, they are still more segregated than White and Latinx Houstonians. Tables 1.2 and 1.3 show the 1990 and 2015 White–Latinx and White–Black dissimilarity scores, a statistic that measures how evenly two groups are spread across a given space, for Houston and several other large metropolitan areas.[7] Values closer to 0 indicate low segregation, whereas values closer to 1 indicate high segregation.

As with many other U.S. metropolitan areas, Houston and the other metro areas represented in Tables 1.2 and 1.3 experienced increases in White–Latinx segregation and slight decreases in White–Black segregation during this time period.[8] Houston's score of 0.52 means that just over half—52 percent—of either White or Latinx individuals would have to move

Table 1.2 White–Latinx Dissimilarity Scores, Selected
U.S. Metropolitan Areas

	1990	2015
Houston	0.48	0.52
Atlanta	0.35	0.49
Chicago	0.61	0.56
Denver	0.47	0.48
Los Angeles	0.60	0.61
Miami	0.33	0.56
New York	0.66	0.61
Washington, DC	0.42	0.48

Sources: The source of White–Latinx 1990 dissimilarity scores is
Frey (2010a). Dissimilarity scores for 2015 were calculated using the
American Community Survey 2011–2015 five-year estimates.

Table 1.3 White–Black Dissimilarity Scores, Selected
U.S. Metropolitan Areas

	1990	2015
Houston	0.66	0.61
Atlanta	0.66	0.59
Chicago	0.84	0.76
Denver	0.65	0.63
Los Angeles	0.73	0.68
Miami	0.71	0.64
New York	0.81	0.77
Washington, DC	0.66	0.62

Sources: The source of White–Black 1990 dissimilarity scores is Frey
(2010b). Dissimilarity scores for 2015 were calculated using the
American Community Survey 2011–2015 five-year estimates.

to a different neighborhood to be evenly distributed across the metro area.
In 2015, the Houston metro area included 2,469,095 non-Hispanic White
residents and 2,432,651 Latinx residents (American Community Survey
2015). Ensuring even distribution across Houston would require a massive
population shift of either 1,283,929 White or 1,264,979 Latinx individuals to
other neighborhoods.

Dissimilarity scores are just one way to measure the extent of racial seg-regation,[9] and as recent work by Logan and Parman (2017) shows, they may dramatically underestimate the extent to which American cities are racially separated. With sociologist Jim Elliott, I used yet another method to examine Houston's racial dynamics over time (Korver-Glenn and Elliott 2016).[10] Our approach emphasized group overrepresentation by measuring groups' presence in individual Houston neighborhoods (i.e., census tracts) relative to their presence in Harris County more broadly. For instance, according to the 2010 census, Harris County had 739,423 Black residents who accounted for 18.7 percent of all county residents. If these residents were distributed equally across the county's census tracts, they would also represent 18.7 per-cent of each tract. (For example, we would expect 748 Black residents to live in a census tract of 4,000 people if the tract reflected the county's Black pop-ulation.) We compared the actual proportion of group members in a given census tract to the proportion of group members in the county to produce a ratio. Ratios higher than 1 and, in particular, higher than 1.5 indicate dis-proportionately high representation of a group within a tract relative to its presence in the county overall.

We found that, in the fifty-year period between 1960 and 2010, White Houstonians were increasingly likely to live in census tracts where Whites were overrepresented relative to their share of the overall county popula-tion. By 2010, 96 percent of White residents in Harris County lived in a tract where Whites were overrepresented. This concentration of Whites in dis-proportionately White spaces increased over time, with White Houstonians living in fewer and more racially concentrated neighborhoods in 2010 than they did in 1960. Meanwhile, during this same time period, Black and Latinx Houstonians were moving across the Houston area. But because their move-ment across the area coincided with White concentration, these groups were still living in tracts where they were overrepresented and separate from White Houstonians.

This racial segregation has coincided with housing market discrimina-tion. Among other entities, the City of Houston's Housing and Community Development Department (HCDD) records and tracks housing discrimina-tion claims filed through its office. Between 2005 and 2014, HCDD closed 887 housing discrimination complaints that alleged 1,151 bases for dis-crimination (e.g., on the basis of race, disability, religion, sex, or familial status). Of these cases, 552, or 48 percent, involved alleged discrimination by race, national origin, or color (Rackleff 2015). These data do not include complaints that victims filed but remained unclosed by HCDD, nor do they include complaints filed with the U.S. Department of Housing and Urban Development or fair housing organizations. Moreover, these complaints are considered to be a conservative estimate of discrimination given fear of retaliation among victims, the costs of filing a complaint in time and money, and cynicism about whether complaints will be taken seriously. At a minimum, then, half of all housing civil rights complaints in Houston involve ethnoracial discrimination.

Alongside such housing inequality and racial segregation, Houston's housing market is one of the most active in the United States. As of this writing, Houston's housing developers and builders construct more new homes each month than any other U.S. city besides Dallas/Fort Worth—a record it has held since 2016. Before that, it held the top position (Metrostudy News 2016a). Between the second quarter of 2015 and the first quarter of 2016 alone (the same period I collected data), 27,263 new homes were started in Houston (Metrostudy News 2016a). In addition to these new homes, thousands of existing homes are bought and sold each year. Between February 2018 and January 2019, for example, 50,234 homes were sold in Harris County, or approximately 1 out of every 16 owner-occupied, single-unit (detached or unattached) homes.[11] In March 2020, the Houston Association of Realtors advertised on its Multiple Listing Service (MLS) press release website that its membership consisted of 37,000 real estate agents who represented 40,932 active listings, 7,566 single-family home sales, and 7,885 single-family pending sales.[12]

In addition, Houston homeowners fared relatively well compared to those in other large markets both during and after the recent housing crash. Homes in Houston lost less value on average than those in many other large cities, and they recovered that lost value more quickly. When comparing the average annual appreciation of home value between March 2010 and December 2016 for the New York, Los Angeles, Chicago, and Houston metropolitan areas, Houston stands out as the most stable. In the Houston metro area, home values depreciated by 2 percent in 2010 and then appreciated an average of 6.2 percent a year between 2011 and 2016. In contrast, homes in New York, Los Angeles, and Chicago depreciated an average of 3.5, 3, and 6.5 percent, respectively, during both 2010 and 2011, and they appreciated 4.75, 7.75, and 4.25 percent a year, respectively, between 2012 and 2016.[13] Houston's very active and ostensibly healthy housing market thus coexists with its marked patterns of racial segregation and housing inequality. And housing market professionals are in the middle, facilitating intense—and racially unequal—housing activity.

Houston Neighborhoods: A Sampler

Housing market professionals interpret racial segregation and housing market trends and apply their understandings to their work (Besbris 2020; Helper 1969; Jackson 1985). Specifically, the real estate professionals I studied used racially coded maps of Houston when they made decisions about where to work, with whom to work, and how to work. These maps were not physical maps covered in red lines but, rather, culturally produced mental maps of which groups live where (see also Bonam et al. 2017; Lipsitz 2011). Professionals then read their maps through the lens of either a racist market or a people-oriented market rubric to determine how different neighborhoods and racial groups made them feel and how they should act. These maps did not necessarily correspond to accurate demographic, cultural, or historical neighborhood characteristics, but the fact that they may have been inaccurate did not make them any less influential. To orient the reader to several Houston neighborhoods—some of which professionals refer to repeatedly throughout the book—Figure 1.3 depicts six areas in terms of their relationship to the broader Houston area. Descriptions of each area, including race and income characteristics, follow.

Denver Harbor

Denver Harbor, also known as El Crisol,[14] is a predominantly working-class and low-income Latinx neighborhood due north of Houston's Ship Channel, northeast of downtown Houston, and north/northeast of other historically Latinx areas, including Second Ward and Magnolia Park. Settled by European immigrants in the late nineteenth and early twentieth centuries, by the 1930s the area had attracted a large number of Latinx (im)migrants because of its proximity to the Southern Pacific railyards and the Houston Ship Channel (San Miguel 2001; Steptoe 2016). By the 1960s, Denver Harbor was one of the primary seats of the local Chicano/a movement.

Denver Harbor was the site of intense organizing surrounding school segregation in the 1970s. As historian Guadalupe San Miguel, Jr., relates,

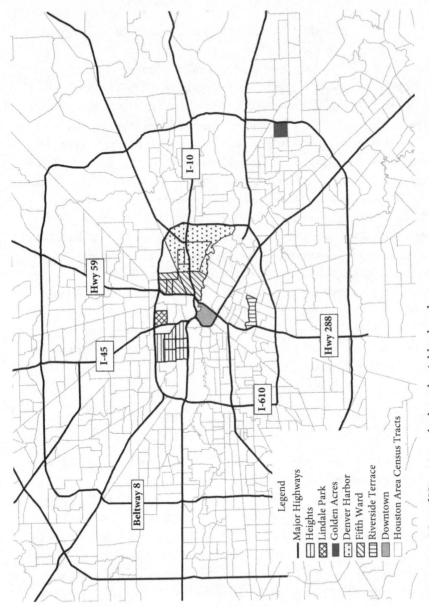

Figure 1.3 Map of Houston and selected neighborhoods.
Source: Map created by Elizabeth Korver-Glenn using GIS software.

Legend

Major Highways
Heights
Lindale Park
Golden Acres
Denver Harbor
Fifth Ward
Riverside Terrace
Downtown
Houston Area Census Tracts

Beltway 8

I-45

Hwy 59

I-10

I-610

Hwy 288

the Houston Independent School District (HISD) tried to avoid desegregating White public schools even after they were court-ordered to do so. The school board, San Miguel writes, "used the White legal status of the growing Mexican American population to circumvent desegregation" (2016:268). In response to the school board's decision to exclude the Whites who made up a large majority of HISD students from the district's desegregation plan, Chicano/a activists organized a boycott of HISD schools. As an alternative, they established *huelga* schools, or "sites of instruction established by community people involved in protesting various forms of social and educational injustices" (San Miguel 2016:266). Denver Harbor was a primary source of enrollment in the *huelgas* that educated students during the boycott: At least 2,000 Denver Harbor students enrolled in the local *huelga* during the first week of the boycott.

Denver Harbor maintained its status as one of Houston's primary barrios through the late twentieth and early twenty-first centuries. As has been the case for so many other Black and Latinx communities in Houston, the city neglected to maintain the streets, drainage and sewer infrastructure, sidewalks, and parks for much of this time, causing these essential infrastructural components to fall into disrepair and exacerbating issues associated with the flooding so common to the Bayou City (Bullard 1987; Feagin 1988). Moreover, the construction of Interstate 10 (I-10; an east–west highway connecting Houston to New Orleans on the east and San Antonio on the west) divided the northern and southern portions of the neighborhood. Despite the presence of a disruptive highway and the absence of city services, local residents continued to build up their community, maintaining bungalow-style, pier-and-beam homes as household funds allowed and preserving minimum-lot size by adopting the Chapter 42 ordinance passed by the City of Houston in 2012 (Sorto 2018). By 2015, when I conducted my study, Denver Harbor was approximately 90 percent Latinx and had a mean family income of $42,000 (American Community Survey 2015).

Fifth Ward

Fifth Ward, a predominantly Black neighborhood, is situated just northeast of downtown Houston and west of Denver Harbor. Soon after the Civil War, approximately half of Fifth Ward's residents were Black and approximately half were White. But, by the 1920s, most White residents had moved away and new Black residents—including several hundred Creole Black migrants who established a four-by-four block area within Fifth Ward known as Frenchtown—had moved in. With easy access to the Southern Pacific railyards that cut through the neighborhood on a northeast–southwest diagonal as well as to the Houston Ship Channel to the southeast, many working-class Black residents lived within walking distance of their work during the early decades of the twentieth century (Kleiner 2010). Lower-middle-class and middle-class Black residents established businesses, including medical practices, a theater, a pharmacy, and barbershops, along Fifth Ward's bustling Lyons Avenue corridor in the years leading up to and following World War II. Single-family homes in the area were typically small. Many of them were built in the "shotgun" style common in cities throughout the South: no more than one room (approximately 12 feet) across and three or four rooms deep. As with many homes in the Houston area, these homes were not constructed on concrete slabs but, rather, rested on pier-and-beam foundations that allowed for the boggy ground underneath to shift without undermining the integrity of the home's structure.

After *Shelley v. Kraemer*, middle-class Black families began to move away from Fifth Ward and into other areas across Houston. At approximately the same time, the Texas Department of Transportation, together with Houston city planners, began constructing Highway 59 (a north–south highway connecting downtown Houston with the northeast suburbs) and I-10. The intersection of these two freeways demolished the economic center of Fifth Ward, destroying homes and businesses and displacing residents and business owners (Feagin 1988). From the 1960s until the early twenty-first century, Fifth Ward experienced increases in poverty and crime as local institutions crumbled and the city all but abandoned infrastructural maintenance or development.

By 2010, however, poverty and crime rates were declining and Latinx residents began to move in. New, albeit modest, homes were constructed, interspersed with the existing, older housing stock, and some existing homes were refurbished in the area of the neighborhood north of I-10. Meanwhile, newly constructed homes eventually began to dominate the landscape of the neighborhood south of I-10. Fifth Ward's proximity to downtown became a useful tool for developers keen to capitalize on the spate of young professionals who wished to live close to downtown amenities without downtown prices. Decades of abandonment by the city, however, meant that Fifth Ward's streets were in disrepair and sidewalks were rare or, when present, in poor condition. Local residents often had to pay someone to maintain and beautify street corners, medians, and parks or do such work themselves. Plenty of local residents walk through the neighborhood, but they encounter few amenities, such as grocery stores, when they do so. By 2015, Fifth Ward was 54 percent Black and 43 percent Latinx, and the mean family income in the area was approximately $35,000 (American Community Survey 2015).

Lindale Park

Lindale Park was developed in the late 1930s and 1940s. A deed-restricted community initially populated almost entirely by White Houstonians, homes in the area are usually brick and built in the cottage, bungalow, or ranch style. Lots are also larger than many found in urban Houston: Most are 7,500 to 10,000 square feet, rather than the 5,000 (or smaller) square-foot lots found in many other areas of the city. All drainage is paved over (unlike many areas of Houston with open drainage ditches). Curbs and tall live oak and magnolia trees line the wide, well-maintained streets.

Between 1970 and 2000, White residents left Lindale Park en masse and were replaced by their Latinx counterparts. During research that I conducted in the area prior to the current study (Korver-Glenn 2014, 2015), I found that many of Lindale Park's residents had roots in and ties to the Near Northside community located just south of the area—in fact, many residents in both Lindale and Near Northside refer to the two areas together as Northside. Yet, because of its middle-class status, deed restrictions, and differences in housing stock (among other reasons), Lindale Park retains a unique identity.

This is an identity that its residents actively cultivate and maintain. For example, when Houston METRO revealed its plan to extend the existing downtown light rail line northward into Near Northside and Lindale Park (as well as other areas north of Lindale Park), the transit agency initially proposed that the line follow Irvington Boulevard. Lindale Park residents fiercely opposed the plan, arguing that it would divide their community essentially in half. Eventually, METRO changed its plan and constructed the light rail such that it followed Fulton Street, which serves as the westernmost boundary of Lindale Park. Lindale Park residents now have easy access to the light rail, which connects them directly to downtown Houston, the museum district, Rice University, the Medical Center, and Reliant Stadium, without what they regarded as the burden of a rail line running through the heart of

the community. When I conducted this research, Lindale Park was 80 percent Latinx and the mean family income was just over $74,000 (American
Community Survey 2015).

The Heights

Grouped together west and southwest of Lindale Park and northwest of
downtown lie the Heights neighborhoods (often referred to colloquially as
one collective neighborhood, "The Heights"). Norhill Heights is a completely
residential, deed-restricted area mainly composed of bungalow-style homes.
Many homeowners here have updated or added on to their homes. Houston
Heights is another deed-restricted area composed of homes of mixed architectural style—modern, bungalow, Victorian, and even Mediterranean. Most
of these homes are modest to large in size and immaculately maintained, with
curated lawns and debris-free streets. Some of the streets have open drainage
ditches, whereas others are covered. Some have sidewalks, and some do not.
In addition to Norhill and Houston Heights, the greater Heights area also
consists of Woodland Heights (south of Norhill) and Sunset Heights (north
of Houston Heights).

Heights Boulevard, a divided four-lane road with large live oak trees and
sculptures created by local artists dotting the median, runs through the heart
of Houston Heights. Large Victorian-era homes with turrets and sweeping
front porches and renovated, enlarged Craftsman-style bungalow homes line
much of the Boulevard. These homes are a continual reminder that Houston
Heights was one of the first planned communities in Texas and of its status
as a white-collar, White "suburb" of Houston (it is now part of Houston's
urban core). Indeed, before Houston cemented its fate as a temple to the car,
Heights Boulevard was the home of the city's first electric street car. Some
of the homes along the street now house businesses, including a bungalow
turned coffee shop where I conducted several interviews.

Some older multifamily dwellings are interspersed among the large single-
family Victorian homes, especially heading south toward I-10. Now, deed
restrictions inhibit landowners from constructing dwellings that would in-
tensify density in the area.[15] In addition, Houston Heights consists of three
historic districts—some of the only such districts in Houston—which re-
strict property owners' ability to demolish or renovate their homes.[16] When
I conducted my research, the Greater Heights area (including Houston,

Norhill, Woodland, and Sunset Heights) was 67 percent non-Hispanic White, and the mean family income was just over $164,000 (American Community Survey 2015).

Riverside Terrace

The Riverside Terrace neighborhood is approximately four miles due south of downtown Houston and is also part of Houston's urban core. Bordered by Brays Bayou—a well-maintained bayou with paved walking and cycling paths—and Third Ward to the north, Riverside Terrace is a predominantly Black neighborhood whose residents are typically middle or upper class. The large, brick, colonial-style mansions and large, midcentury modern homes that line its main thoroughfare, S. MacGregor Way, are immaculate. Large live oak trees, closely cut grass, and decorous shrubs frame homes.

Riverside Terrace was formerly known as the "Jewish River Oaks": By "gentlemen's agreement," Jewish individuals were not allowed to purchase homes in the White, wealthy River Oaks neighborhood, so wealthy Jewish families settled in Riverside Terrace instead (Kaplan 1981). When the first Black family moved into Riverside Terrace in 1953, their home was bombed (Feagin 1988). Eventually, however, middle-class Black Houstonians' desire for high-quality housing overtook the very real fears of violence at the hands of White neighbors. Over time, Black residents moved into new suburbs such as Missouri City as well as existing White middle- or upper-class neighborhoods—even those such as Riverside Terrace with a history of violence against Black newcomers.

By the 1980s, Jewish and White Riverside Terrace residents were moving out of the neighborhood as Black middle- and upper-class newcomers moved in. These newcomers had and continue to have relatively easy access to amenities in nearby neighborhoods, including the Houston Medical Center (now the largest medical center in the world). The community is near wealthy White areas, such as West University Place, that offer the full array of neighborhood services. With the exception of churches, gas stations, and convenience stores, however, few amenities are located directly within or immediately adjacent to the neighborhood. In 2015, Riverside Terrace had a mean family income of approximately $95,500 and was approximately 79 percent Black (American Community Survey 2015).

Golden Acres, Pasadena

Southeast of downtown in Pasadena, Texas—one of Houston's largest proximate suburbs—is the Golden Acres neighborhood, a largely White, low-
income, and working-class area. The housing stock in Golden Acres is
very mixed, including single-family and multifamily homes. Most single-
family homes are small, ranch or bungalow style. Some homes in the area
are manufactured. The streets have open drainage and no sidewalks or
curbs, and it is not uncommon to spot an old recreational vehicle or truck
rusting in a driveway. But several amenities are located just across the
highway from Golden Acres, near Pasadena's middle- and upper-class White
neighborhoods, including a Cinemark theater, several fast-food restaurants,
a Hobby Lobby, and an Amegy Bank branch.

Initially founded as a farming community in the late nineteenth century,
Pasadena's working-class White residents were incorporated into Houston's
emerging, booming oil and shipping economy during and after World War
II (Pomeroy, n.d.). Like other Texas cities, Pasadena imposed residential segregation and banned Spanish-language instruction in public schools. By the
1980s, Pasadena was the headquarters of the Texas branch of the Ku Klux
Klan (Ura 2017a).

Eventually, attracted by local economic opportunities, blue-collar Mexican
American families began moving into the northwest Pasadena area; by 2010,
they comprised the numerical majority of the City of Pasadena. In the midst
of these changing demographics, Johnny Isbell, the White then-mayor of
Pasadena, cast the tie-breaking vote to put Proposition 1 to a general vote. The
proposition would change two of the eight single-member city districts (each
responsible for electing its own city council member) to two at-large council
seats, who would be elected by the city as a whole. The White-majority elec-
torate passed the proposition in 2013. Then, in 2014, five Pasadena residents,
represented by the Mexican American Legal Defense and Education Fund,
filed a lawsuit against the City of Pasadena, arguing that this redistricting
diluted the local Latinx vote. In 2017, a federal judge ruled that the City of
Pasadena had violated the Voting Rights Act and ordered the city to come
back under federal supervision—the only city in Texas thus far to regress to
the pre-2013 status of federal voting supervision (Davies 2014; Ura 2017a,
2017b). When I conducted my research in 2015, soon after the lawsuit had
been filed and before the federal judge's decision, Pasadena's White-headed
households comprised 40 percent of this Houston suburb, with an average

income of approximately $71,900. Within Golden Acres, however, 56 per-
cent of households were classified as White-headed, and the mean family
income was approximately $42,800 (American Community Survey 2015).

* * *

The six areas discussed in this chapter exemplify some of the local dynamics common to Houston's three largest racial groups—Black, Latinx, and
White—across the city's hundreds of neighborhoods. Most of them appear
multiple times in the pages that follow. And, as part of the fabric of Houston's
housing context, they were key to housing market professionals' and consumers' use of the racist and people-oriented market rubrics and racially
coded maps of the city. These maps were important for all of the professionals
I studied, including housing developers. Let us now turn our attention to
these professionals, who often jumpstart the exchange of homes through
selecting neighborhoods to develop and then choosing specific plots of land
to target for development purposes.

2

Building Homes

Every home has a beginning. In the United States, that beginning usually starts with housing developers and builders, who typically plan and construct new homes before they are sold to individuals or families. Since 1974, developers have constructed more than 31 million new single-family (one-unit) homes for Americans to purchase.[1] In recent years, Houston has led the nation in new home construction: In 2015, the year I conducted my research, Houston-area builders and developers finished constructing more than 27,000 new homes.[2] To start, finish, and ultimately sell a home to a buyer, developers must make many choices leading up to and during construction. These choices include architectural style (Will the home reflect Craftsman or Mediterranean Revival sensibilities?), the quality of such construction materials as lumber and windows, and whom they will hire to do the actual building work. But perhaps the most important choice developers make—at least from their perspective—is where to build.

The decision about where to build was particularly important to the urban housing developers I studied. Unlike their suburban or exurban counterparts, they typically did not construct homes on newly developed or undeveloped land. Rather, developers working in central Houston were building homes in areas with much longer histories. They looked for opportunities for "infill," by which they meant purchasing vacant lots for new construction, or for "teardowns," the process of tearing down existing, older homes and building new ones in their place.[3] Developers in my study navigated these histories by making their where-to-build decisions at two levels: the neighborhood and the individual plot of land. Neighborhoods are an important part of urban history, and neighborhood racial composition (itself a product of historic and contemporary processes) was a key indicator developers used to make their choices about where to build. When it comes to deciding which specific plots of land to purchase, developers must interact with the individuals who already own them. The developers I studied based their decisions about which homeowners to approach and how to approach them on racialized assumptions about these owners, engaging in *reverse blockbusting*.[4]

Race Brokers. Elizabeth Korver-Glenn, Oxford University Press (2021). © Oxford University Press.
DOI: 10.1093/oso/9780190063863.003.0003

Thus, from the very beginning of the housing exchange process—the actual planning and construction of homes—developers brokered race by building racism into the urban landscape. That is, more often than not, they used racist ideas about specific places and people, or the racist market rubric, to interpret their racially coded mental maps of Houston (see Bonam et al. 2017; Lipsitz 2011). They then purchased land, invested resources, and developed homes for sale or rent based on their interpretations. Such practices did not represent the bad habits of a few bad apples. Instead, residential developers in Houston systematically favored White neighborhoods, building more new homes in these areas than in Black and Latinx neighborhoods even after accounting for other neighborhood characteristics (Korver-Glenn and Elliott 2016). Developers' racist choices to prioritize White neighborhoods and White home buyers, reproduced at scale, turned their racially coded mental maps into racially unequal neighborhoods: Among other benefits, neighborhoods with more newer homes have newer infrastructure (e.g., drains, sewers, and sidewalks) and higher home values.

Working against the grain of this larger pattern, a small number of builders pursued development projects in Black and Latinx neighborhoods because they believed these areas deserved investment, were appealing to many home buyers, and were profitable. Using the people-oriented market rubric to interpret their racially coded mental maps of Houston, these builders demonstrated that other developers' decisions to build racism into the urban landscape were not simply an economically rational response to consumer demand. (Indeed, consumer demand was lower in White Houston neighborhoods than in otherwise comparable Black and Latinx neighborhoods at the time of the study (Howell and Korver-Glenn 2018).) Each of the developers in my study used their resources to play an active role in creating the Houston housing market—a market that theoretically serves a population that is predominantly Black and Latinx. But most of the developers I interviewed and observed used the racist market rubric to pursue projects in White neighborhoods and for White home buyers. In doing so, they were the on-the-ground people sustaining and exacerbating the racially unequal housing landscape perpetuated by the Houston residential development industry more broadly (Feagin 1988; Korver-Glenn and Elliott 2016).

Choosing Neighborhoods

In terms of where to build, the first stage of decision-making often occurs at the neighborhood level. That is, urban housing developers in the United States first consider which neighborhoods will be best for their new home plans prior to purchasing individual plots of land on which to build. Developers have many tools at their disposal to evaluate neighborhoods. In addition to using quantitative measures of housing demand, they may consider proximity to local business districts, amenities, utilities, and transportation infrastructures (Goldberg 1974; Jackson 1985; Logan and Molotch 1987; Kummerow and Lun 2005). Housing developers, like commercial real estate developers, may also lean heavily on their local relationships to learn more subjective information about local areas (see Kimelberg's (2011) discussion of commercial development processes).

Neighborhood reputation, or the socially constructed "memory" of a community as desirable or undesirable, is a subjective component of developers' decisions. Neighborhood reputation includes perceptions of local amenities and appeal. It also includes the (historical) social status of neighborhood residents—perhaps, especially, their race (Bell 2020a, 2020b; Wells 2018). But developers, like other individuals, do not interpret neighborhood reputation and, in particular, neighborhood racial desirability or appeal in a uniform way. Rather, they interpret and respond to neighborhoods through other cross-cutting factors, such as their own experiences of racial privilege or discrimination and their interactions with home buyers and local residents. Depending on how these factors intersect, developers can interpret the same neighborhood in different ways. They may ultimately move forward with their plans to build new homes or, alternatively, decide to avoid the area altogether.

Choosing White Neighborhoods

The majority of developers in my study approached the task of selecting neighborhoods by recalling their racially coded mental map of Houston and then interpreting specific neighborhoods through the lens of the racist market rubric. That is, developers called to mind specific Houston neighborhoods, imagined local racial composition, then interpreted each area as desirable if White or as undesirable or less desirable if not White.

Developers believed White neighborhoods were the most desirable neighborhoods. They also believed White new home buyers were the most desirable consumers, and that these buyers found White neighborhoods the most desirable. In this way, developers' understandings of White buyers and White neighborhoods reinforced each other. By deciding where to build through this racist market rubric, developers built racism—their own or White buyers'—into the urban landscape. Doing so reinforced neighborhood racial inequality by ensuring that new homes were concentrated within White or increasingly White areas. Moreover, when they did (rarely) build new homes in neighborhoods of color, developers using this approach managed such developments in racialized ways, particularly through their policing of local residents who already lived in these areas.

Jesse, a White, small-time housing developer active in the Heights and Lindale Park neighborhoods, explained how he puts his racially coded mental map of Houston to work through the racist market rubric. He began by describing what made Houston's housing market unique:

> People don't care where they live. That's what's unique about it. People will buy anything anywhere. Since we don't have zoning, buyers cannot be choosy. So it creates this whole different vibe, feel, whatever you want to call it, and it's like anything goes. We don't care about the traffic, we don't care about the sewer system, we don't care about the loss of trees, the quality of life. So yeah, anything goes. And it sucks. And you know, I'm here to make money or I'd live somewhere else.

But, later on in our interview, Jesse explained one way in which he believed his home-buying customers *are* "choosy": They care about who their neighbors will be or who they *think* their neighbors will be, particularly with respect to their future neighbors' racial identity. Jesse then made major decisions about where to build based on his White customers' racial prejudices. He illustrated this in discussing Fifth Ward—a place he would "never" choose to purchase land for residential development:

> I know that I would never purchase anything in Fifth Ward at this point, because I don't know it. I think it's Black. I think it's heavily populated with Hispanics and maybe some Blacks. And my clientele, the people that are going to buy my house, they're not Black or Hispanic. That's the reality. I'm

not discriminating; that is the reality. People who are going to buy my house are typically White.

Although Jesse said he did not "know" Fifth Ward, he did know that the neighborhood was predominantly Black and Latinx.[5] This detail was the one he singled out as key for his where-to-build decision. Jesse believed White home buyers—whom he assumed comprised the possible buyer pool—*would* care that the neighborhood was Black and Latinx, even if they did not really care about train tracks, sewers, or trees. He thought they would care so much that they would simply refuse to purchase a new home in a Black and Latinx area. Jesse then used this belief to justify not building new homes in Fifth Ward. In other words, to make his decisions about where to build, Jesse read his racially coded mental map of Houston through the racist market rubric.

Brad, a White, middle-aged developer and real estate agent active in the predominantly White Heights neighborhood and other White areas, also illustrated this approach. He explained:

BRAD: [The Northside neighborhood]'s a working-class, Hispanic neighborhood. You know, you can get a deal [on land]. But, the truth is there's too much low-income to push out right now. But you can't change the culture in the neighborhood, really, anymore. I'm too conservative to build anything nice in there. [But] the White people will move into a Mexican neighborhood. They will not move into a Black neighborhood. Straight up, it never happens. Um, White people can assimilate with Mexicans because they generally are family-oriented. They generally are religious, they're hard-working. So you can relate to them, you can generally get along with them.

EKG: Why won't White people move into a Black neighborhood?

BRAD: Because it's too much of a cultural difference. Um, it's not safe, generally. Um, they are generally, you know, single parents raising kids that are crazy, because they're just wild animals. I'm just telling you what people— this is perception. Um, and Black people, culturally, they're really tight. And so, they're not gonna assimilate very well with White people. White people need to feel safe. Mexicans, on the other hand, they could move into a Black neighborhood, and kind of stick with their own and not really care.

In this quote, it is clear that Brad was sharing his own opinions about neighborhoods of color as well as his understandings of how White buyers perceive these neighborhoods. Because he perceived neighborhoods of color in racist ways and because he prioritized White buyers and *their* perceptions of these areas, he decided to avoid building new homes in these communities. Brad and other developers believed that the most profitable and least financially risky housing development plan was to build in areas where there would be demand for White buyers: assuredly not in Black neighborhoods, possibly in Latinx neighborhoods, and definitely in White neighborhoods.

Stan, a Hispanic developer and real estate agent active in the Heights and several other White Houston neighborhoods, described his development strategy in a similar manner:

> We're not really allowed to talk about it, but the reality is people—how do I say this tactfully? People won't buy in Black areas. They'll buy in Hispanic areas—you know—reluctantly. And as a business person, I've got to build what people will buy. There are just certain areas you just don't go into. But more what we see is the Hispanic areas get redeveloped. People don't seem to mind as much living around Hispanic families, poor Hispanics, and it's just pure, unadulterated racism. I can't say it's anything other than that. There is degrees of—you know—just flat out racism to others that say, "Well, it's a big investment. It's too risky."

Stan's decisions about where to purchase and redevelop land were influenced by his understandings of Whites ("people") as the most desirable home buyers. Stan believed he had to cater to White buyers' racially prejudiced views of Black and Latinx neighborhoods in order to build a profitable business.

Later on in his interview, Stan also illustrated a view common among the small-to-midsize developers in my study. He and his counterparts believed that until a large Houston-area developer (e.g., Lovett Homes, Perry Homes, or David Weekley Homes) decided to develop multiple tracts of land in a Latinx or Black neighborhood, they could not afford to take what they perceived to be an enormous financial risk by building where they thought White people would not want to buy. Stan, like Jesse, self-identified as a leftist liberal and demonstrated an awareness of racism in housing development. Yet, Stan, Jesse, and Brad (who identified as politically conservative) all made neighborhood development decisions using the racist market rubric.

They believed White neighborhoods had positive reputations and Black and Latinx neighborhoods had negative reputations among White buyers. Then, because they prioritized White new home buyers as the most desirable and because they themselves viewed White areas as more desirable, they decided to develop in White areas and to avoid developing in Black and Latinx communities. Moreover, Stan demonstrated how complicit racism works within the context of housing development. He called out racism in the housing market *and* he engaged in development placement decisions that reified such racism.

Developers' racialized neighborhood perceptions were at times more coded than overt. For example, during his interview, Tony, a Mexican American developer and real estate agent whom I went on to shadow during the next year, used words like "rough" to describe Latinx and Black areas such as Near Northside and Fifth Ward, respectively. To Tony, these areas were places where only a few home-buying "mavericks" and "trailblazers" would buy, making them a risk for a small-to-midsize developer such as him. As we sat together in his office near downtown, Tony pointed to a map of these nearby neighborhoods to discuss his evaluation of their promise for development:

> But if you go back several years I mean this [Near Northside] is [a] pretty rough area. Now not so much, right? Because Hardy [Street] used to be, you don't want to go over there. You know you don't want to be driving around or messing around if you don't know anybody over there. Today it's not like that. I mean, you drive through there and yeah, you're not going to see what's happening in the Heights. But there are signs of development. You have some mavericks, right, some trailblazers that say "Yeah, I'll go over there, I'll live there, I don't mind," you know. You know I can wait until the area changes. Now Fifth Ward has that same um—that same appeal because it's just that close to downtown. Now I think it may take a little bit longer here [in Fifth Ward] than over here [in Near Northside] simply because you really don't want to mess around over here [in Fifth Ward] at night if there's no reason for you to be over there. Um and, you know, that limits the amount of people who are willing to go in there, especially when there are other areas, you know, that are ideal for development.

Although Tony did not explicitly refer to racial categories in his evaluation of these areas, through his coded references to Near Northside and Fifth Ward as rough neighborhoods where "you really don't want to mess around," he made it clear that he believed the number of White people who would be willing to live in these areas was too low to balance the risks of building there. Instead, other White(r) areas were "ideal for development." Throughout my fieldwork, Tony was actively involved in development projects in established White areas (e.g., the Heights) and in neighborhoods with recent rapid increases in the White population.

Tony, Jesse, Stan, and Brad's decisions to build in White neighborhoods animated the broader Houston residential development industry, which disproportionately concentrates new homes in White neighborhoods (Korver-Glenn and Elliott 2016; see also Feagin (1988) on the historic role the Houston development industry played in cementing racial segregation).

Developers' use of the racist market rubric did not stop at the where-to-build decision. Even on the rare occasions they ultimately decided to develop housing in neighborhoods of color, they used the racist market rubric to police residents of their developments as a way to make these developments more desirable to (prospective) White consumers. In my research, this occurred most frequently among developers who built multifamily rental housing in neighborhoods of color. For example, Shawn, a White developer with land holdings throughout Houston, was in the process of developing land in Latinx Near Northside and had recently developed multifamily rental housing in a Black Houston neighborhood.[6] When I asked him about land value differences across the areas, he used coded language to describe the Black neighborhood as dangerous and unkempt, but referred explicitly to Near Northside as Latinx to justify value differences across these areas:

> I think it's just how the communities are and how the people within the communities maintain themselves. I hate to say. You know, this has a lot of political undertones to it. It's how people are but when I drive through the Near Northside, which is predominantly a Hispanic area of town, you can get a feel, you can look at the houses, you can look at the yards, you can look at how things are maintained. Versus if I go into [the Black neighborhood]. And I'll be frank. I mean, just being very open. You know, I watch myself more in [the Black] area than I do in my Near Northside [property]. I have a concealed handgun license and I make sure I always carry my handgun when I'm in [the Black neighborhood].

During his interview, Shawn indicated that he believed Near Northside was "transitioning" and that his development project there would capitalize on that change by bringing in housing consumers who, like him, felt comfortable enough in a predominantly Latinx space. In his view, the Black neighborhood was only profitable in terms of the rent that could be extracted from the already-present Black community—again recycling racist ideas about Black neighborhoods and their residents (see also Rosen 2014). He believed Near Northside was less desirable than White neighborhoods, but it was still more desirable than the Black neighborhood where one of his other rental housing development projects was located.

Shawn's explanation also shows how developers used the logic of the racist market rubric to manage their development projects once they decided where to build. In Shawn's case, he both disparaged what he perceived to be Black tenants' lack of maintenance of the property and characterized the neighborhood's Black residents as violent to justify his hyperpolicing of this development. In reality, the neighborhood in question had a violent crime rate lower than that of the Houston average in 2014.[7] Nevertheless, Shawn actively policed his Black tenants, bringing his gun with him when he visited his rental apartment project.

Ken, a developer of color with many development projects throughout the Houston area, also illustrated how the racist market rubric affected his understanding of neighborhood racial reputation, where-to-build decisions, and the management of development projects. Ken, like most other developers in my study, viewed Black and Latinx neighborhoods as undesirable. But he believed he could make them desirable by attracting and retaining White newcomers, particularly by managing and policing his residential development sites in certain ways. For example, Ken had recently decided to develop a mixed-income, scattered-site residential complex in a Black Houston neighborhood. His perception of the area was that "there's nothing there, lots of beat-up homes," which he contrasted with his planned development: "What we're doing is leased, subsidized housing that is architecturally correct." Ken's rhetorical contrast—which hearkens to other research describing how developers view neighborhoods of color as invisible or obsolete (McFarlane 1999; Seamster 2015)—downplayed the worth of the existing Black neighborhood in order to foreground what Ken believed was a better plan for the neighborhood.

Ken described his plan to manage the development in ways that would make the neighborhood more desirable, and therefore more valuable, to both himself and future White residents:

> Hopefully we'll be having positive activity and we'll be able to attract a better group of tenants. We're going to be a little bit stricter. They'll hopefully take care of their yards, and these tenants will all want to live there. If I have a better pool of tenants, then the market rate people won't mind. They don't mind living next to a secretary that works. The problem with subsidized housing is when people don't go to work, there's ten kids, that kind of situation.

Drawing from racist tropes of Black families, Ken contrasted his perceptions of the neighborhood with what he envisioned would be a "better" pool of subsidized tenants. He and his company would manage these tenants with stricter leasing requirements in hopes of attracting the "market rate people" (i.e., Whites) who would make the area "positive." Together with the other developers in my study and the stark pattern of unequal new home construction that exists across Houston, Ken's narrative laid bare the racist foundation of the housing development industry—in particular, its anti-Black orientation.

Choosing Neighborhoods of Color

The second, more unusual, approach developers took in choosing where to build new homes was to interpret neighborhoods of color through the people-oriented market rubric. These developers, like those who used the racist market rubric, called to mind specific Houston neighborhoods and interpreted them through a racially coded mental map of the city. Yet rather than prioritizing White neighborhoods and White buyers as the most desirable, these developers viewed neighborhoods of color and all prospective home buyers as desirable. They then chose to purchase land and construct new homes in Black and Latinx neighborhoods throughout Houston. They catered to buyers of color as well as White buyers in their development pursuits. Two developers of color in my study used this approach to build profitable real estate development businesses. In doing so, they further exposed the racist rationale behind the economic justification other developers used for avoiding neighborhoods of color—that White buyers were the ones with money and that, without them, it would be too financially risky to invest in Black and Latinx neighborhoods.

Ramon and Pablo, both middle-aged men, actively developed homes in neighborhoods of color throughout Houston. Ramon, a Mexican American developer who began his career in the housing market as a real estate agent selling foreclosed properties in a White neighborhood, eventually became a developer as well. Pablo, a Hispanic developer, began his career as an engineer but then transitioned to managing a residential development company. Both of these developers emphasized the welcoming nature, deservingness, and profitability of neighborhoods of color; that is, they used the people-oriented market rubric to justify and guide their work.

Ramon, for example, became convinced that other real estate professionals ignored or provided poor service to Latinx renters, buyers, and sellers. Unlike most of the other developers I studied, he rejected the racist logic that only White neighborhoods were profitable for residential development purposes. Instead, believing that Latinx communities deserved better service and that he could make more money by establishing a niche with Spanish-speaking Latinx consumers, Ramon got into the real estate development business. He began his career by scouring Latinx communities for highly motivated home sellers—for example, those with a death in the family or who were getting a divorce—and offering them a guarantee to sell within forty-five days, with no fee to be paid if he did not sell the home. Then, he began buying, renovating, and selling properties in these communities. Eventually, he began buying land to develop in these areas, working with a local architect and real estate agent to plan, design, construct, and sell new homes. Over the years, Ramon has (re)developed and sold more than 1,000 homes—almost all in Latinx neighborhoods—by adopting this approach.

Pablo managed a development company somewhat larger than Ramon's outfit. Similar to Ramon, Pablo was aware of neighborhood racial reputations and other developers' consistently negative assumptions about Black and Latinx areas. And, like Ramon, Pablo rejected these racist perceptions and instead emphasized that such communities were desirable for Black, Latinx, and White first-time home buyers. In May 2015, Pablo showed me around a couple of new homes he was building in a Black Houston neighborhood. As we walked up the stairs of a home still under construction, he described how he decided where to build:

Our strategy has always been where there's land, and strong community, and to work with the neighborhood. We buy empty land, and we don't knock on people's doors, because I think that's disrespectful. We noticed that between here and [Camden Street], it seemed like more of a neighborhood feel. And the neighborhood is welcoming.

When I asked him who was buying the new homes his company was building, Pablo replied, "I'd say young, urban professionals, first-time home buyers, many of them moving to the neighborhood for the first time. Although I did have one couple, African American, they bought one, and they're moving back to the area." He then went on to describe the racial identity of the buyers who had most recently purchased newly constructed homes in the immediate area: "For these, we had an African American woman in one, then a Hispanic woman buy another, then three Hispanic men—two were from Colombia—and then one White male." During my fieldwork, Pablo's developments in this one Black neighborhood were so successful that all but one of the newly constructed homes sold prior to their completion. This mirrored the success of his residential development projects in other neighborhoods of color.

Ramon and Pablo understood neighborhood racial reputation in dramatically different ways from many of their counterparts. These two developers viewed Black and Latinx individuals and neighborhoods as welcoming, desirable, and profitable. They thus chose to build new homes in these areas, and in so doing they subverted the assumed logic of White desirability present among the other developers in my study. In addition to adding new housing stock to these areas, Pablo and Ramon also built up local infrastructure. For example, Pablo's company improved a drainage system and repaved part of a street in a Black neighborhood where they were building several new homes. Moreover, Pablo and Ramon profited from their endeavors, building successful businesses that allowed them to accrue wealth and further grow their respective companies. Their reflective choices to develop homes for sale in neighborhoods of color are a sharp foil to the other developers, who portrayed their choices to avoid these neighborhoods as economically necessary or otherwise appropriate responses to White buyer demand and widely shared presumptions of Latinx and, especially, Black neighborhood inferiority. Pablo and Ramon showed that other developers' choices about where to build—and where to *not* build—are not economically necessary. Instead, other developers' choices often unfairly privileged White neighborhoods and consumers while excluding neighborhoods and consumers of color from housing opportunities.

Reverse Blockbusting: Acquiring Land for Development

Once developers decide on the neighborhood(s) where they are going to build, they have to purchase specific plots of land. In urban settings, these plots are sometimes empty, but more frequently, they contain residential or commercial structures. Urban developers often purchase existing homes and then tear them down to make way for new development. Alternately, they may decide to renovate or expand the existing structure(s) when building a new home. Either way, developers working in urban areas often find homes that are already for sale or approach homeowners whose homes are not for sale and try to persuade them to sell.

Housing developers in my study engaged in reverse blockbusting as they attempted to acquire urban land for (re)development. Whether by contacting specific homeowners (in person or via mailers) or placing signs advertising home purchasing services, developers relied on racist ideas about Latinx and Black homeowners as gullible or as having little knowledge of housing market dynamics. They did so because they believed they could purchase these homes for bargain prices—particularly in areas they believed Whites were (increasingly) buying. Their aim was to purchase low, develop the land for White consumption, and sell high.

Reverse blockbusting is a close cousin to what is known as "blockbusting," a now-illegal practice real estate agents used in early and mid-twentieth century American cities. Real estate agents would go door-to-door on city residential blocks, targeting White homeowners and telling them about newcomers, usually new Black residents, to the area. They convinced these homeowners that the presence of residents of color in the area would drive down home values. They also convinced them to sell their homes quickly to avoid catastrophic drops in value. Afraid of what the future would hold, White homeowners sold their homes for bargain prices to these real estate agents, who then turned around and sold these homes for much higher prices to home buyers of color (Garb 2006).

In contrast to this practice from decades past, housing developers in my study targeted homeowners of color, reversing the flow of targeting and property turnover. This reversal constituted what Seamster and

Charron-Chénier (2017) and Taylor (2019) have called "predatory inclusion," or the "process whereby members of a marginalized group are provided with access to a good, service, or opportunity from which they have historically been excluded but under conditions that jeopardize the benefits of access" (Seamster and Charron-Chénier 2017:199–200). Developers in my study did not bank on homeowners' racist fears, as did their real estate agent counterparts in the era before fair housing laws. Rather, they assumed these homeowners would be the least likely to understand housing market dynamics and would be the most likely to be in a precarious economic position that would motivate them to sell their homes at a below-market price. What blockbusting and reverse blockbusting have in common is that they both rely on racist ideas that relegate individuals of color to the lowest rungs of the social hierarchy and do so in order to extract wealth.

For example, in my fieldwork with Mateo, a Latino developer and real estate agent, I found that he strategically used his co-ethnic and co-linguistic status to persuade Latinx homeowners who lived in White areas to sell him their homes at bargain prices. One day after visiting a local flooring supplier, Mateo and I sat debriefing in the lobby of a high-rise condo in Houston's Galleria/Uptown district. As we chatted, Mateo told me that when he immigrated to the United States, his parents were afraid that he would experience discrimination, but this had not happened even though he had lived in predominantly White areas. As we ended our conversation, which had touched on topics related to race and discrimination in his own personal history, Mateo lit up a cigarette and I asked him when he wanted me to get in touch next. He replied, "Actually, I'm going to negotiate a deal on [Bravo] Street tomorrow." "Can I come?" I asked. "Actually," he laughed,

> because of what we were just talking about, no [you can't come], because it's a sweet old Hispanic lady. Why? Because she only wants to sell to other Latinos? Because she's afraid you'll take advantage of her? I mean, I'm not gonna wear this [pointing to his expensive, tailored suit], I'm gonna wear jeans or something, too.

In contrast to Pablo, who believed that knocking on homeowners' doors to ask them to sell their property was "disrespectful," Mateo actively went to Latinx individuals' homes to persuade them to sell. And, he did not allow me to observe his attempt to connect with this specific Latina homeowner, whom he planned to meet wearing jeans rather than his usual tailored dress pants. In his view, having me (a White person) tag along might make the prospective home seller suspicious she was being taken advantage of, and thus less likely to sell her home for the amount Mateo proposed.

Brad lacked Mateo's cultural and symbolic capital, but he similarly targeted Latinx homeowners in White areas to find homes at bargain prices that he could tear down to make room for new development. When I asked Brad about why Latinx individuals were moving out of the Heights neighborhood, he explained, "Because they get bought-out, right? I mean, I buy houses every day from Hispanics. They move somewhere else, we take their property, destroy it, and build a house for a rich White family to move in." When I asked him where he thought the Latinx families moved, he first said he did not know, but then he guessed they moved to Katy, Texas (a large Houston suburb). He then rationalized his strategy of targeting Latinx homeowners for land acquisition by positing that these families had made "good money" and could move to the suburbs:

> They'll just move out to the suburbs, or Katy. I mean, they make good money. Usually their properties are paid for, and they make $300,000 to $400,000 to go buy a really nice house in Katy. So they can get out of their two-bedroom-bath bungalow that's falling down.

Apparently, it did not occur to Brad—who was also active as a licensed real estate agent and had at least one real estate agent working for him—to represent these Latinx families when they purchased $300,000 to $400,000 homes in Houston's suburbs. Developers' choices, including those regarding reverse blockbusting, were about maintaining a *racial*-economic order and not just maximizing economic efficiency.

In addition to contacting Latinx homeowners in person, developers sometimes made contact by mailing letters and flyers advertising services to specific homeowners. Mateo, for example, kept the form letter depicted in Figure 2.1 in his files. In addition to providing details about two options for selling the home, the letter reflected Mateo's desire to build a sense of shared purpose with prospective Latinx sellers, which he emphasized by including his name[8] and personal cell phone number (not pictured) at the bottom of the letter.

In addition to mailing form letters to targeted homeowners, developers also mailed or hand-delivered brightly colored flyers. These flyers displayed developers' phone numbers and often included such sales pitches as "We pay

Dear Homeowner,

I'm sure you're tired of getting letters from investors and builders, asking you to sell them your property. These letters probably do not offer you what you think your house is worth.

<u>I know that is probably frustrating.</u>

So, I want to offer you the opportunity to sell your house at a price you think is reasonable, with the chance to make an additional profit once your house has been rehabilitated to sell at a higher price.

Here are two options I'd like to extend you:

Option 1: You sell your house to me for **$270 per square foot**, for a total price of **$297,000** (for your 1100 square foot house). This is higher than what you would receive if you put your house on the market right now.

Option 2: You sell your house to me for **$225 per square foot**, for a total price of **$247,500** (for your 1100 square foot house). Then, as part of your buyer contract, I will agree to pay you **10% of the price I receive when I sell your renovated house.** For example, if the renovated house sells for $500,000, I would pay you $50,000. If it sells for $600,000, you would receive $60,000, and so on. In this market, I would expect your renovated home to sell for around $550,000, giving you a profit of $55,000 in addition to the $247,500 I pay you for the home initially.

If you are interested in either of these incredible offers, please act now by calling or texting me at the number listed below.

I welcome any questions you have and look forward to working with you!

Sincerely,

Mateo Alfaro, Broker

Figure 2.1 Form letter for obtaining property for housing development.
Source: Mateo Alfaro, Developer. (Note that "Mateo Alfaro" is a pseudonym and I have removed from view the cell phone number Mateo placed at the bottom of each letter.)

cash for houses!!!" Figure 2.2 illustrates one such flyer mailed to residents in the Latinx Near Northside neighborhood.

Besides approaching Latinx or other homeowners of color, other strategies for targeting these populations included placing informal, often handwritten, signs in Latinx and Black areas. These signs were scattered throughout Lindale Park, Near Northside, Fifth Ward, and other Black and Latinx neighborhoods. Some developers had placed such signs in areas with a large presence of residents of color that were adjacent to White neighborhoods, such as the Brooke Smith area near the Heights. These signs often stated something along the lines of "We Buy Houses—Any Condition"

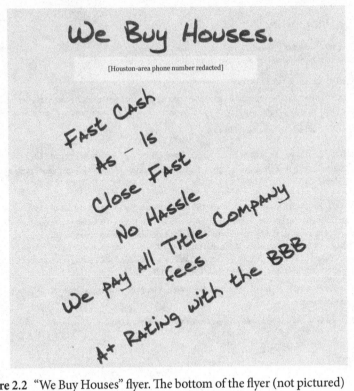

Figure 2.2 "We Buy Houses" flyer. The bottom of the flyer (not pictured) included the developer's business name and address.

(often in English on one side and Spanish on the other), followed by a local phone number (Figure 2.3).

Tony described these informal signs as signals of off-the-market transactions between local liaisons, investors, and developers that would become a "grassroots effort" to obtain homes in these areas at a low cost to later sell high. During his interview, Tony explained:

> You may not see a lot on the market but, you know, you got people over there. I mean if you drive through you see signs, "we buy houses," stuff like that, and a lot of that is the precursor of—you got guys that have contacts with investors, developers, and that's the way that they go in. That's kind of like the grass roots effort. You know you have somebody that lives there and it's like, "Hey I need to sell my house," they see the sign, they call. That's how it works. Or they get a letter in the mail and it's like, you know, most

Figure 2.3 Handmade sign, "Compramos Casas" ("We Buy Houses"), in Northside, Houston.
Source: Photograph by Elizabeth Korver-Glenn.

times they throw it away but you get that right person that's like, "Hey, you know I owe two years' worth of taxes." That's what happens in these areas [of color].

Although Tony did not create and scatter handmade signs, he did have one of his assistants regularly send out form letters to specific homeowners in communities of color and those with tax delinquencies, as did Mateo. Occasionally, when I stopped by his office, there were stacks of envelopes—hand addressed by his assistant Meg to provide a personal touch—stuffed with these letters, waiting to be stamped and mailed out. One such day, Meg and I watched as Tony used the HAR.com website to search for potential land to (re)develop in a Latinx neighborhood. He explained, "From a development perspective, you can look at the homes around . . . and figure out where you're going to build. If you want to know more about the property, you can go to HCAD [Harris County Appraisal District]." To illustrate, Tony then went to HCAD's website to search for a specific property within the neighborhood, typed in the property's address, and viewed the results, which indicated the property was an "estate." Tony then opened a new tab and typed the property's address into Google Street View. Meg, looking over Tony's shoulder, noted, "That's why it's so run-down, because it's in an estate." As Tony perused both the HCAD and Google Street View information, he called out, "Hey, Meg, send these people a letter." "I've already got it written down," she responded.

If not licensed real estate agents themselves (Brad, Tony, and Mateo all held real estate licenses), housing developers often hired and worked closely with real estate agents or other local stakeholders who assisted them in purchasing specific homes for redevelopment and selling newly constructed homes. These stakeholders understood that developers targeted specific homeowners for their housing development plans, and at times connected such targeting back to racist ideas about Latinx and Black people.

I shadowed Jay, a White real estate agent, during my year of fieldwork. In addition to working in suburban areas of Houston, Jay represented buyers and sellers in urban areas where housing development, at least on a small scale, was somewhat common, including the Near Northside, Heights, and Eado ("East Downtown") neighborhoods. One day, I met him in the Montrose neighborhood at the local brokerage where he based his work. As we sat chatting in the small conference room, catching up and debriefing about recent events tied to a Near Northside property he had listed for a Latinx homeowner, Jay interjected with an explanation of his understanding of the development process:

> These [Latinx] folks are living hand to mouth. They don't have a mortgage, so they have no escrow. But when they get their new [tax] bill next year and it's $5,000 instead of $3,000, it's going to be difficult to pay that. [Developers are] working on this demographic that's vulnerable to that.

Jay then clarified his understanding of predatory development tactics even further, explaining,

> One of my fears for [Near Northside] is that the families won't pay their taxes, and they'll get a lien from a predator [developer], who will sit on eight properties on the block and then tell them, "Get out." I think, you know, "You need to get your kids to work, they don't need to drive around in that nice car."

At the same time that Jay expressed fears that Latinx homeowners were being targeted by predatory developers searching for a bargain, he deployed racist tropes about Latinx homeowners. He believed these homeowners were poor *and* that they wasted money on unnecessary commodities such as "nice" cars for their children.

Another example of how other involved stakeholders understood and influenced reverse blockbusting emerged during an August 2015 meeting between Casey, a Black developer informant working in a predominantly Black

Houston neighborhood, and Rob, a White planning consultant. During the meeting, held at Casey's office, Rob repeatedly emphasized Casey's need for a better, more concrete plan to acquire land for housing development moving forward. His advice was to use Casey's local knowledge of the neighborhood to "hold on to land, target particular areas, before speculation [by other developers] happens." At the same time, he recommended bringing in an outside consultant who would help implement this plan, moving forward in acquiring land from a list of specific properties they had already created. It was important to hire this outside person soon, he said, because "we need to get that land now, so that we can sell it privately at a nice profit. We need someone [to do the plan] that isn't tied to race, class, socioeconomic status *baggage*." In other words, Rob was proposing that because of his and Casey's local ties—specifically, the "baggage" of their interracial, intraracial, and interclass dynamics and relationships—none of those present in the room could themselves target the Black homeowners on the list. Instead, an outside person would be better positioned to take what he viewed as a necessary step in making development profitable: acquiring property at a low price in order to sell high, exploiting Black homeowners in the process.

Building Race and Racism into Urban Landscapes

Housing developers often built race into the urban landscape by first assuming that White neighborhoods and home buyers were the most desirable and then choosing to build new homes in White neighborhoods for White buyers. In other words, they read their racially coded mental maps of Houston according to the logic of the racist market rubric, rationalizing their active neighborhood choices as an economically necessary and appropriate response to White buyer demand. These developers actively build a racist housing market by prioritizing White spaces and White people. Yet Pablo's and Ramon's development practices and experiences exposed and denaturalized this racist-economic logic by pursuing equitable, people-affirming development strategies. They prioritized neighborhoods of color and residents in those neighborhoods, whom they interpreted through the people-oriented market rubric. And, their developments were profitable.

Developers also used the racist market rubric when they engaged in reverse blockbusting. They used racist ideas about Black and Latinx homeowners to justify targeting these residents, offering to purchase their homes for below-market prices with the goal of redeveloping and selling high to White buyers. (Note that although some of the reverse blockbusting I observed occurred in lower income or working-class communities of color such as Near Northside, some also occurred in working- and middle-class neighborhoods of color, including Lindale Park. This suggests reverse blockbusting is not simply a mechanism of gentrification; it is also a tool for making neighborhoods White(r) regardless of their socioeconomic status.) In doing so, developers illustrated how the buying, selling, and (re)development of land and homes incorporated homeowners of color into the housing market in predatory ways—ways "*fundamentally* distorted by racism" (Taylor 2019:8, italics in original).

Developers' choices about where to build and who to target for land acquisition have significant implications for the processes that help prop up racial segregation and neighborhood racial inequality. First, most developers I studied, especially those who identified as White, made conscious decisions to cater to White buyers and chose to develop homes in White areas (or areas to which Whites were increasingly moving). Their decisions animated the broader landscape of racially unequal residential development in Houston, in which new homes are built at systematically higher rates in White neighborhoods than in otherwise comparable neighborhoods of color (Korver-Glenn and Elliott 2016). Their choices matter for real outcomes, such as local home values. The more new homes there are in an area, for example, the higher the home values in that area will be (Howell and Korver-Glenn 2018). By choosing to concentrate new home construction in White neighborhoods, developers thus directly contributed to ongoing differences in home value and wealth accumulation between White neighborhoods and neighborhoods of color. Through their building choices, they created the market they imagined.

It was not only White real estate developers who behaved this way. Several developers who identified as people of color used components of the racist market rubric to select neighborhoods and target homeowners of color. Their choices to view White neighborhoods and home buyers as most desirable were not simply cases of internalized racism—that is, racism that racially oppressed people have (unintentionally) accepted or adopted in how they view themselves and other racially oppressed people.[9] Instead, these developers made their choices at the intersections of White racism and unequal economic opportunity. To the extent that White consumers are socially and economically invested in Whiteness and demonstrate this investment by seeking out homes in White neighborhoods, developers, regardless of their own race, can generate economic profit from White buyers' racist prejudices. These developers, like their White counterparts, can also profit from the racialized system of valuation that hypervalues homes in White areas (see Chapter 5; Howell and Korver-Glenn 2018; Thomas et al. 2018). This quest for profit can subject developers who identify as people of color to discrimination in White spaces during the development process. For example, a prominent White architect refused to work with Tony on a development project in a White neighborhood. Tony was also profiled by police when he reported a break-in at one of his properties, still under construction and located in a White neighborhood. Yet Tony still profited from developing homes in this White area, where new home values were consistently higher than in many of Houston's neighborhoods of color. Whether or not housing developers of color directly experience the constraints of White prejudice as Tony did, they can still profit from the structural racism that re-creates economic advantage within White spaces (see Harris 1993).

A second key implication of my findings is that developers' policing of residents in neighborhoods of color and reverse blockbusting can contribute to gentrification and neighborhood racial turnover. Even when developers decided to build homes in neighborhoods of color, they policed or micromanaged local residents of color, whether because of their own fears or because they wanted to make the neighborhood more attractive for White residents. Such behavior demeans and antagonizes residents of color, perhaps prompting them to move elsewhere. Furthermore, developers engaged in reverse blockbusting in both lower income and middle-class neighborhoods of color, which could help explain how rapid socioeconomic and racial turnover occurs (see Rucks-Ahidiana (forthcoming) for more on neighborhood race and class differences in gentrification processes). Some of the developers I studied, including Shawn and Ken, did not avoid neighborhoods of color altogether but, rather, exploited them for the explicit purposes of extracting rent from residents of color or by attracting White residents to live there.

Taken together, housing developers' choices about where to build and whom to target for land acquisition reinforce racial inequality for both individuals and neighborhoods from the very beginning stages of the housing exchange process. Every home has a beginning, and at least in Houston, developers build new homes on racist foundations.

3

Brokering Sales

Once homes are built, they are bought and sold on the housing market. American home buyers purchase hundreds of thousands of new homes and millions of existing homes each year. Between February 2015 and January 2016, the period that overlaps with my study, almost 5.5 million existing homes were bought and sold in the United States.[1] During the same period, more than 64,000 existing homes were sold in Houston.[2] But home buyers and sellers do not typically strike out on their own when it comes to marketing or finding their homes. Rather, real estate agents facilitate the vast majority of these home sale transactions.

Whether representing home sellers or buyers, real estate agents occupy center stage in home sales (Besbris 2016, 2020). Of all housing market professionals, they spend the most time with home buyers and sellers. Among other activities, listing agents provide assistance and advice to home sellers. Such help includes counseling sellers on how to best "stage" their home or prepare it for sale. These agents take photos and prepare descriptions of the home and then post these photos and descriptions on the Multiple Listing Service (MLS) when they list the home for sale. They host open houses and send information about the home to other agents and housing consumers they know. Listing agents sometimes advertise the for-sale home on flyers or mailers that they send to people in their networks. They may even post their listings on social media, using apps such as Facebook and Instagram to generate interest. Buyer's agents (who are sometimes also listing agents) provide assistance and advice to home buyers. They help buyers locate homes that fit or exceed their budgets and connect buyers to other housing professionals, including contractors, inspectors, and mortgage bankers (Besbris 2020). Buyer's agents accompany home buyers to open houses, make appointments for buyers to see for-sale homes and show them these homes, negotiate on behalf of buyers, and offer buyers moral support through the close of the transaction.

Real estate agents learn the best routines for buying and selling real estate from other agents, real estate brokers, and housing market professionals as

Race Brokers. Elizabeth Korver-Glenn, Oxford University Press (2021). © Oxford University Press.
DOI: 10.1093/oso/9780190063863.003.0004

well as from their occupational organizations, including brokerages and real estate boards. Unlike housing developers, who do not need to possess a license or work with someone who does, agents must have a real estate license and work under a real estate broker (often in a real estate brokerage company). Or, they must have their own real estate broker license, a credential that requires more education, certification, and experience than a standard real estate license. Brokers are responsible for training agents and reviewing and approving their transactions. Although agents are not required to become members of local or national real estate organizations, they frequently join local real estate boards in order to access the MLS or participate in national organizations, such as the National Association of Realtors (NAR).[3] Real estate brokerages, boards, and organizations shape agents' practices and enhance agent authority and legitimacy through professional licensure; networking opportunities; continuing education and certifications; and access to legal counsel, among other resources.[4]

In my study, real estate brokerages, boards, and other related organizations pressured or encouraged agents to become economically successful through networking, percentage-based commissions, marketing, and risk management routines. Most agents I studied adopted these organizational routines. But agents also had the ability to adopt routines that fell outside of organizational pressures, including not listing homes for sale in a public forum such as the MLS. On this particular routine, Houston-area real estate organizations were silent.

At first blush, these organizational routines may seem race-neutral, as though pressuring agents to pursue particular strategies or remaining silent when they chose alternate routes did not involve racism. But in practice, the real estate agents I studied interpreted organizational pressures through either the racist market rubric or the people-oriented market rubric. And they interpreted organizational silence on certain alternate marketing techniques as approval, creating racialized flows of housing opportunity in the process. Thus, when they followed brokerage expectations and viewed networking and the percentage-based commission as the best ways to generate profit, they adhered to the belief that they should cultivate *networks of value*. How they interpreted value, and how they accomplished their jobs through networking, depended on whether they interpreted clients and prospective clients through the racist or the people-oriented market rubric. When they advertised homes on the local real estate board's MLS, the MLS software automatically assigned individual homes to market areas that dramatically diverged along racial lines. When they gauged whether prospective clients were low risk or high risk, they often drew on the racist market rubric, making snap judgments about whether a prospective client was putting them in physical danger or would simply be a waste of time. And, when White agents chose not to advertise on the MLS and instead used *pocket listings*— that is, homes marketed via word-of-mouth instead of public channels— they funneled knowledge about for-sale homes to their White networks, excluding buyers and agents of color from accessing these homes.

Real estate agents facilitate millions of home sale transactions every year. How they do so—the subject of this chapter—has significant import for persistent housing inequality and racial segregation.

Cultivating Networks of Value

From the national organizational leader in real estate brokerage to large brokerage franchises and local brokerage firms, the real estate organizations I encountered in my study encouraged agents to generate business through their social networks. Through online, hard copy, and face-to-face training, such organizations urged agents to cultivate their networks through mining their "sphere of influence" and to build their influence through community participation. For example, in an online training module, NAR emphasized that interacting face-to-face and networking were more likely to be profitable than print or online advertising:

> While your print and online advertising communicate your marketing message powerfully, you can make a better case personally for your skills and ability to represent prospects. Remember not to forego community events or other neighborhood involvement—where you can meet prospects in person. Those activities are vital components of a business plan that puts you in front of potential customers.[5]

Houston-area brokerages also urged their agents to recruit clients through networking:

> Expanding the quality and quantity of your personal "sphere of influence" *for business* is *the most* important factor to generating income. It's all about prospecting. . . . You are building your own book of business that will grow

through repeat business and referrals—it takes time, effort and patience! [Italics in original][6]

Real estate agents in my study adopted the networking approach that their brokerages and other real estate organizations encouraged. Indeed, most of them fiercely advocated for this practice: They professed a belief that they *had* to build their businesses through their social networks to become economically successful. Whether new to the profession or experienced, real estate agents reported that it was the people within their own personal social networks, client referrals, and repeat clients that accounted for the majority of their business. Almost all of the agents I interviewed or shadowed reported that at least 50 percent of their business came through referrals or repeat clients, and more than half reported that at least 70 percent of their business came through referrals or repeats (Korver-Glenn 2018a).[7]

In addition to urging social networking, real estate brokerages maintained another key policy that remained informal and unwritten: percentage-based commission. Although it is illegal for groups of realtors to formalize a fixed percent at which real estate agents are to be paid, real estate brokers and brokerages often set the commission through in-house conversations and through policing agent behavior. Agents who deviate or think about deviating from the local rate are called out.[8] In practice, agents were routinely paid and expected to be paid a percentage of the home's sale price in return for their services. They also made sure that other agents conformed to brokerage commission expectations. The commission rate in the United States is typically 5–7 percent of the sold home's price, which is then usually split 50–50 between the buyer's agent and the listing agent. Each agent then pays a cut of their earnings to their respective brokerage, although the amount of this cut varies across brokerages.

Almost all of the agents I studied adopted the percentage-based commission standard, regardless of their race. Several were zealously committed to the Houston-standard 6 percent commission. For example, one day Michael, a middle-aged White real estate agent and informant, told me about another agent at his brokerage who had broken with the commission standard. This agent had recently convinced a builder to use him as the listing agent for a new home in a development. As Michael drove me to a large, expensive home he had just listed in the White Heights neighborhood, he said, "[That agent]'s a real douche bag. I made a big stink about him at [my brokerage], because how he got the [home] listing was he went and reduced his commission."[9]

Michael reported the other agent's behavior to his broker, confident that his broker would censure the agent and prevent him from reducing his commission again.

Jane, a middle-aged White real estate broker and informant, also policed the commission of the agents who worked under her supervision. During a visit to her brokerage one afternoon, Jane explained to me that I had just missed a visit from one of her agents, who had come to her for advice. As I got out my notebook and sat down in an empty chair near Jane's desk, she explained:

JANE: Yeah, an agent of ours just came in. She had some clients come in right before closing and they tried to strong-arm her into giving back $1,000 of her commission . . .
EKG: Wow! Was she afraid she'll lose the deal if she doesn't give it to them?
JANE: No, I think she was more afraid in terms of the future impact, as in no referrals from them. But I told her, "These are not the people you want referrals from. These are people you say, 'Bye-bye, have a nice life.'"

Jane believed that maintaining the standard commission rate—and finding clients who would pay the full commission—was more important than this one transaction. Indeed, in Jane's view, it was important to find the kind of people who would *not* attempt to negotiate the commission and *would* provide future referrals to others who would also pay full price.

Other agents also defended the local 6 percent commission rate. Although perhaps they were less zealous than either Michael or Jane, they still worked to replicate the percentage-based commission norm. For example, when I interviewed Jeanette, a middle-aged Black real estate agent, she staunchly defended the percentage-based commission:

But on the listing side—you know—you want to be able to provide a great service to your client. And depending on what kind of home or establishment you have, you want to be able to market it so it can get sold. But when you have those different little flat rates, it makes it hard when you're a buyer's agent. Because when you get in and see 2 percent on that listing, that that's what you're going to get, it's really hard because—you know—we're doing the best job that we can, and it's a job. And other agents that want it discounted, whatever, it's a disservice to other agents because we do work hard. We don't just collect a check. We go through the first step explaining, educating. And, I mean, I've taken calls ten, eleven o'clock at night from clients where they have a question or whatever the issue is. I'm not saying I want to be available every night at ten or eleven, but I want to make it where if they have a question, hey, I'm going to call them back or let them know. But it makes it hard when they say 2 percent to the buyer's agent and that's all you're getting.

In Jeanette's view, flat fee or discount brokers made work difficult for the agent working the other side of the deal. Jeanette argued that "discounted" commissions limited her ability to devote resources for marketing and devalued the time agents spent with clients—in her case, working with them after hours, late at night, and over the phone. Jeanette and other agents expressed a desire to avoid working with agents who gave "discounted" service. Such ostracism was another way that Houston agents pressured or attempted to pressure other agents to stick to the widely accepted 6 percent rate.

Encouraged or pressured by their brokerages and other real estate agents, the agents I studied tended to adopt both social networking and percentage-based commissions as the ideal way to become good, economically successful real estate agents. On their own, these routines appeared to be race-neutral—ostensibly not racist or not related to sustained housing inequality or racial segregation. But in reality, agents merged these two organizational routines in ways that inadvertently or intentionally allowed overt and color-blind racist ideas to influence how they finessed and maintained their networks.

Finessing Networks of Value

Agents' approach to social networking operated in tandem with the percentage-based commission.[10] Together, these organizational routines pressured real estate agents to finesse *networks of value*—that is, to network with the clients who they believed would produce the most income with the fewest number of headaches. In practice, almost all the White agents in my study understood prospective clients' value in part or wholly through the racist market rubric. That is, because White agents viewed networking as key to economic success and because they were paid a percentage of a home's sale price, they attempted to work with White clients. They did so because they believed Whites were "high value." From their perspective, White individuals had more money to spend, their homes were worth more, they were more educated about the home-buying or -selling process, and they ultimately would bring the least amount of trouble to a transaction. Furthermore, White agents believed their White clients would refer them to other White clients and assumed these other White clients would also be "high value." At the same time, White real estate agents assumed buyers and sellers of color were lower income or had bad credit, would require more work to educate, had poorly maintained and low-value homes, or would expect them to reduce the commission. White agents believed that clients of color would ultimately bring with them problems that the agents did not want to handle. These agents also thought that clients of color would refer them to other clients of color, whom they also assumed would share these characteristics. For all of these reasons, White agents avoided networking with prospective clients of color. In short, White agents finessed their networks of value through the racist market rubric.

Frank, a late middle-aged White agent and broker, explained these common racial beliefs as the "pecking order" within real estate brokerage. In his words,

> The Hispanics can afford a little more than the Blacks can afford. Okay. I've found that, um, credit worthiness, you know, in a pecking order. . . . It seems like, you know, it's the Asians, Caucasians, it's the Hispanics and the Blacks. If you wanted to do it, you know, in that order of educational situations and, really, their ability to purchase.

White agents applied this racist market rubric to their networking routines. One day I waited with David, a White middle-aged associate broker working in Jane's brokerage, as Jane made a few phone calls. As we waited, David told me more about the brokerage's approach to networking. He emphasized that they did *not* finesse their networks around race. At the same time, he used racist ideas to explain how they finessed their networks. David said that real estate agents do not attempt to network with residents of Black and Latinx neighborhoods such as Fifth Ward, Third Ward, and Near Northside and, instead, actively exclude these individuals from their networks

> not because of ethnicity, you know why that is? Price. You have to do 15 percent more work, for houses under $200,000. The people over there aren't qualified [for mortgages], their houses haven't been maintained, and it's just a headache. A $1 million house is a different type of work, but

you know that it won't take three contracts to get it to stick. It's just sheer remuneration. I'll give you an example. This lady called not too long ago and wanted to look at a house in Third Ward. She said she had a good job and everything. I asked her if she was [pre-]qualified, and she said no, and I explained that she needed to talk to a lender to find out what she would be pre-qualified for, and that I would send her a list of lenders, and then she got all defensive! I mean I'll show her the house because it could result in a sale. But I know she's not qualified. And it's not because of race, it's because she doesn't know anything about the process, doesn't know about property taxes, and so on.

David said their exclusionary networking routine was not about "ethnicity" but, rather, about price. At the same time, David assumed that prices were lower in neighborhoods of color and did not bother to check the actual prices of homes in these areas. He also assumed buyers of color would not qualify for mortgages and would be uneducated about the home-buying or -selling process, thus bringing with them more "headaches." When interacting with this prospective buyer, he expressed such a view despite her protests and insistence on her economic stability and ability to purchase a home. Indeed, the woman's defensiveness suggests that she understood David's remarks as thinly veiled racism.

David's comments were emblematic of how White real estate agents used the racist market rubric to interpret prospective Black and Latinx clients. They believed these home buyers and sellers were "low value" and avoided seeking out their business. That is, White agents believed prospective clients of color had less money to spend or had homes that were worth little money *and* that these consumers would bring with them problems that agents did not care to address or solve. Even as David denied that race had anything to do with the brokerage firm's networking routine, he explained that he and Jane do not seek out Black and Latinx clients precisely because of these racist assumptions.

Grady, another White real estate agent, told me that at least 80 percent of his clients were White because, as he explained, they were highly educated and had more money to spend on more expensive homes. By contrast, in describing consumers of color, he had this to say:

There's a lack of education for lower income people. And there's entitlement reform where your reform needs to happen because people, in my opinion, they're not—there's no drive for them: "Why go work at McDonald's when I make the same or more by not working at all?" I don't know. There's just a lot wrong with the country. And there's a lot good about the country, too. It's a great country—best country in the world. So, I guess it's hard to get it all right. I don't think it's racially driven or ethnically driven at all. I think it's all dependent upon your education level. Because, if you have a higher education, you can afford more and you buy more, you want more for your kids and that's where you end up.

Grady immediately assumed Black and Latinx individuals were low-income and had little education. By doing so, he illustrated a rhetorical move common within color-blind discourse—to emphasize other assumed social or cultural traits of groups of color to explain some aspect of inequality (Bonilla-Silva 2006). In addition, he drew on a well-established—and false—racialized trope surrounding welfare dependency to describe individuals of color as unmotivated to become socially mobile. Enabled by the organizational pressure to cultivate and finesse networks of value, Grady and other White agents used these racist ideas to justify pursuing White clients and avoiding Black and Latinx clients.

White agents also finessed their networks by avoiding prospective Asian clients. Although White agents tended to agree that Asian clients were wealthy or had money (e.g., Frank's "pecking order"), they still avoided networking with them. White agents avoided Asian clients because they believed these consumers would pressure them to reduce their expected pay (i.e., their percentage-based commission) or would otherwise waste their time. During her interview, Kate, a White real estate agent in her thirties, explained:

> I believe I've heard that they've—I don't know if it's just Chinese or if it's Asian where it comes from. But they expect that you drop the commission lower, so therefore they're not having to pay it. So they'll blatantly ask you that you lower your commission.

Kate continued her narrative by explaining that White real estate agents avoided Asian clients because of these stereotypes.

Thus, even when White agents perceived a racial group of color as having monetary value—in this case a group they broadly categorized as "Asian"—they relied on other stereotypes drawn from the racist market rubric to finesse their networks. White agents in particular viewed White consumers as unilaterally high value, in terms of both their monetary worth and their intangible or intrinsic worth. In these ways, White agents shaped their networks toward White consumers and away from consumers of color.

Like White real estate agents, most Black and Latinx real estate agents also defended and relied on networking and the percentage-based commission to become economically successful. In contrast to White agents, however, agents of color deployed the people-oriented market rubric when evaluating prospective clients of color. They upheld the social, cultural, and economic value of people of color, which they juxtaposed with the racial discrimination they and their clients had experienced from White professionals and consumers (see Clergé 2019; Jung 2015). At the same time, agents of color perceived White consumers as high value and attempted to network with them. Accordingly, they attempted to network with home-buying and -selling consumers of color as well as White home-buying and -selling consumers, and many built thriving real estate businesses doing so. Moreover, Black and Latinx agents occasionally departed from the percentage-based commission norm.[11] They did so to carve out competitive niches among consumers of color that White agents did not control and to enable underserved buyers of color to access homeownership opportunities from which they had previously been locked out.

Kevin, a middle-aged Black real estate agent I observed during my year of ethnographic research, was active across the Houston metropolitan area. He networked with Black, Latinx, and White clients who ranged from lower middle class to wealthy, taking advantage of his relatively racially and socioeconomically diverse church and his connections with for-profit and nonprofit housing developers to do so. When I interacted with him during fieldwork, Kevin repeatedly emphasized, "To me, it's not about the commission. It's about the people." Unlike most White agents I studied, Kevin perceived cultural and symbolic value in clients even when he did not see monetary value. His beliefs about prospective clients prompted him to finesse his networks in a much more expansive way than did his White counterparts.

Ramon, the Hispanic developer introduced in Chapter 2, was also a licensed real estate agent who had previously spent most of his time on the real estate brokerage side of the business. He explained that he had become a licensed real estate agent in order to service a largely Spanish-speaking clientele—people he believed had been underserviced and neglected by other real estate agents. Ramon said that his approach had been to charge a flat fee (rather than a percentage-based commission) and guarantee fast results to his clients. One day, as we waited for a city inspector to arrive at one of Ramon's newly constructed homes, Ramon explained his approach in more detail:

> But what I would do is I would target highly motivated sellers: people going through a divorce, people with a death in the family. And I would tell them, I'll take forty-five days to sell your home for $60,000, all based on a handshake, they haven't signed anything. If they decided they wanted me to sell, I would say, "Okay, my fee is $6,000," there would be no percentage. Then I would go out and match private lenders with the house. But I would make it happen.

Ramon's deal with his home sellers was that they did not have to pay him a dime if he did not provide a buyer within forty-five days of listing the home. Then, once they had agreed to the terms, Ramon worked aggressively on behalf of these sellers, whom other real estate agents had largely ignored or poorly serviced. To receive high-quality service, the sellers in the example Ramon provided actually paid him substantially more than the going percentage-based commission rate and were very happy with the service he provided. These sellers recommended Ramon to their networks because he delivered high-quality service, time after time.

Like Ramon, Candace, a middle-aged Black real estate agent active in Fifth Ward and other areas of metropolitan Houston, regularly departed from the standard 6 percent commission model adopted by almost all of her peers. Like Kevin, Candace explained this flexibility in terms of her desire to assist her clients—people she knew would otherwise be marginalized. During her interview, held at her brokerage in suburban Houston, she explained:

> If I've known you for years, I might say, "I'll sell it for a dollar." It depends on the rapport you have. And then each case is case-by-case, but we don't have a set rate. Everybody here charges 6 percent, of course. Sometimes I may go 4 percent, 5 percent if I have a buyer that's marginal, I'll give in. We're not supposed to, but I do, because I'm a social worker at heart. I want people to get into their homes. I want to put a family into a home, so sometimes I have to bite the bullet.

Candace, Ramon, Kevin, and other real estate agents of color intentionally networked with consumers of color because they perceived these buyers and sellers as economically, culturally, and symbolically valuable. Although agents of color often viewed White consumers as high value, their shared experiences and awareness of housing market exclusion and discrimination also shaped how they understood value and finessed their networks. Unlike White agents, who assumed that *only* White prospective clients were high value, agents of color saw both monetary and social value in cultivating diverse client networks.

Maintaining Networks of Value

Networks, once established, must be maintained. Agents maintained their networks by demonstrating their clients could trust them. To inspire trust, real estate agents offered information or opinions about local schools and neighborhood racial composition to familiar clients and tolerated or anticipated their clients' racial prejudices or preferences. In particular, White agents accommodated and anticipated their White clients' racial prejudices, or negative bias against non-White groups, when they were in one-on-one or all-White spaces (see Korver-Glenn 2018b; Krysan 2008; Picca and Feagin 2007). Agents of color sometimes accommodated their clients' racial preferences—that is, the desire to be around racially similar others—but they did not report experiences with clients who expressed prejudice against other racial groups.

One example of how White agents secured trust with their White clients emerged during my interview with Grady. When I asked Grady to explain the relationship between schools and housing and how consumers evaluate school quality, he responded as follows:

GRADY: Word of mouth, you know. As like part of like ethics and, you know, guidelines and stuff, we can't tell people, "This is a great school, your kids can go to school here." Or, "I would never send my kids there." You can't say that kind of stuff. So, probably the greatest resource that's surfaced recently is greatschools.com or greatschools.org, whatever it is. It rates [schools] on a scale of one-to-ten. And seemingly from our client base, anything above a seven is considered acceptable. From our clients. You know, if it's below seven—it's a six—they're like, "Eh, why is it a six?" And they start digging deeper. Maybe six is acceptable, maybe it's not.

EKG: Okay. So if they directly asked you, "Would you send your kids here?" What do you say in response to that?

GRADY: If they ask me? Umm, and I know the answer? I'll tell them. I'm not gonna be advertising it, you know. And sometimes depending upon if it's a really good friend of mine, I can be a little more honest and they're not going to go running back to TREC [Texas Real Estate Commission] and report me, right? But if it's like a lead off the internet, and they say something about, "Would you send your kids to school here?" I may say something like, you know, "Actually, my wife and I have already engaged in a private school and we're going to send our kids to school there no matter where we live." I'd give a very diplomatic answer.

Grady explained that White housing consumers determine school quality by asking the opinion of other White individuals ("word of mouth"), checking a school rating website, and asking him what he thinks (see Holme 2002; Wells et al. 2014). Moreover, Grady acknowledged that it was unethical for him to weigh in on school quality, which is why he instead points his clients to online resources. Then, he explained that this practice differs when he is maintaining his already established relationships (as a reminder, Grady estimated that at least 80 percent of his existing clients were White). Although he feared that unfamiliar clients would report him if he provided his "real" opinion about schools, he said he "honest[ly]" evaluates school quality among clients he knows. Such forthrightness was a way to demonstrate that he trusts his clients and that his clients can trust him to tell them what he really thinks.

White agents also maintained trust by acting on their White clients' racial prejudices (overt or coded) or what they believed those prejudices would be. This was particularly true when they answered their clients' explicit or coded questions or comments about neighborhood racial composition. My interview with Amanda, a White real estate agent in her thirties, illustrates this dynamic. I met Amanda at an open house I attended in late February 2015. The following week, I interviewed her in a conference room at her brokerage. During her interview, Amanda described observing racism in the housing market. Then, after our interview ended, Amanda continued discussing some of the race-related dynamics she had mentioned during the interview. As we left the conference room and walked down the hallway, then stepped back out into the warm Houston day, Amanda told me that her White clients regularly ask her about neighborhood racial composition.[12] Amanda then explained how she responds to these questions, signaling that her clients can trust her without referring to explicit racial categories. According to Amanda,

> People ask me *all* the time, "Is this a Black neighborhood? Is this area Black?" *All. The. Time* [emphasizing each word]. And it's hard! I just tell them to drive around. "Oh, look! There's a 'tires and tamales,' all under one roof" [as though she's pointing this out to a client.]. "Oh, okay" [client responds].

Although Amanda specifically mentioned client queries about Black neighborhoods, her response ("tires and tamales") indicated how White agents perceived and described Latinx neighborhoods. Whether Amanda lumped Black and Latinx neighborhoods together in answering client questions or whether her clients asked her specifically about Latinx neighborhoods in addition to Black neighborhoods, Amanda illustrated two dynamics key to understanding how White agents maintained trust with White clients. First, White clients felt comfortable asking White agents explicit questions about neighborhood racial composition. Second, White agents answered these inquiries in ways that were clear enough for White clients to understand their racial meaning.

Jesse, the White real estate agent and housing developer introduced in Chapter 2, also demonstrated how White agents built trust and maintained relationships with White clients in these ways. When I initially interviewed him, Jesse told me about a property he was trying to sell near the Heights neighborhood. He subsequently kept in touch to give me updates on the home. Three months after our interview, Jesse contacted me to let me know the house had finally sold,

> but it wasn't without some pretty astonishing comments by [real estate agents]. I believe that the reason it took a while to sell was because the potential buyers did not want to live next door to an apartment complex occupied by people who did not look like them. The apartment complex next door bothered every potential buyer except the folks that ended up buying [it]. And who knows . . . maybe it bugged them too, but not enough to not buy the house. One [agent] asked me what life was like next door [in the apartments] on Sundays. His clients were from NYC and they wanted to know. Were folks grilling chicken and listening to Latin music like in NYC

in the Puerto Rican neighborhoods. This seems like a harmless comment except that the clients from NYC didn't want any part of that. Other potential clients were concerned about their safety and that of their children because of the apartments.

From Jesse's encounters, it was clear that the White real estate agents and White prospective home buyers they represented had explicitly discussed the local neighborhood's racial dynamics. Compared to Amanda's approach, which was to answer client questions in coded ways, one agent Jesse encountered took his clients' racist interests a step further. This agent felt comfortable enough to ask Jesse about the racial composition of the nearby apartment complex outright. In doing so, he explained that he was representing his clients' explicit desire to avoid the kinds of neighbors who grilled chicken and listened to Latin music. These interactions indicated that White agents maintain their networks of value, or what they interpret as White networks, by fielding their White clients' inquiries about neighborhood racial composition and by relying on other White professionals to give them relevant information to do so.

In addition to fielding White buyers' questions about neighborhood racial dynamics, White agents also tolerated their White home-selling clients' racial prejudice. White real estate agents I interviewed told me they had White sellers who did not want to sell to Black buyers, for example, because they assumed this would mean a decrease in property value for their White neighbors. One White real estate agent had a White client who refused to sell his home to a Middle Eastern buyer because he did not want to "support terrorists." Another White real estate agent explained, "[Sellers] have asked me, 'Well are these people Black or White or Mexican?' They're just curious, or they may have good friends in the neighborhood and they all don't want, you know, people [of color] moving in." By tolerating their home-selling clients' explicit racial prejudice—only rarely reminding clients they could not talk about race and always continuing to represent them despite these explicit comments—White real estate agents signaled that their clients could trust them, banking on that trust to secure future business.

During fieldwork, I also observed how White real estate agents drew on the racist market rubric when they interacted with their White clients, even outside of housing-related events. Doing so was a way for them to continue building rapport. In late May 2015, I met Jane and the buyers she was representing at a title company to observe a home sale closing. The buyers,

Bob and Deborah, were a middle-aged White couple currently working in the oil and gas industry in Saudi Arabia. The home they were purchasing in Houston was a second home in which they planned to stay when they visited the United States. In addition to Jane, Bob, Deborah, and I, one White escrow officer attended the closing. Once the sale had closed, Bob and Deborah continued chatting with Jane about their plans for their new home: new paint, eventually, and a new refrigerator they had bought for a steal at Home Depot because it had dents on the side and lacked shelf brackets.

As they talked, Bob explained a little more about the work he did for the oil and gas company, and he described working in Saudi Arabia. Then Jane jumped in. "Saudis are rude and arrogant," she said. Deborah quickly joined in: "I've been terrified of what would happen if the police saw me without my hair covered, because you hear horror stories." Bob and Deborah then both became frustrated as they described how daily prayers interrupted their schedules. There was no shopping, for example, because all the stores were closed during prayer times. Bob and Jane then continued chatting about Bob's job; Deborah listened as she clutched the deep purple gift bag that contained wine Jane had purchased for them. After Jane, Bob, and Deborah exchanged goodbyes, we all went our separate ways. Jane, Bob, and Deborah did not share their negative views of Saudi Arabians within a specifically housing-related event; the couple had already purchased their home. But Jane preempted her clients' racist stereotypes and, in doing so, validated their understandings of race in this casual conversation. Sharing these stereotypes freely with each other was one way to build trust and had the function of reifying racist ideas about Saudi Arabians. For Jane and other White agents, these types of conversations with each other and with their White clients were also a way of doing business. They used race as a tool to maintain their relationships with clients they perceived as valuable.

Unlike White agents' descriptions of interacting with White home buyers and sellers, agents of color did not report fielding racist questions or accommodating racial prejudice. Rather, on occasion (and infrequently compared to their White counterparts), they reported that some clients of color told them that they preferred to live near racially or ethnically similar neighbors. These agents said that their clients expressed such preferences because they wanted to live near family or to access cultural goods such as food. One Black real estate agent explained, "You end up showing homes to people in areas that they've chosen; so once again, people still want to live close to people that kind of think and feel and kind of the same energy that they do." This sentiment was echoed and explained in more detail by two more agents of color, Central American agent Hector and Vietnamese agent Teague:

> They want their own people. And that's the way I feel. Honestly speaking you want to stay around your people. If they're Hispanic, I'm Hispanic, and we speak the same language, they can help each other out. If they're Black, they're Black. They're similar habits.
>
> —Hector

> I had a family that they're from Mexico. They did really well. They were ready to buy a house, but they wanted to be closer to a lot of other Mexicans because they want either the food or the restaurants or the shopping. Asians are like that, too. I helped [a] Vietnamese family that just came in from Vietnam. But he's been in Houston for five or six years—American citizen now. He just wanted to be around a lot of Asians, a lot of Vietnamese because he wants to be close to the shops and the restaurants.
>
> —Teague

Agents of color assisted their clients in finding homes in clients' preferred areas, thus building client trust and maintaining their relationships with their clients.

Under pressure from brokerages and other real estate organizations, real estate agents believed they had to maintain their networks of value to be successful in the business. White real estate agents often maintained their relationships with White clients by acting on White home buyers' and sellers' racial prejudices, even if such prejudices were not overt. Although White agents appeared at times exasperated by their clients' comments and queries, they used their responses to these queries as a way to demonstrate their clients could trust them. Also, although real estate agents are bound by a code of ethics and fair housing law, White agents never reported discontinuing their relationships with White clients who asked them about schools, neighborhood racial dynamics, or home buyer race. Even on the rare occasions White agents acknowledged or expressed angst about their White clients' racism, they turned it into an opportunity to shore up their business, an example of complicit racism. By contrast, agents of color at times maintained their relationships with clients of color by accommodating clients' racial or ethnic preferences. But such behavior was not exclusionary; it was in stark contrast to White agents who avoided and excluded neighborhoods and buyers of color to accommodate their White buyers' and sellers' racist prejudice.

Marketing Inequality

Once real estate agents and clients establish their relationship, agents begin providing relevant real estate brokerage services. Buyer's agents help home buyers through the housing search process. Buyer's agents and buyers often begin this part of the process by identifying potential neighborhoods. Typically, they choose neighborhoods they already know (Krysan and Crowder 2017). But their search for homes is also dependent on whether and how listing agents market homes for sale.

Just as organizational pressures shape agents' networking practices, two organizational routines influence listing agents' marketing practices. And, like social networking and percentage-based commissions, these routines could claim to be race-neutral but in reality created unequal opportunities for White neighborhoods and consumers and neighborhoods and consumers of color. The first involves mapping; the second, risk.

First, the Houston-area real estate board, the Houston Association of Realtors (HAR), required listing agents to use an HAR-drawn market area map when they listed homes for sale on the HAR-owned MLS.[13] This map reinforced a spatial hierarchy of race and set majority-White areas apart as unique or "special." Second, real estate boards and other organizations emphasized that agents must continuously gauge their own financial and safety risks when "in the field" (i.e., working). This emphasis primed agents to pull from the racist market rubric in their marketing efforts. In particular, White real estate agents thought that they were reducing risk by avoiding or excluding specific racial groups from their home-selling and -marketing efforts.

Houston-area real estate organizations also remained silent about a widely shared, alternate marketing routine that could not even pretend to be race-neutral. White agents in particular sometimes marketed homes for sale through pocket listings—that is, nonpublic listings shared within their networks. Because White agents' networks were predominantly White, this practice disproportionately excluded agents and home buyers of color from learning about or accessing these for-sale homes. During my research, I did not encounter a single Houston real estate organization that weighed in on or attempted to curtail pocket listings, despite their implications for housing inequality and segregation.[14] But whether operating under explicit organizational pressures or silence, real estate agents must still actively choose how to interpret norms and the people they encounter. As the gatekeepers of the market, their choices either exacerbate or mitigate racial housing inequality.

Mapping Home Location

For real estate agents participating in the open market, the first major step in advertising a home for sale is to list it on the MLS. This is, of course, why agents refer to homes for sale as "listings." In Houston, all MLS listings appear on HAR's website (https://www.HAR.com). When agents use the online MLS interface to list homes for sale, the MLS software automatically assigns each home to an HAR-drawn market area.[15] HAR's market area boundaries map Houston in a way that reinforces racial homogeneity within communities and hides class and other forms of heterogeneity within Black and Latinx areas. These boundaries also signal the heightened, specialized marketing of White space. In this way, the Houston real estate board requires agents who list homes for sale publicly to implement a racialized map in their marketing.

During the research period, ninety-eight HAR market areas were within or overlapped the City of Houston boundaries. Overall, the area encompassed by these ninety-eight market areas was 20 percent Black, 41 percent Latinx, and 31 percent White. Unsurprisingly, given the long history of racial segregation, more than two-thirds (seventy) of these market areas were predominantly one race—majority Black, Latinx, or White. If these seventy majority-race market areas were divvied in ways that actually represented the Black, Latinx, and White proportions for the entire area, we would expect fourteen majority-Black, twenty-nine majority-Latinx, and twenty-one majority-White market areas. But this was not the case. Rather, there were *fifty* majority-White market areas (2.4 times more than expected)! These areas had approximately 20,000 residents on average. By contrast, there were only four majority-Black and fourteen majority-Latinx market areas (3.5 and 1.8 times less than expected, respectively)! These areas had an average of approximately 61,000 and 88,000 residents, respectively. The extreme overrepresentation of majority-White and underrepresentation of majority-Black and -Latinx market areas as well as vast differences in population size across these areas indicated greater marketing specialization for

White areas, even relative to high-income characteristics. (See Table 3.1 for a summary of market area race and income characteristics, as well as average total population.)

Using these market areas was mandatory for real estate agents who wished to list a home for sale on HAR's MLS. One day, I met Chase, a White real estate agent informant, at a coffee shop in Eado. He wanted to show me the process of loading a residential listing to the online MLS system. He pulled up the listing on his laptop and then opened a separate tab to show me the market area map. Chase then showed me that when he put the home's address into the online system, it automatically populated a market area number. He switched back to the market area map tab, then explained,

Table 3.1 Race and Income Characteristics for the Houston Association of Realtors' Market Areas

Race and Income Characteristics	n	Average Total Population
Majority Black	4	61,191
Majority Black and majority high-income households (>$100,000)	0	
Majority Black and at least 30% of families below poverty level	1	47,121
Majority Hispanic	16	88,232
Majority Hispanic and majority high-income households (>$100,000)	1	3,452
Majority Hispanic and at least 30% of families below poverty level	5	93,057
Majority non-Hispanic White	50	19,663
Majority non-Hispanic White and majority high-income households (>$100,000)	14	17,050
Majority non-Hispanic White and at least 30% of families below poverty level	0	
Total market areas with racial majority	70	37,709
Total market areas with no racial majority	28	51,617
Total market areas	98	50,607

Note: I layered demographic data onto the market areas using ArcGIS software and 2010 Census (blocks) and 2010–2014 American Community Survey five-year estimates (block groups). The table only includes information regarding market areas internal to or overlapping the City of Houston boundaries.

People used to fudge when they were putting in the [market] area on the listing. If the listing was actually in, say 24 [pointing to map on computer screen], but no one wants to live in 24, but maybe it's next to 23, well then they would put 23 just to get someone to look at the listing and maybe get them hooked. But then HAR started policing that. Then they came out with the Geo Market Area, which are smaller areas, about two years ago. It's much more specific.

By automating the assignment of market areas, HAR prohibited real estate agents from tinkering with area boundaries. At the same time, it required listing agents to advertise homes for sale in a spatially and racially unequal manner.

Managing Physical and Financial Risk

Real estate organizations also shaped listing agents' marketing practices by emphasizing the need for agents to gauge prospective buyer "riskiness." Such risk was often framed in terms of agents' physical and financial safety. For example, NAR reinforced a sense of fear regarding agents' physical safety. In one online publication, NAR (n.d. (a)) emphasized that

> working in real estate involves many inherent risks. From showing clients vacant properties to hosting open houses and disclosing personal information in your online marketing, *your well-being is at stake every time you go out into the field* [italics added].[16]

Similarly, HAR's training school for real estate agents offers a slew of continuing education courses.[17] One such course, approved by TREC, was titled "Open Houses, Open Doors."[18] The description of the course stated the following:

> In this 3-hour course, the REALTOR member will learn how to successfully input, promote, market, host and draw leads from an Open House. You will learn step-by-step how to use Open Houses as a tool for agent success, *while maintaining agent safety* and integrating new technology that's cutting edge for today's millennial agent [italics added].

Likewise, Champions School of Real Estate, a Houston-area real estate school that billed itself as the "largest real estate school in Texas," offered many TREC-approved continuing education courses. One such course was titled "10-Hour Risk Reduction Assessment." The purpose of this course was "to help brokers and sales agents *recognize and assess the risks involved in the everyday operations* and transactions taking place in their real estate brokerages [italics added]."[19]

White real estate agents in particular took these warnings and concerns to heart. They worried about risk and used the racist market rubric to look out for and minimize the perceived risks their brokerages and continuing education experiences had warned them about. That is, White agents interpreted individuals and neighborhoods of color as posing safety or financial risks and then avoided or excluded them when marketing homes for sale because they thought that doing so would reduce risk. White agents primarily reported believing that prospective Asian clients would be financial risks—a perceived waste of time and, thus, money—whereas prospective Black clients might pose safety risks.

Even when Black buyers scheduled appointments to view homes, they sometimes encountered White agents and White sellers who interpreted them as risks and locked them out of for-sale homes or followed them throughout the showing. During her interview, Traci, a middle-aged Black real estate broker, related an experience she had when she brought one of her Black, wealthy clients to view a new Perry Homes property:[20]

> I went to a Perry Homes [house] to show a Black woman—smoker—but I said, "You can't smoke around here." She did look like she had a lot of money. She had a lot of money. She had money, and the man closed the door on us, locked the door at Perry Homes. And I called and turned him in. Of course, he's still there [working at the company]. He wouldn't let her in to see the model home.

Although the prospective buyer's dress and mannerisms communicated her wealth, Traci worried that if the buyer were seen smoking, she would be treated negatively. Traci thus warned her client not to smoke when they got near the home, but her warning and the buyer's presentation of wealth were not enough to get the buyer through the door. The Perry Homes real estate agent still locked them out, even though Traci had made them an appointment.

Blake, a forty-year-old White agent, described how he had represented wealthy Black buyers—former residents of River Oaks, one of Houston's wealthiest, Whitest neighborhoods—who wanted to downsize after they became empty nesters. He scheduled an appointment for them to view a home in the Willowbend area, south of Houston's Galleria/Uptown area, Bellaire, and West University Place. The first thing Blake noticed when he and his Black clients arrived for their appointment was that the White sellers were still there. Moreover, he explained,

> Me and my Black clients are walking on the front yard headed up towards the front door and the seller comes out the front door and asked who we were. And I was like "Oh, I'm [Blake], I have an appointment to show this house," you know, blah, blah. And he [the White homeowner] was pretty shocked. I mean he showed surprise on his face, but they weren't rude. You know they didn't say anything, but they gave us weird looks the whole time. I mean it was uncomfortable. I mean they made it uncomfortable. I was uncomfortable. My clients were uncomfortable. They were uncomfortable for no reason.

Usually, a seller leaves the house before a showing. If they have forgotten about the appointment, they generally make themselves scarce when a real estate agent shows up. In this case, however, these White home sellers stayed home for the entirety of the Black buyers' appointment. They shadowed the buyers throughout their home, repeatedly giving them "weird looks" as a way to reinforce that they viewed these Black buyers as a risk and were watching their every move. Blake acknowledged that this encounter was uncomfortable and told me about it to illustrate it as a form of discrimination, explaining that it was a completely unnecessary show of aggression by the White home sellers (i.e., why the Black buyers were uncomfortable for "no reason"). But Blake did nothing to assuage his clients' discomfort. Instead, he chose to accommodate the White home sellers' fears by not confronting them about their behavior, even though he could have used his status as the White market "expert" to suggest that the sellers give the buyers some space. Moreover, when speaking with me, he *excused* these White home sellers by remarking "they weren't rude." In this way, Blake exercised complicit racism, expressing disgust for the encounter and allowing the White home sellers to police buyers they viewed as risks to their property rather than representing the best interests of his Black home-buying clients.

Like the White home sellers Blake described, Anthony, a White escrow officer and former real estate agent, explained how he had observed White agents gauging both Asian and Black client risk:

> When I was in real estate, there was something called prime desks. So you would be on the desk and then if a call came into the company for someone saying, "Hey, I'm looking at this house. I'm driving by this house and want to know about this property," and if you'd get a call and it was an Asian person you'd usually take the number and you'd never call them back. Because they'd get all the information, you may go show them the house, and then they'd come back later with their cousin or their aunt or their uncle. Yeah, I mean I think about when I worked at my big firm down here and it just— there were a lot of things that were said and done that were—I mean, an African American would call or come to an open house. First of all, they would think they were there to steal and they would usually call someone for backup because it was like "Uh-uh!" [startled sound], you know, and many times, they wouldn't take that person seriously, or they wouldn't put the time into it, or they wouldn't take the call.

As Anthony explained it, White real estate agents avoided marketing homes to potential Asian clients because they believed Asian buyers took advantage of White real estate agents and then retained agents within their own ethnic networks. In addition, Anthony's coworkers called for "backup" when potential Black buyers—whom they perceived as dangerous and a risk to personal safety—attempted to attend an open house.

Another example of how White agents' marketing practices affect buyer access happened one Sunday afternoon, when I was doing fieldwork with White agent Jane while she hosted an open house at a million-dollar home in a White neighborhood. Multiple White couples came in during the course of the open house, and Jane answered each of their questions. Several times, she told these couples to call her if they had any questions or needed assistance. Then, a Black couple came in to view the home. Like their White home-buying counterparts, they toured the property and spoke briefly with Jane. The man mentioned the name of his wife's company—a well-known economic powerhouse in Houston—during that interaction. Then, at one point when the couple went upstairs, Jane remarked to me, "I wonder what she does at her company . . ." as she trailed off, not expecting me to answer. The couple were the last ones at the property at 2:00 p.m., the time the open house was scheduled to close. Although Jane did not call for backup, she did tell them she had to leave, briskly ushered them out of the house, and locked the door behind them. She did not offer to answer any questions or be of assistance to them as she had with multiple White prospective buyers who had come through earlier that afternoon. Instead, by questioning the woman's occupation, ushering the couple quickly out of the house, and not actively marketing the home to them or answering their questions, Jane demonstrated that she interpreted these prospective Black buyers as both a financial and physical risk. By contrast, she did take the White buyers who had come through the open house seriously and marketed the home to them more aggressively.

Real estate agents felt the need to assess financial and safety risks. To do so, they often drew on specific risk-related stereotypes embedded in the racist market rubric—such as Asian buyers being difficult or unemotional, or Black individuals being dangerous—to determine the marketing practices that would minimize such perceived risk. From the time that a home is listed for sale, these marketing practices shape a stream of unequal housing opportunities for White buyers and sellers, on the one hand, and buyers and sellers of color, on the other hand.

Pocket Listings

Not all Houston real estate agents conformed to organizational marketing routines. In particular, White real estate agents frequently reported an alternate means of marketing homes for sale that did not rely on the local real estate board or the MLS at all. This alternate marketing routine, which they called pocket listings, was very common among the White real estate agents in my study; only one agent of color reported ever using this routine. Houston-area real estate organizations were notably silent on the issue of pocket listings during my study, at least in publicly released statements or other media. That is, HAR neither encouraged nor inhibited agents from using pocket listings.[21]

Pocket listings are home-sale listings that real estate agents kept "in their pocket." Instead of listing the home on the MLS, these agents only shared information about the for-sale home to people within their networks. White real estate agents sent pocket listings not only to former clients but also to friends, family, mortgage bankers, and builders. These agents told me they used pocket listings to generate heightened interest in a property—a social-psychological incentive to have access to something before anyone else—as well as to preserve their clients' privacy.

The White real estate agents I interviewed reported using pocket listings on a regular basis. Jordan, for example, stated that 50 percent of his predominantly White clientele consider selling their homes as pocket listings. In fact, at the time of our interview, one home-selling couple was under contract for a $525,000 offer on their house through Jordan's use of the pocket listing routine. When I asked Grant, another White agent I interviewed, if he was familiar with pocket listings, he replied, "Sure, I do them all the time. I have one now that's being shown even as we speak." Yet another White agent I interviewed, Marie, explained,

> Sometimes the sellers don't want a sign in their yard so they just want you to spread the word. Sometimes it's that the seller just wants to feel what the market would do. So they're like, "If you could get me this for my house then I would sell it." So then as a realtor you might call your friends and say, "Hey, do you have anybody that wants a three-bedroom, two-bath house that's about $600,000?" More times than not it's listings that we're getting ready for market. So right now I probably have five houses I'm getting ready for market. So if an agent says, "Hey, do you have this, this, this?" And I say, "Oh yeah, I do have one, it's coming up in two weeks." They'll say, "Can I get in to see it [before it goes to market]?"

Of my informants, Jane, Michael, and Chase regularly used pocket listings, and they referred to other White agents who used them too. Michael, for example, used his pocket listings and his connections with other White agents who had pocket listings to reassure a pair of White first-time home buyers that he had the inside track on the market. Likewise, Chase explained,

> When it's a pocket listing, I've told the buyers, "Look, you have an opportunity to get it now before it goes live and the whole city sees it's for sale." So it was easier to kind of get terms that would have been typically difficult to get on the open market just because buyers had the pressure of, "Oh my god, I'd better do it or they're going to put it on the market, and who knows what's going to happen?"

By drawing attention to the increased competition buyers may face on an "open market," Chase highlights that pocket listings are a *closed* market routine.

White agents throughout Houston used the pocket listing routine. During my study, the *Houston Chronicle* reported on how falling oil prices were weakening the Houston housing market. The report highlighted a local real estate agent who was "coping with the shift [in the market] . . . by keeping some of the houses he's trying to sell off listing websites, so in case they don't sell right away the public won't see them as tainted" (Sarnoff 2015).

In contrast, the Black and Latinx real estate agents in my study did not use pocket listings, perhaps because—as one Black agent stated—they "never heard of them" or because they believed in the economic logic of an open market. One Black agent explained,

> I don't understand why [other real estate agents] would do that. And I'll tell you why. MLS—everybody can see it. Every agent can see it. That's like our go-to guide. If there's a good point of properties listed on MLS, any property you want is there. And that's the way we do business.

As this agent implied, pocket listings had the consequence—whether intended or unintended—of excluding most of the general public from access to a for-sale home advertised only through informal, network-based means. White real estate agents who cultivated networks of value through the racist market rubric had predominantly White networks. Thus, when they engaged pocket listings, they disproportionately excluded prospective agents and home buyers of color from accessing the home or even knowing that it was for sale. Even if agents of color were to engage pocket listings, the practice would not have the same exclusionary effects because their client and colleague networks were much more racially diverse than those of White agents.

Organizations, Agents, and Inequality

Real estate organizations such as brokerages and real estate boards maintained the front lines of segregating American cities by race and class in the early and mid-twentieth century (Garb 2006; Gotham 2014; Helper 1969; Taylor 2019). They did so by underwriting real estate agents' explicitly racist tactics to create and keep White neighborhoods White and make a profit while doing so. After the U.S. Congress began to pass fair housing laws in 1968, many of these organizations began to adopt codes of ethics that affirmed the real estate brokerage industry's commitment to fair housing, at least on paper.

Despite their stated commitment to equal housing opportunity, the twenty-first-century real estate organizations in my study continued to underwrite housing inequality and segregation.[22] They shaped agents' racialized practices in two key ways. One was through pressuring agents to pursue particular routines to become economically successful. These routines, including networking, percentage-based commissions, required market area mapping, and gauging financial and safety risk, were racialized. That is, they primed agents to act in ways that contributed to the racially unequal distribution of resources. In other words, although brokerages and real estate boards did not explicitly tell agents to network with White consumers or to police or exclude consumers of color, they did encourage them to cultivate networks of value and to view prospective buyers as potential risks. Then, White agents in particular drew from cognitively and emotionally available racist stereotypes that entwined hierarchical ideas about class and culture to interpret people and neighborhoods and enact these organizational expectations in overt and subtle ways (see Ray 2019). Meanwhile, many real estate agents of color interpreted people and neighborhoods as equals and deserving of equal opportunity. Their enactment of—or departure from—organizational routines reflected these equitable, people-affirming ideas.

In addition, although the Houston-area real estate board did not use discursive means to overtly downgrade or marginalize Black and Latinx Houston neighborhoods, its market area map—required for all homes listed for sale on its MLS—did marginalize these areas in spatially explicit ways. The HAR market area map grouped Black and Latinx neighborhoods according to their racial status and ignored many forms of local heterogeneity. By contrast, the same map differentiated smaller White areas with far fewer numbers of residents, playing up the White racial status of these areas and highlighting their uniqueness.

The second way real estate organizations shaped agents' practices was through remaining silent about or not curtailing the widespread, if unofficial, pocket listing marketing routine. Silence and inactivity in this case also promoted racialized agent behavior. Almost all the agents in my study who used pocket listings were White. And, because most of their clients were also White, they made some homes available to a primarily White home-buyer base while excluding people of color who were not in their networks. Real estate brokerages, boards, and associations could, in theory, prohibit or regulate the pocket listing routine (see endnote 14 in this chapter, which describes a recent attempt by NAR to do just that). During the course of my study, however, I did not encounter a single Houston-area real estate organization that warned agents against pocket listings or attempted to curtail their use, despite their obvious connection to unequal housing opportunities.

Real estate agents actively chose how to interpret organizational pressures or silence. Organizations often pressured them to act in particular ways, but individuals decided what routines meant, and they relied on their understandings of who people are to do so. White agents and agents of color tended to enact similar organizational routines, but because they interpreted their customers and prospective clients through distinct rubrics, they acted in ways that either reinforced privilege and advantage for White individuals and neighborhoods (White agents using the racist market rubric) or expanded opportunities for individuals and neighborhoods of color (agents of color using the people-oriented market rubric). Both White agents and agents of color worked within organizational contexts that emphasized finessing and maintaining networks of value, and both worked within organizations that pushed particular marketing strategies and approaches to gauging risk. But these agents diverged fundamentally in how they viewed people, specifically with respect to race. Their understandings of race then shaped *how* they finessed and maintained networks of value (and whether they broke from this routine), *how* they marketed homes for sale, and *to whom* they extended housing opportunities.

Real estate agents are central housing market gatekeepers. As such, the intersection of real estate organization routines and agents' use of the racist or the people-oriented market rubric has significant implications for whether housing consumers have access to housing opportunities and under what conditions that access is granted. Indeed, real estate agents are so key to the housing market that they also shape the mortgage loan process, a necessary next step that most U.S. home buyers take once they have begun working with a real estate agent.

4

Lending Capital

Most Americans who purchase homes obtain a mortgage loan to do so (U.S. Census Bureau 2017).[1] For most of these individuals, the mortgage loan is the largest amount of money they will ever encounter within a single transaction and represents a massive commitment in terms of money and time. Most mortgage borrowers pay at least three percent of the home's value up front. After signing the loan, they must make regular monthly payments toward the loan principal and interest or risk foreclosure. The monthly median mortgage payment for American homeowners is $1,100; the median length of a mortgage is thirty years (U.S. Census Bureau 2017).[2] In return, the mortgage loan grants buyers access to a place to live and an investment that often appreciates in value. It also unlocks a major cultural achievement: Homeownership is a significant part of the American dream (McCabe 2016, 2018). Moreover, homeownership is often the main means for Americans, particularly Black and Latinx families, to accumulate wealth (Faber 2018). Whether housing consumers gain access to mortgage loans and under what conditions they do so thus have significant implications for their current and future quality of life.

To get a mortgage loan, home buyers must connect with a mortgage lender (i.e., the financial entity that funds the loan), usually through either a mortgage broker or a mortgage banker (both classified as loan officers by the federal Bureau of Labor Statistics).[3] As part of making this connection, buyers must apply for a mortgage loan to determine their eligibility and the terms under which the loan will be granted.[4] The application process requires buyers to provide extremely detailed information on their employment, income, and expenses. Loan officers can assist and advise buyers through this process. Once applications are complete and include the necessary supporting materials (e.g., pay stubs), mortgage bankers send applications on to mortgage loan underwriters, who assess applicant and property risk before approving or denying the loan. Mortgage bankers, like real estate agents, typically receive a percentage of the mortgage loan value as commission when the sale of the home is complete.

Race Brokers. Elizabeth Korver-Glenn, Oxford University Press (2021). © Oxford University Press.
DOI: 10.1093/oso/9780190063863.003.0005

Home buyers often find their mortgage bankers the same way they find their real estate agents: Someone else refers them. Likewise, mortgage bankers often connect with home buyers when someone else refers them. For both buyers and mortgage bankers, that "someone else" is often a real estate agent. Real estate agents connect mortgage bankers to buyers; they are often the point of entry for home buyers seeking a mortgage loan. For this reason, mortgage bankers actively attempt to network with real estate agents, reasoning that strong relationships with a small number of real estate agents will end up bringing them far more business than networking with many dozens of individual housing consumers. Indeed, mortgage lending professionals view relationships with real estate agents as central to their professional success. In reporting for the Mortgage Professional America association, Smith (2017) states that "good relationships with real estate agents are among the most important assets" for loan officers.

The mortgage bankers and real estate agents I studied networked with each other as a way to achieve professional success. Mortgage bankers viewed real estate agents as crucial to expanding their loan applicant portfolios, and real estate agents viewed relationships with mortgage bankers as an important service they offered their clients. But most White mortgage bankers and real estate agents took this interindustry networking and made it exclusionary, avoiding professionals of color and pursuing connections with White real estate agents and mortgage bankers, respectively. They assumed that doing so would return higher yields. Such *segregated interindustry networking* was remarkably similar to how White real estate agents cultivated networks of value among housing consumers. Segregated interindustry networking resulted in racially segregated professional and client networks for mortgage bankers and jump-started mortgage inequality before mortgage borrowers ever encountered loan officers or loan products. By contrast, although mortgage bankers and real estate agents of color were also looking for profitable professional relationships, they pursued interindustry networking across racial lines. They saw social and economic value in this strategy and used it as a way to minimize the discrimination their clients would face in the housing market.

Moreover, in the same way that real estate agents exercise choice in deciding which clients to take on, mortgage bankers have discretion in whether and how they assist buyers and interpret their applications (see Stuart 2003). The White mortgage bankers I studied exercised *racialized discretion* in interpreting buyers, their applications, and the properties they hoped to purchase.[5] That is, at multiple points during the loan application process, White mortgage bankers had the opportunity to use their own judgment in making decisions about mortgage borrowers, and they often did so by interpreting buyer and property risk through the racist market rubric.

All of the mortgage bankers in my study pursued interindustry networking and exercised discretion in interpreting mortgage loan applicants. Yet these professional routines intersected with mortgage bankers' racial heuristics. Mortgage bankers and real estate agents of color and some White professionals drew from the people-oriented market rubric to *de*segregate interindustry networking or to attempt to protect prospective mortgage borrowers of color from discrimination. By contrast, White mortgage bankers and real estate agents used their professional power to segregate interindustry connections and discriminate against prospective mortgage borrowers of color by relying on the racist market rubric to interpret other professionals and housing consumers. Thus, White mortgage bankers and agents in particular contributed to a lending structure that provides fundamentally unequal access to mortgage loans by embedding racism in their everyday professional routines. In doing so, these professionals made racism seem like a normal and appropriate way to conduct housing business and preserved the housing market status quo (Taylor 2019).

Loans, Racial Segregation, and the Racial Wealth Gap

Mortgage lending has long played a direct role in fostering racial segregation and racial wealth inequality. Prior to the passage of fair housing law, mortgage lenders actively engaged in redlining, the practice of excluding neighborhoods and borrowers of color from accessing mortgage loans. (The term derives from the specific practice of shading neighborhoods of color red on city maps, delineating these areas as "hazardous," or extremely risky for lenders.) These local policies dovetailed with federal housing policy. The Home Owners' Loan Corporation and, subsequently, the Federal Housing Administration (among other federal programs) institutionalized redlining through the adoption of similar racially exclusionary maps (Faber 2020; Jackson 1985; Rothstein 2017; Stuart 2003). Redlining hardened patterns of racial segregation by not allowing borrowers of color to purchase homes via established financial institutions or with federally backed mortgages, regardless of the neighborhood in question, and by not providing White borrowers access to mortgage loans in neighborhoods of color. Redlining thus cemented patterns of racial segregation and exacerbated racial wealth inequalities by ensuring White families had access to a financial instrument that allowed them to build wealth and families of color did not (Aaronson et al. 2017; Faber 2020; Jackson 1985; Rothstein 2017; Oliver and Shapiro 2006).

Although the Fair Housing Act (1968) ostensibly attempted to interfere in discriminatory mortgage lending practices such as redlining, prospective Black home buyers continued to encounter many barriers in accessing mortgages or building home equity through the 1970s and 1980s. Federal and local governments as well as private organizations and individuals erected or maintained these barriers. For example, the 1968 Housing and Urban Development Act encouraged housing market professionals to become active in low-income urban housing markets by removing the risks real estate and banking industries had long attributed to these areas. In doing so, however, the federal government created the conditions under which real estate agents, inspectors, appraisers, and bankers exploited low-income African American home buyers, trapping them in distressed homes and bad loans (Taylor 2019). Such ongoing discrimination in part prompted the passage of additional legislation, including the Equal Opportunity Credit Act (1974), the Home Mortgage Disclosure Act (1975), the Community Reinvestment Act (1977), the Fair Housing Amendments Act (1988), and the Federal Housing Enterprises Financial Safety and Soundness Act (1992) (Sharp and Hall 2014). Thus, at least through the 1980s, mortgage lenders continued to exclude Black home buyers and other buyers of color from owning a home and accumulating wealth or to include them in homeownership using a variety of predatory mechanisms that virtually ensured negative outcomes (e.g., foreclosure) (Taylor 2019).

Then, in the 1990s, lawmakers began dismantling the mortgage loan industry's regulatory scaffolding, even as fair housing legislation remained on the books. One such relevant change included removing ceilings on interest rates: By the mid-1990s, there was no limit on the interest rates lenders could charge, and such rates could move up and down (Campen 1998). Within the context of deregulation, subprime, or risky, high-cost lending flourished. Lenders began to develop new kinds of exploitative loan products and marketed them specifically to borrowers and neighborhoods of color (Massey et al. 2016; Steil et al. 2018; Williams et al. 2005). In this new world of high-risk lending, a buyer could purchase a home with little or no money down and artificially low introductory interest rates on the premise that they could refinance later with equity obtained through the magic of appreciating home values. Through this predatory inclusion, mortgage lenders disproportionately strapped borrowers of color with unfavorable, high-cost loan terms, such as ballooning interest rates.

In large part because of these and other strategies lenders pursued in the wake of deregulation, the housing market crashed in 2008. In the aftermath, many homeowners with subprime loans found themselves "underwater"— in debt for more than their houses were worth—and unable to keep up with payments tied to climbing interest rates. Borrowers and neighborhoods of color were more likely to experience foreclosure and subsequent wealth loss (Rugh et al. 2015). For example, sociologist Jacob Rugh and colleagues (2015) estimated that in Baltimore, Maryland, individual Black borrowers living in Black neighborhoods who borrowed between 2000 and 2008 would pay excess costs of approximately $16,000 over a thirty-year loan. They also estimated that the Black Baltimore borrowers in their sample experienced a total excess loss of approximately $2.1 million through foreclosure and repossession by the end of 2012.

In their response to the housing crash, the Department of Justice and other fair housing organizations filed suit against mortgage banks such as Wells Fargo—reaching landmark settlements for affected Black and Latinx borrowers in some cases (U.S. Department of Justice 2012). Meanwhile, lawmakers focused on the regulatory lapses that had made the bubble possible rather than the conditions that had made it possible for lenders to target Black and Latinx borrowers. The Dodd–Frank Act (2010), for example, required a third party to oversee the relationship between mortgage lenders and appraisers in an attempt to minimize collusion between these two industries (U.S. Government Accountability Office 2012). By 2014, four years after the passage of Dodd–Frank and the lowest point in the post-crash recession, the housing market was in full recovery mode (Faber 2018).

Even as the overall market recovered, racial inequality persisted in mortgage loan access, in part because Dodd–Frank did not directly address the racialized nature of predatory lending practices before, during, and after the housing crash. For instance, using Home Mortgage Disclosure Act data, sociologist Jacob William Faber (2018) found that Asian, Black, and Latinx borrowers were significantly less likely to be approved for a mortgage loan in 2014 than their White counterparts. He also found that Black and Latinx borrowers were more likely to receive high-cost loans than their White counterparts.[6] Findings such as these and others (e.g., Haupert

2019) indicate that discrimination continues to happen at some point(s) in the loan application or evaluation process. Moreover, mortgage lending discrimination seems likely to continue or even get worse as lawmakers dismantle requirements for transparency in mortgage lending: In 2018, the U.S. Senate repealed aspects of Dodd–Frank, among other banking rules, including its requirements for more detailed reporting on borrower and loan characteristics, such as more information about their credit scores and interest rates (Jan 2018).

How Mortgage Bankers and Real Estate Agents Shape Consumer Loan Opportunities

How does mortgage loan inequality take place post-recession? My encounters with mortgage bankers and real estate agents in Houston suggest that the foundation for mortgage loan inequality is laid prior to borrowers filling out a mortgage loan application. Mortgage bankers intentionally networked with real estate agents to gain access to agents' clientele and pad their loan portfolios. White mortgage bankers usually pursued exclusionary and segregated interindustry networking in ways that reproduced racially segregated home buyer–agent–mortgage banker networks.[7] Likewise—and in even more racially restrictive ways—White real estate agents connected with White mortgage bankers as a way to expand the package of services they offered their White home-buying clients and locked mortgage bankers of color out of their networks. Occasionally, they pursued such racially segregated networking in obvious ways through relying on the racist market rubric.

By contrast, Black, Latinx, and, rarely, White mortgage bankers networked with Black and Latinx real estate agents and developers, who also referred home-buying clients to mortgage bankers. And, Black and Latinx real estate agents networked with Black, Latinx, and White mortgage bankers. Occasionally, Black and Latinx agents cautioned their home buyers of color away from particular (White) mortgage bankers because of their discriminatory track record. For these bankers and agents, the undergirding sense of or aspiration toward racial equality crucial to the people-oriented market rubric informed their interindustry networking and relationships with home buyers. As a result, these individuals formed racially diverse professional networks and attempted to get around the racism they knew constrained mortgage opportunities for home buyers of color.

These differences in interindustry networking—exclusionary, segregated networking across White housing market professionals and diverse networking across professionals of color—meant home buyers had different mortgage opportunities. Specifically, home buyers of color and White buyers were exposed to different streams of mortgage bankers through these backstage, preloan networking routines, even if mortgage bankers and real estate agents did not intend or state their intention of creating these circumstances. Home buyers in my study did not observe these networking efforts and typically did not question agents' referrals to specific mortgage bankers, suggesting that buyers may be unaware of how other key market professionals shape the housing exchange process behind the scenes.

Early on a Tuesday morning in April 2015, I met Michael (the White real estate agent introduced in Chapter 3) at a bungalow-style home converted into a coffee shop in the Heights neighborhood. We were there to meet some of Michael's newest clients, a White husband and wife couple who were purchasing their first home. While we waited for the couple, Dave and Shanna, to arrive, Michael and I sipped coffee and chatted for a few minutes. Michael told me that Dave and Shanna had been referred to him by both an interior designer they knew as well as Shanna's hair dresser. The couple, who currently rented in the Montrose neighborhood, had told Michael they wanted to purchase a home in the Heights. A few moments later, Dave and Shanna arrived, and we exchanged introductions and greetings. "Tell me a little bit about where you are in the process," Michael invited as we all took a seat. "We started looking about six months ago generally in the Heights to get a sense of what the area is like. We want to find a renovated bungalow, maybe a 2/2 or a 2/1½," Dave began.[8] "Do schools matter?" asked Michael. "No," replied Dave. Michael continued asking probing questions in this manner, eliciting more specific information about the homes Dave and Shanna would consider.

Eventually, Michael asked, "Have you gotten preapproved [for a mortgage loan]?" "No," replied Dave, "do we need to do that?" "Yes," said Michael, "you can't really submit an offer until you're preapproved.[9] You figure out what you can afford first and then what you're comfortable spending." Shanna jumped in to ask for Michael's advice: "Do you recommend shopping for a preapproval?" Michael responded affirmatively, telling the couple that the important thing was to find a local mortgage banker. "I recommend Cole Greenwich," Michael continued, "and we don't get anything from him, no kickbacks or anything, we just know he gives good rates and is easy to work with. Just don't walk into a big bank without knowing a private banker there."

As the couple continued discussing some of the practicalities of the home search process, Michael emphasized two more times that the couple should work with a local mortgage banker. The second time, Michael gave them a hypothetical example to hammer this point home even more strongly: "As a listing agent, if I received three offers and one had a local lender, I would go with the [offer with the] local lender, because they work with appraisers that are familiar with the area and are specialists." Shanna, perhaps feeling a little concerned or uncertain about finding a local mortgage banker, asked, "Well, we bank with Wells Fargo, so what should we do?" Michael quickly stepped in with another specific mortgage banker to recommend. "We know Brandon Duke at Wells Fargo, he's a private banker at [a local Wells Fargo] office. But we'll send you a list of lenders."

Michael's and other agents' ability to rattle of a list of mortgage bankers was in part possible because of mortgage professionals' networking efforts. During my fieldwork, I observed Cole and Brandon, the two mortgage bankers Michael mentioned, actively pursuing relationships with Michael and other White real estate agents and housing developers. Cole, for example, attended a client appreciation event that Michael hosted for approximately fifty of his consumer clients and professional acquaintances (including other agents, developers, and mortgage bankers, almost all of whom were White). Cole worked the crowd, rekindling connections with people he had met previously and introducing himself to other professionals and consumers he did not know. At a separate event—a broker open house that Michael hosted—Brandon attended and networked with Michael and several other White real estate agents present; no agents of color were present. Brandon also attended a public open house hosted by Jane, another White real estate agent introduced in Chapter 3. As he introduced himself to her and advertised his mortgage services, Brandon made sure to give Jane a firm handshake and a business card. Throughout my year of fieldwork, I never observed any of the White real estate agent informants in my study refer a home-buying client of any race or ethnicity to a mortgage banker of color.[10]

Segregated interindustry networking between White mortgage bankers and White agents meant that most White mortgage bankers worked primarily with White home buyers. Of the nine White mortgage bankers I formally interviewed, six reported that the vast majority of their clients were White, two declined to answer, and one reported that a plurality (40 percent) of their clients were White.[11] To answer my question about the racial composition of his clientele, one White mortgage banker turned toward his computer screen during our interview and told me he would read me who was in his day's lineup, beginning the list by describing it as "pretty diverse":

I would say [my clientele is] pretty diverse, but probably—how about I go over my pipeline and I'll tell you right now. And this will give you a perspective, okay? So we have Hispanic, Caucasian, Caucasian, Caucasian, Caucasian, Indian, Pacific Islander, right? Caucasian, Caucasian, Caucasian, Caucasian, Caucasian, Hispanic, Caucasian, Hispanic, Pacific Islander, Lithuanian, Caucasian, Caucasian, you know? Hispanic? So, there's some mix, but you can see it is highly Caucasian. I do, typically, I think maybe more Caucasian than some in a highly diverse area because I do [work] the Inner Loop and I think the Inner Loop is a little bit more— yeah—a little bit more frosty.

Another White mortgage banker reported that 80 percent of his borrowing clients were White, then explained, "That's not by my choice . . . that's just who the realtors are and who—what lands."

Mortgage bankers of color had markedly different experiences when they attempted to network with White agents. In mid-October 2015, I arrived at Jane's brokerage office after a prior fieldwork appointment and, realizing I had missed the start of a bimonthly staff meeting, waited outside in the broiling ninety-two-degree heat until the meeting ended. About twenty minutes later, the door opened and several agents exited the office on their way to listing appointments and other activities. After the initial flow of agents stopped, I stepped inside to see Jane chatting with two other White agents, David and Suzie, and her assistant, Grace. To my right was a small kitchenette. Foil-wrapped breakfast tacos and tomatillo salsa from a popular local restaurant rested in a heaping pile on the kitchen counter. In front of me were several heavy wooden desks. Jane, David, Suzie, and Grace were gathered around one of these desks.

As I took a seat nearby, I overheard Jane asking her colleagues, "Do you think we should go to a once a month meeting?" "I think twice a month is really better," replied David, "One of [the meetings] can be sponsored, and the other just a short forty-five-minute check-in." Grace joined in, affirming David's assessment: "That's the feedback we've been getting from the agents." Jane confirmed this move to only one sponsored meeting a month while also describing what she believed was the problem with sponsored meetings:

So a sponsored meeting once a month. The problem is that the sponsors come in and keep talking longer than they're supposed to. Lenders will be the sponsors, but then they'll have insurance buy the food, so then insurance also thinks they can talk, too. What we need to do is make sure that it's just one sponsor up front.

The breakfast tacos had been purchased by a local mortgage banker and a homeowners insurance provider. These two professionals had been attempting to network with the agents at Jane's brokerage and sell their services to these agents.

Local mortgage bankers and insurance providers regularly attempted to sponsor meetings at Jane's brokerage in order to gain access to these networking opportunities with White real estate agents. As the conversation continued, however, it became clear that Jane and her White colleagues[12] excluded certain mortgage bankers and other housing industry professionals. Suzie turned to Jane and complained that she had been getting calls from someone who had been hired by a mortgage banker to call agents on their behalf. "It's like, 'Piss off!' " Suzie exclaimed, "If you want to meet me, call me yourself." Jane commiserated, telling a story about a mortgage banker who had hired someone to make calls for them. According to Jane, the person making the calls, the "dialer," would call her three or four times a week, even after Jane requested multiple times that the mortgage banker take her off her call list. "The lender was an idiot," Jane commented, "She could barely speak English. Eventually, I had to get in touch with the president of the company. It's like, you know, you've turned your business over to someone with a fourth-grade education"—"And didn't speak English, either!" Suzie interrupted. "The president ended up making a donation to the charity of my choice, and the calls stopped after that," Jane concluded with a chuckle.

This mortgage banker was unsuccessful in her attempts to network with Jane. Beyond that, Jane reported her to the president of her mortgage company, who attempted to smooth things over. Although Jane did not specify the mortgage banker's race, Jane and Suzie both emphasized the entwined tropes of "uneducated" and "non-English speaking" common to the racist market rubric to mark this individual as not White and therefore unworthy of their professional time. Moreover, in Jane's narrative, this mortgage banker violated an established norm of interindustry networking by calling her, or having the dialer call her, too many times. After this set of phone interactions, in which Jane repeatedly applied racist understandings of English-speaking ability and education to the mortgage banker, it is reasonable to conclude that Jane would never refer any of her home-buying clients to this banker. Furthermore, Jane reiterated and validated these components of the racist market rubric to the other agents still in the room, who worked under her supervision. Such exclusionary, segregated interindustry networking among White mortgage bankers and White agents proceeded apace, with both types of professionals giving each other the benefit of the doubt and assuming the best outcomes from such networking. But White agents only rarely reached across racial lines. Instead, they avoided or excluded mortgage bankers of color even as they allowed and encouraged White bankers' networking efforts and gave them access to their White clientele.

By contrast, mortgage bankers and real estate agents of color and, occasionally, White mortgage bankers pursued interindustry networking across racial lines, drawing from the people-oriented market rubric to emphasize the social and economic value of these connections. For example, Pablo, the Hispanic developer introduced in Chapter 2, invited me to the construction site of a home he was building in a Black Houston neighborhood in late September 2015. When I arrived, he explained that we were waiting on his residential construction banker as well as a mortgage banker who worked at the same bank with the construction financier. "[The construction banker] wants to introduce me to the lady that does mortgage lending. . . . Anyway, we met her a couple of weeks ago, and now she wants to see the properties." Pablo, whose pool of home buyers was almost as diverse as the city of Houston, went on to explain that his hope was that he would be able to start referring the individuals buying his newly constructed homes to this mortgage banker. Soon after, the construction financier and the mortgage banker—both White—arrived.

A couple of months later, I interviewed Melinda, the White mortgage banker Pablo had introduced to me, at her bank in west Houston. She told me that 30 percent of her mortgage business was through referrals from builders or developers such as Pablo, whereas 20 percent came through referrals from real estate agents and 50 percent via referrals from past home-buying clients. Reflecting the interindustry networking routine, she explained her business approach, was to "develop a relationship with realtors who are working with buyers . . . [and a] relationship with builders." She estimated that half of the builders with whom she intentionally cultivated relationships were Latinx, like Pablo, and the other half were White. Melinda explained that she has pursued relationships with Latinx developers and builders because "people love [their] work, [they] just do a great job" and because, like Pablo, these developers would refer her to mortgage borrowing clients.

Not long after Pablo had introduced me to these mortgage lending professionals, I met Tony, the Mexican American real estate agent and developer introduced in Chapter 2, at his main office. With him were Jake, a Black mortgage banker, and Shawna, a Black real estate agent. After Tony showed Jake and Shawna some of his strategies for prospecting for land using the public interface of HAR.com (rather than the agent-oriented version that required agents to log in to the website), Jake instructed Tony to visit NARRPR. com and showed him how to navigate the website to find out "more info about the neighborhood" where properties were located. After this back-and-forth, Tony asked, "So what do y'all want to talk about?" "I wanted to introduce you to Shawna," Jake responded, "and we've got Manny, who's our contractor, and then Drew is the architect. I know you said you usually use two architects, but it's kind of like producing albums, you want to have different options for producing the right sound." "Yeah, I gotcha," Tony affirmed. Shawna jumped in: "We're a group of three. I do the real estate, Jake works on mortgage, and then we have someone working on marketing. We're hopefully trying to take responsibility, and just get out there and work up business."

"So what are y'all wanting to do?" asked Tony. "We're trying to get out and partner up with developers," Shawna responded. Jake joined in: "We know you're an actual realtor—and you have a lot of responsibilities. Maybe Shawna can help you push those properties faster. . . . She uses a lot of social media—Instagram, Tumblr, Facebook, Twitter. . . ." "Traditionally," Tony interjected,

> I do my own listings. I have my broker's license and I have a couple of agents under me. Meg is my right-hand, she does marketing. And without even trying, we have ten to fifteen listings in addition to the new construction. So putting a sign in the ground and doing open houses, that doesn't really work for me. *But* if I can teach you how to look for land . . .

Tony trailed off as he turned back to his computer screen. As he walked through the process of prospecting for land using several online tools, including HAR.com, he explained how a collaborative relationship with Jake and Shawna could work, if it involved Shawna finding plots of land to (re) develop and Jake providing mortgage financing to prospective home buyers. Unlike Jane, who had forcefully excluded at least one non-White mortgage banker from networking with her, Tony used his time with Shawna and Jake to capitalize on a possible partnership moving forward.

Similar interindustry networking across real estate agents, developers, and mortgage bankers of color occurred throughout my fieldwork. For example, Mateo, the Latino real estate agent and developer introduced in Chapter 2, hosted broker open houses at properties that he had developed and listed for sale. In addition, he invited a diverse crowd of mortgage bankers, brokers, and real estate agents to attend. One of these broker open houses, held in November 2015, was a swanky event at a luxury home in a White neighborhood.[13] Young Asian and Latinx women wearing form-fitting skirts and blouses offered champagne and delicate hors d'oeuvres to guests, all of whom Mateo had specifically invited. One of these guests was a Latino mortgage banker, who had come to network with the racially diverse crowd of agents present at the event.

Networking among mortgage bankers, agents, and developers of color also occurred at home buyer education classes, which were regularly held in Black and Latinx neighborhoods throughout Houston. These events were often sponsored by local nonprofit organizations, developers, or the "diversity" arm of banks such as Wells Fargo. Prospective home buyers of color were the primary attendees at these classes, which were regularly led by Black and Latinx real estate agents and mortgage bankers. These professionals used the classes as opportunities to network not only with prospective home buyers but also with each other. One such class I attended in a Black neighborhood was sponsored by Casey, a Black developer and informant, who had invited a Black real estate agent and a Latina mortgage banker to help lead the informational session for a group of thirteen prospective home buyers (four Latinx and nine Black). Of the three such classes or workshops I attended as part of my fieldwork, none were led by White mortgage bankers or real estate agents; only a handful of White prospective home buyers attended.

When real estate agents of color pursued or reflected on their interindustry networking, they often noted the racial discrimination they had witnessed, heard about, or experienced within the mortgage lending industry and affirmed their commitment to facilitating equal housing opportunities for home buyers of color. Their awareness of such discrimination and determination to facilitate equal housing opportunities shaped how they perceived mortgage bankers and the mortgage recommendations they made to their home-buying clients. Melissa, a Black real estate agent I interviewed and later shadowed, described two examples of racial discrimination within the context of home buyer–mortgage banker interactions. One of these involved an interracial home-buying couple applying for a mortgage loan. In Melissa's words,

> She was Black, he was Hispanic, and they were trying to get a house. And their credit was okay. Everything was fine, and I did tell them, "Don't go out and buy anything. You don't want to change your ratios if you know—if they're running your credit now, they're going to run it again in thirty days." They did not listen to what I said. They went and bought some furniture, and it threw their ratios off. Well, that shouldn't have been a deal buster for them. They should have been able to explain that and then maybe wait a few more days or a few more weeks for the ratios to be okay. But the bank decided not to give them the loan. I look at a lot of people now who are looking to refile or to get modifications, and I believe modifications were given out disproportionately more to White people than they are to people that are Black.

This experience and others similar to it guided the mortgage banker recommendations real estate agents of color made. These agents cautioned their home-buying clients away from specific mortgage bankers, such as the one Melissa described, because they believed these professionals would discriminate against their clients of color. Janice, for example, another Black real estate agent, described how she actively avoided large banks with mortgage lending arms, such as Bank of America and Wells Fargo, in part because of their widely known track record of racial discrimination. As she explained it,

> The racial prejudices [in mortgage lending] exist. And you really can't get into the heart of a lender as to why they turn down certain people. Just about four years ago, Bank of America was charged and Wells Fargo was fined because of racial discrimination and then somebody came forth at Bank of America, some little White guy—I hope he's still alive—and exposed that they were foreclosing ten times more on Blacks than on Whites illegally. Homes were being foreclosed on in a record number. I don't deal with Bank of America or Wells Fargo. I know the history. They don't deal with Black or Hispanic people or poor Whites. I deal with [local and regional lenders]—ones who I have long-term rapport with, that I have a history of helping people get a loan. I never, I don't ever refer to Bank of America

or Wells Fargo because the big guys do not care a thing about the little guy, unfortunately.

Janice went on to describe how her own negative personal experience with Bank of America also influenced her practice of never referring clients to these large banks:

> And I've had such bad luck with those two, although my home loan is with Bank of America. Bank of America overcharged me for my loan. And then I found out, after five years after fighting them, that I overpaid them by over $9000. I was so exhausted from the fight, I said, "You know what. I still might go pursue it and still try to find a lawyer to go over it." I was so upset. Bank of America is known for not giving minorities loans.

Janice, Melissa, and other agents of color believed their buyers deserved a fair shot, and they made mortgage recommendations accordingly. Real estate agents of color thus tended to refer their clients to mortgage bankers of color and particular White mortgage bankers who they believed would not discriminate.

In short, interindustry networking is not a racially neutral professional activity. Instead, White mortgage bankers and agents tended to build relationships with each other while excluding real estate professionals of color. Often, their segregated interindustry networking reflected their activation of the racist market rubric. By contrast, mortgage bankers, real estate agents, and other housing market professionals of color tended to work together as well as with White professionals. Although their interindustry networking reflected in part the discrimination they had experienced when attempting to network with White professionals (e.g., Tony's encounter with a White architect who refused to work with him), it also was informed by the principle of equity undergirding the people-oriented market rubric.

Thus, even before the initial contact point between home buyers and mortgage bankers takes place, interindustry networking happening behind the scenes between mortgage bankers and real estate agents can shape buyers' pathways into homeownership—perhaps without their knowledge. In Houston, at least, segregated interindustry networking between White mortgage bankers and real estate agents means that White mortgage bankers rarely encounter borrowers of color, whereas bankers and other professionals of color have more diverse professional and consumer connections. In turn,

White-segregated mortgage borrower–mortgage banker relationships are a key part of the context in which prospective home buyer and property risk are evaluated.

Racialized Discretion in Determining Applicant Risk

Mortgage bankers exercise discretion in many areas of their work. As Stuart (2003) argues, discretion helps hold the mortgage lending industry together, ensuring that mortgage bankers can navigate the plethora of governmental and organizational rules they regularly encounter. In particular, mortgage bankers exercise discretion in deciding what sorts of applicants merit loans. Within the set of existing rules, they have wiggle room for screening and working with applicants and interpreting situations and individuals that these rules do not cover. Lenders use their judgment to evaluate whether applicants conform to rule standards and have a good chance of being "low risk." They also exercise discretion in deciding whether to advise their applicants on how best to complete their applications so as to appear "low risk" to others.

The White mortgage bankers I studied exercised racialized discretion when recording mortgage loan applicant race and ethnicity and when determining risk for applicants of color. That is, they first inferred applicant race and ethnicity and then recorded them on the Uniform Residential Loan Application. They then interpreted applicant race or ethnicity when evaluating an applicant's income, employment, or credit characteristics to make judgments about the risk level of an applicant. When assessing applicants of color, White bankers drew on widely shared, negative racial stereotypes to inform their decisions about applicant risk (i.e., the racist market rubric). Racialized discretion was embedded in the context of White-segregated mortgage borrower–mortgage banker relationships. White bankers rarely encountered borrowers of color or borrowers purchasing homes in neighborhoods of color, lessening their encounters with individuals or areas that theoretically could counter the widely shared race and class stereotypes prevalent in the racist market rubric. Thus, even on the rare occasions when they did have these encounters and were presented with evidence of these borrowers' qualifications for mortgage loans, bankers reverted to the racist market rubric to justify decisions that excluded these borrowers from loan opportunities.[14]

For the White mortgage bankers I studied, racialized discretion began at one of the earliest stages of the mortgage loan application process: assessing borrower race/ethnicity as per the instructions on the Uniform Residential Loan Application (Form 1003). In addition to filling out information about employment, monthly income and expenses, and assets and liabilities, Form 1003 asks (but does not require) borrowers to fill in their ethnicity, race, and sex for government monitoring purposes. If the borrower does not fill in this information, the form indicates that the loan officer or loan originator is required to fill in the requested information if the borrower completed the form in person. Form 1003 instructs the mortgage banker to use "visual appearance and surname" to "note" the borrower's ethnicity, race, and sex. Figure 4.1 shows this section of Form 1003.

Of the mortgage bankers I interviewed, most reported filling out borrower race and ethnicity even if the borrower was not completing the application in person. To infer and report this information, mortgage bankers used linguistic cues such as borrower accent if they had spoken to the borrower over the phone; borrower name(s); and visual cues from driver's licenses or other identification that borrowers faxed or emailed. Whether self-reported or selected by the mortgage banker, borrower ethnicity, race, and sex were not concealed during the underwriting stage of the loan application process.

Because borrower name, race, and ethnicity were not concealed, mortgage bankers interpreted this information as part of their discretionary assessments of applicant risk during the underwriting stage of the loan application process. Racialized discretion at the underwriting stage emerged from mortgage bankers' interpretations of Black and Latinx borrowers as being low income or having poor credit and little financial awareness—and thus high risk. Brandon, the White mortgage banker who actively sought to network with both Michael and Jane, used three widely shared racist tropes when describing Black borrowers as high risk:

X. INFORMATION FOR GOVERNMENT MONITORING PURPOSES

The following information is requested by the Federal Government for certain types of loans related to a dwelling in order to monitor the lender's compliance with equal credit opportunity, fair housing and home mortgage disclosure laws. You are not required to furnish this information, but are encouraged to do so. The law provides that a lender may not discriminate either on the basis of this information, or on whether you choose to furnish it. If you furnish the information, please provide both ethnicity and race. For race, you may check more than one designation. If you do not furnish ethnicity, race, or sex, under Federal regulations, this lender is required to note the information on the basis of visual observation and surname if you have made this application in person. If you do not wish to furnish the information, please check the box below. (Lender must review the above material to assure that the disclosures satisfy all requirements to which the lender is subject under applicable state law for the particular type of loan applied for.)

BORROWER	☐ I do not wish to furnish this information			CO-BORROWER	☐ I do not wish to furnish this information		
Ethnicity:	☐ Hispanic or Latino	☐ Not Hispanic or Latino		Ethnicity:	☐ Hispanic or Latino	☐ Not Hispanic or Latino	
Race:	☐ American Indian or Alaska Native ☐ Native Hawaiian or Other Pacific Islander	☐ Asian ☐ White	☐ Black or African American	Race:	☐ American Indian or Alaska Native ☐ Native Hawaiian or Other Pacific Islander	☐ Asian ☐ White	☐ Black or African American
Sex:	☐ Female	☐ Male		Sex:	☐ Female	☐ Male	

Figure 4.1 Excerpt from the Uniform Residential Loan Application (Form 1003).

So I mean I feel like, I mean I see a lot of instances that—African Americans that are applying for a mortgage—that more often than anything else, than any other race, I believe there's more um—a term that we use, a little bit more hair on the deal. Um like credit, right, when they're trying to reach more for their property. As well as the fact that they're just not as familiar with it.

That is, Brandon believed Black mortgage borrowers were more likely to have problematic loan applications, whether because they had low credit, were trying to purchase a home outside of their means, or were unfamiliar with the mortgage process. These beliefs functioned as red flags for Brandon, such that he became suspicious of borrowers' credit risk once he knew they were Black. Similarly, Perry, a White mortgage banker, believed Black and Latinx borrowers do not make it through underwriting as easily as White borrowers because of "credit history, credit scores. You can get approved with a score as low as 580, so if your score is below that, then you must have seriously abused your credit." Yet another White mortgage banker, Austin, reported he had a colleague who was actively trying to avoid Latinx clients because "they're very hard to work with in that their paperwork is never in line." By this, Austin and other mortgage bankers who made similar statements referred to their stereotypical understandings of Latinx home buyers, whom they assumed were paid under the table and did not have a trail of paperwork to support their income claims.

White mortgage bankers' racialized perceptions of borrowers of color were so entrenched that they routinely refused the possibility that racial discrimination was still happening in the mortgage loan process even as they reproduced such discrimination. For instance, after White mortgage bankers interpreted Black and Latinx borrowers as high risk (as all but one of them did), I shared findings from recent sociological studies of racial inequality in mortgage lending. Specifically, I explained that Black and Latinx borrowers are less likely to get approved for prime mortgage loans than their White counterparts, even when income, credit score, and other key characteristics are held constant. After presenting them with this information, I asked them how they would explain these racial differences in loan outcomes. Upon answering, most White mortgage bankers explicitly stated that racial bias was simply not part of the process and instead came up with additional racialized justifications for loan inequality that placed the blame on borrowers of color.

For example, Adam, a White mortgage banker, first stated that mortgages were all about sales. By this, he meant that loan officers, being paid by commission, are unlikely to get in the way of a deal. Thus, he reasoned, any inequality in the underwriting and loan approval process would not stem from racial bias but, rather, from differences in credit scores and other markers of risk:

> I don't see any of that [racial bias] and I've never seen that in my career. The way loan officers and even real estate agents interact—we're salespeople and at the core of that there's this need for money. Even if there are people that I and other loan officers haven't liked and we'll still do the transaction for them 'cause at the end of the day that's the how we get compensated.

After I explained that mortgage loan outcomes continue to be racially unequal even after accounting for income and credit scores, he replied,

> I wonder what they're shopping. I wonder how the White person is being compared to how many lenders they'll talk to, to compare interest rates; whereas opposed to the minority? In the Hispanic culture, I see more of a trust like, "Hey, I like you. I want to work with you," the Asian community as well. So maybe there's not that shopping. Where [the] majority of the clients that will shop me are Caucasian White clients. "Is that the best rate you can get me? Well, I want to call my bank. They have different options."

Adam's response—to continue to find fault with borrowers of color (specifically Asian and Latinx borrowers) and to blame mortgage loan outcomes on what he believed were their shortcomings—was emblematic of other White mortgage bankers.

Such racialization of prospective mortgage borrowers of color happened in tandem with the discretion mortgage bankers exercised as they processed the loan application. For example, Jason, a White mortgage banker, described how a Black home-buying couple he knew had been turned down for their loan, despite having "good" income, employment, credit, and savings, thus countering prevailing stereotypes. According to Jason, this happened because

> [underwriting] came up with an underwriting guideline at their discretion to decline the loan. So, they got declined, it's a good loan. Um, from a legal

standpoint, it was sort of that gray area of, uh, you know, kind of, under-writer discretion.

Jason went on to explain that despite the guidelines put in place to prevent discrimination, "there's still room for the underwriter to just not feel com-fortable about it." He emphasized that this exercise of discretion, although a "gray area," was a "legal" practice. Similarly, another White mortgage banker explained to Melissa, the Black real estate agent introduced previously, that "if your name is racially ambiguous it's okay. But if you have a name that's— you know—ethnic—it sounds ethnic, *they could find a way to not give you the loan* [italics added]." White mortgage bankers used the racist market rubric when exercising their professional discretion to deem mortgage borrowers of color as "high risk" or in some way deficient. This racialized discretion also shaped how they interpreted property risk.

Racialized Discretion in Determining Property Risk

During the mortgage loan application process, lenders evaluate the property being purchased as well as the applicant hoping to buy it. Lenders deter-mined property risk by ordering appraisals of for-sale homes.[15] I found that lending professionals exercised racialized discretion when anticipating and interpreting these appraisals. Moreover, because home appraisals are contin-gent on values in the surrounding neighborhood (see Chapter 5), mortgage bankers understood individual for-sale homes—those with the potential of being mortgaged—as inextricable from their local neighborhood contexts.

Mortgage bankers thought about appraisals regularly, even when unre-lated to a specific home. For example, I encountered Lucy, a Black mortgage banker, during fieldwork. Lucy mentioned in passing that for-sale homes in neighborhoods of color were "struggling with appraisal values," meaning that appraisers frequently landed at a dollar value lower than what buyers had offered to pay. In these cases, mortgage bankers will generally not lend buyers the full amount of the mortgage they initially applied for. The deal will likely fall through unless the seller lowers their asking price, the buyer offers more cash up front, or the buyer requests another appraisal that ends up valuing the home at or above the contract price. Lucy went on to speculate that local housing advocates and nonprofit developers in these areas could potentially get into the "assumption business, which is when buyers assume a mortgage already in place."

The topic of appraisals also arose when I met Pablo, his residential construction banker Andy, and Melinda, the mortgage banker, at the construction site mentioned previously. Andy explained as an aside to me that he was there to check in on the home's progress: "Whenever [Pablo] gets a construction loan from us, each time he's requesting monies, we have to make sure that he's using the money to do the work." As Andy and Pablo talked shop, Andy explained that there would be an appraisal issue with building numerous new homes all at once. "If we do fourteen units, we're gonna run into the bulk appraisal issue," Andy commented, "If it's appraised on its own, it will be appraised at $205,000, but if you do them all together, it will be $180,000." (Here, Andy was referring to the discounts that appraisers make when they assess the collective value of multiple new homes that are part of what is considered the same development.[16]) They continued their conversation by discussing how they could avoid the discounted valuation for the homes Pablo was building in this Black Houston neighborhood. Unfortunately, I did not hear what, if any, final strategy they decided upon because Melinda began to speak with me and then their conversation took a turn.

White mortgage bankers exercised racialized discretion when anticipating or interpreting appraisals and considering property risk. They drew on the racist market rubric when interpreting the for-sale homes borrowers hoped to purchase as well as the neighborhoods in which these homes were located. These lending professionals assumed that homes would be lower risk and higher value in White areas because they perceived these areas as having low crime, excellent schools, and high demand. To them, these signals indicated stable or rising property values. Mortgage bankers simultaneously expressed concern about appraisals in neighborhoods of color. That is, they worried whether the assessed value of the home would meet or exceed the home's contract price and mortgage loan amount, or whether appraisers would flag these properties as high risk. White mortgage bankers, in other words, worried that these homes might be overpriced or that they might decline in value.

When White mortgage bankers described homes they believed were low risk, or homes that would maintain their value and appreciate over time, they located these hypothetical homes in White neighborhoods. For example, Kenneth, a White mortgage banker, explained that "some areas are more, uh, desirable than others, obviously. People will start looking for houses right in there [points to a White neighborhood on a map of Houston laid out in front of us]. They wanna get zoned at that right school." Kenneth pointed to a White neighborhood on a map and then used coded language to describe this area as exemplary of those he believed were low risk for mortgages. From his perspective, they were low risk because they were "desirable" and had "good" or "right" schools and would "obviously . . . maintain a good value . . . increasing over the lifetime [of the loan]." White lending professionals believed homes in White neighborhoods were low risk. Thus, when they evaluated properties located in White neighborhoods, they did not anticipate the appraiser would flag the mortgage loan amount as risky.

But mortgage bankers interpreted properties in neighborhoods of color in an opposite way. Austin, the White mortgage banker who complained about Latinx borrowers' paperwork, explained that his first response when he receives a mortgage loan application for a home in a neighborhood of color (or what he calls "demographic areas"), is concern about the appraisal. From Austin's perspective,

> So there's a lot of sociological questions that come up in those demographic areas. It hasn't really affected anything I think that I've dealt with, except for the sense that I know that now when you're buying there, I used to think, "Okay we're buying in the 135 to 195 range [$135,000–$195,000]." [Now] where you're seeing someone just came, flipped the house, and now they're buying a remodeled house, and it's 225, 275 [$225,000, $275,000]. Sometimes even more than that. And my first thought is, "Hey, is it going to appraise? And do they actually know the understanding of the area that they're getting into?" That's my thought.

Austin's narrative illustrates how mortgage bankers entwined the (assumed) race and class composition of neighborhoods when considering appraisals. Furthermore, he demonstrated how this entwinement could affect their assessments of property risk. He assumed that homes in neighborhoods of color should be in the low range of the price spectrum and that home values in these areas would not show rapid appreciation, even if remodeled or redeveloped. For these reasons, Austin explained, he suspected appraisals in neighborhoods of color would not meet or exceed the contract price and even questioned buyers' decisions to purchase homes in these communities. In other words, on the rare occasions that White mortgage bankers encountered buyers attempting to purchase homes in neighborhoods of color, they were exercising racialized discretion in the background, assuming higher property risk and anticipating potential loan failure.

People in numerous contemporary bureaucratic settings rely on discretion as a way to navigate the multitude of rules they encounter in their work (Lipsky 2010). This includes mortgage lending professionals (Stuart 2003). The White mortgage bankers I studied exercised discretion through a racialized lens to make sense of mortgage borrower and property risk. They interpreted Black and Latinx mortgage borrowers and homes in Black and Latinx neighborhoods as high risk because they interpreted these individuals and homes through widely shared racist tropes that entwined racial status with what they perceived as economic, moral, and cultural shortcomings. Racialized discretion in interpreting applicant and property risk affects borrowers' access to mortgage loans—theoretically, a major wealth-building tool.

The Visible Hands of the Housing Market

Brandon, the White mortgage banker I had encountered during fieldwork with Michael and Jane, agreed to an interview with me in early May 2015. It was during this interview that he described Black mortgage borrowers as coming with a "little more hair on the deal" (discussed previously). As we sat together inside a bustling restaurant near Houston's wealthy, White River Oaks neighborhood, I asked him one last question: "Have you ever witnessed any kind of racial discrimination in the housing market?" He replied,

> I can't say without a doubt that I've seen any kind of discrimination or any kind of attitude, you know. It's all been very, very good here. I think people kind of see, and when it comes to maybe your subject, people kind of see like the invisible hand moving things, you know. You know I guess transitioning things. People in the real estate industry see that, you know, 'cause we're all, you know, in business for ourselves. I like it when home values are higher because it increases my opportunity to be successful.

In his assessment of whether and how racial discrimination may be at play in mortgage lending processes, Brandon drew on a phrase often used to explain economic markets: the "invisible hand." Here, Brandon was referring specifically to how people get mortgages and purchase homes. He said he had not observed any racist intent or discrimination in his career; thus, he believed that any differences in mortgage loan outcomes and where people live were a natural result of impersonal economic forces.

Yet Brandon's own account of his professional work as a mortgage banker as well as the professional routines that I observed first-hand in my field-work did not support the logic of an invisible hand. Rather, White mortgage bankers such as Brandon, as well as real estate agents and other market professionals, were the very *visible* hands of the housing market. More often than not, these hands do their work using racist tools. With respect to seg-regated interindustry networking, White mortgage bankers and agents pur-sued relationships with each other as well as with White clients because they perceived relationships with other White individuals as easier and more prof-itable. At times, White agents did not network with and sometimes explicitly excluded mortgage bankers of color through appeals to racist justifications.

Meanwhile, Black and Latinx mortgage bankers and agents—also visibly shaping the housing market—typically worked with one another, in part because of such exclusion and in part to pursue opportunities for them-selves and to support each other. Agents of color also counseled their home-buying clients of color away from particular White mortgage bankers or lending institutions. They did so because they wanted their clients to avoid experiencing racism during the mortgage lending process. They believed their clients of color deserved fair treatment and did not want to see them discriminated against by mortgage bankers they did not trust. In short, mortgage bankers' and real estate agents' interindustry networking routines shaped distinct connections and loan opportunities for home buyers prior to the actual mortgage loan application process. Yet it was White-segregated banker–agent networking that reinforced exclusion and embedded racism in this process.

Once mortgage bankers and home buyers connected, White mort-gage bankers exercised racialized discretion in evaluating buyers' loan applications. These professionals suspected borrowers of color would be high-risk candidates for mortgage loans based on stereotypical assumptions about Black and Latinx borrowers' income, credit scores, and financial pre-paredness. These and other suspicions persisted even when White mortgage bankers were presented with evidence of racial bias or the financial fitness of the potential borrower. White bankers also exercised racialized discretion when they gauged property risk. In particular, they perceived homes in White neighborhoods as low risk, but they expressed concern about mortgage risk for homes located in neighborhoods of color. White mortgage bankers' exercise of racialized discretion in evaluating mortgage loan applicants and property risk indicates how unequal access to mortgage loans occurs after the application process begins. Such racialized discretion bleeds into one of the final stages of the housing exchange process—when mortgage bankers order appraisals and appraisers determine home value.

5

Appraising Value

For homes purchased with a mortgage loan, the appraisal is one of the final, key steps in the housing exchange process.[1] As discussed in Chapter 4, lenders order appraisals—that is, professional assessments of the for-sale home's value—to help them determine the property risk associated with a loan. These assessments are conducted by appraisers, a group of real estate professionals overseen by state licensing boards and the federal government.[2] If an appraiser arrives at a home value that is at or above the contract price— that is, the price at which the buyer proposes to purchase the home—lenders typically view the property as low risk. If an appraiser decides the home value is lower than the contract price, lenders view the property as high risk. In these cases, the lender can deny the loan or require that the buyer covers the difference between the appraised value and the contract price in their down payment.[3] If the buyer cannot or will not put more down, the seller has to decide whether they want to drop the sale price to meet the appraised value or risk losing the buyer. Either way, the lender ends up loaning less money, thus lowering the risk they believe they are taking on with the property.[4] Appraisers thus play a key role in determining whether and under what conditions a home sale can proceed. Appraisers' assessments also influence how much money sellers can make on the sale of their home.

Contemporary appraisers typically use the *sales comparison approach* to assess a home's value. Although specific aspects of the sales comparison approach have changed with the passage of fair housing legislation, appraisers have been using the same general technique for almost as long as banks have offered mortgages. Before 1968, federal and industry rules explicitly required appraisers to assess individual home values by comparing each for-sale home to other previously sold homes located within the same neighborhood or in other neighborhoods with similar race and class profiles. These rules primed appraisers to use White homeowners' and buyers' racial prejudices as the standard for determining home and neighborhood desirability. A combination of fair housing legislation and lawsuits against the appraisal industry resulted in these explicit rules being removed from appraisal forms and

Race Brokers. Elizabeth Korver-Glenn, Oxford University Press (2021). © Oxford University Press.
DOI: 10.1093/oso/9780190063863.003.0006

training materials. But even with the explicitly racist rules off the books, the appraisers in my study used racist ideas about neighborhoods and people (i.e., the racist market rubric) to fill in the blanks created by deleted appraisal criteria. In particular, they believed that White neighborhoods were the best, most desirable neighborhoods and that neighborhoods of color were less desirable. They also assumed that White buyers were the "typical buyers" whose taste would determine what was and was not "desirable" and that "typical buyers" would match neighborhood race. For these reasons, appraisers did not compare homes across White and not-White neighborhoods, ensuring that the highest values were reserved for homes in White areas.

The appraisers in my study were not just racist outliers. After examining all single-family home values in Houston in 2015, sociologist Junia Howell and I found that homes in White neighborhoods were worth approximately twice as much as homes in Black and Latinx neighborhoods, even when considering such important variables as individual home quality and size and other key neighborhood characteristics, including poverty and crime (Howell and Korver-Glenn 2018). At the very least, my data indicate that appraisers' ongoing use of the sales comparison approach recycles home values that were initially determined under the explicitly racist appraisal criteria used prior to the 1960s and 1970s. This recycling process maintains unequal home values. But the degree of home value inequality across White neighborhoods and neighborhoods of color has not remained constant. Instead, the level of inequality in home values across racially distinct neighborhoods has increased during the past several decades—and, net of historic appraisals, contemporary appraisals have played a key role in this increase (Howell and Korver-Glenn, forthcoming). My data suggest that appraisers have contributed to this growing inequality through their use of racist, if unofficial, appraisal logic and methods.

The Racist History and Legacy of the Sales Comparison Approach

Some historical background is useful to understand how the sales comparison approach continues to contribute to racial segregation and economic inequality. Beginning in the 1930s, the U.S. federal government and professional appraisers sought to systematize the appraisal industry by adopting a "scientific" approach to appraising. At the time, appraisers were using a variety of logics and methods to assess home value. For example, prior to the establishment of the Federal Housing Administration (FHA) and the Home Owners' Loan Corporation (HOLC) in the 1930s, the most common way to appraise was the cost approach. This approach emphasized individual home structure and lot as the most important components of determining home value. When using the cost approach, appraisers "estimated the value of a property by calculating the reproduction cost of the building (minus physical depreciation) plus the value of the land" (Stuart 2003:31).

The two new federal agencies endorsed an alternative method of appraising: the sales comparison approach. This approach tasked appraisers with using prior home sales in the vicinity of the for-sale home as the main determinant of the for-sale home's value. That is, appraisers were to examine the prices of previously sold homes to gauge the value of the for-sale home. These previously sold homes were to be similar to and near the for-sale home. Unlike the cost approach, the sales comparison approach elevated the neighborhoods in which individual homes were located as equally or more important than the structure or condition of individual homes (Koopman 2019; Stuart 2003; Woods 2012).

Three components of this historical approach laid the foundation for the contemporary appraisal practices I observed during my fieldwork and interviews. One was the theory of value adopted and implemented by the FHA, which stated that homogeneous or uniform neighborhoods were the most desirable. That is, homogeneous neighborhoods had the highest value and lowest risk. Thus, homes within these areas had higher values than otherwise similar homes located in diverse or mixed neighborhoods. In fact, their definition of "neighborhood" assumed homogeneity. According to the FHA's *Underwriting Manual* (1938: part II, paragraph 903(d), italics in original),

> *Neighborhood* is defined as a single area composed of locations separated only by publicly used land, the residential portions of which exhibit a degree of homogeneity. In general, a neighborhood is available for, or improved with, dwellings of more or less similar character, age, and quality.

Likewise, the *Underwriting Manual* (FHA 1936: part I, paragraph 316) stated,

> The best type of residential district is one in which the values of the individual properties vary within comparatively narrow limits. In such a district one is likely to find people whose living standards likewise are

substantially the same.... Such a district is characterized by uniformity and is much more likely to enjoy relatively great stability and permanence of desirability, utility, and value than a district in which the residential values are found to vary within wider limits.

In other words, rather than choosing an approach that prioritized individual home characteristics, the newly formed appraisal profession—strongly influenced by federal underwriting guidelines—promoted neighborhoods as the driving factor in determining individual property risk. Then, it defined neighborhoods as homogeneous and assumed such areas were more desirable and presented lower property risk. Other diverse or mixed areas did not fit the definition of neighborhood; thus, appraisers believed these areas were less desirable and higher risk. Appraisers assigned higher values to homes in (uniform) neighborhoods and lower values to homes in diverse or mixed areas.

A second key aspect of the historical sales comparison approach that framed how appraisers in my study used this method was that appraisers explicitly defined neighborhood homogeneity as uniformly White and/or high income through the FHA's risk rating system (Stuart 2003; Woods 2012). Frederick Babcock, the architect of the FHA's initial *Underwriting Manual*, viewed the risk rating system as a logically necessary complement to his valuation theory, given the inherent uncertainty of assessing (future) value. The neighborhood risk rating system—likely influenced by HOLC's redlining strategy (Woods 2012)—was explicitly racist and classist. For example, the *Underwriting Manual* (FHA 1936: part II, paragraph 233) stated,

> The Valuator should investigate areas surrounding the location [individual home being appraised] to determine whether or not incompatible racial and social groups are present, to the end that an intelligent prediction may be made regarding the possibility or probability of the location being invaded by such groups. If a neighborhood is to retain stability it is necessary that properties shall continue to be occupied by the same social and racial classes. A change in social and racial occupancy generally leads to instability and a reduction in values.

Appraisers assumed that home values would decline in White neighborhoods with increasing numbers of non-White individuals (the "racial groups" seen as "invading" White territory) and in high-income neighborhoods with increasing numbers of low-income individuals (see Taylor 2019).

The official Appraisal Report created by the FHA reflected these racist and classist assumptions about neighborhoods, their residents, and home values. This report, shown in Figure 5.1, required appraisers to rate the location of the individual home they were assessing. Specifically, the form required appraisers to assign the neighborhood numerical values with scaled weights in eight categories designed to assess the location's desirability, ranging from its convenience to transportation and freedom from "special hazards" to more subjective issues such as "relative economic stability" and "appeal."

Given that several of these categories were open to interpretation, the FHA *Underwriting Manual* provided instructions. Under "Appeal," for example, the manual directed appraisers to measure the "social attractiveness" of the home's location. Specifically, it outlined that "satisfaction, contentment, and comfort result from association with persons of similar attributes. Families enjoy social relationships with other families whose education, abilities, mode of living, and racial characteristics are similar to their own" (FHA

Rating of Location

FEATURE	REJECT	1	2	3	4	5	RATING
Relative Economic Stability		4	8	12	16	20	
Protection from Adverse Influences		1	2	3	4	5	
Freedom from Special Hazards		1	2	3	4	5	
Adequacy of Civic, Social, and Commercial Centers		2	4	1	8	10	
Adequacy of Transportation		1	2	3	4	5	
Sufficiency of Utilities and Conveniences		1	2	3	4	5	
Level of Taxes and Special Assessments		2	4	6	8	10	
Appeal							
TOTAL RATING OF LOCATION							

Figure 5.1 "Rating of Location" report established in the FHA's 1938 *Underwriting Manual*.

1938: part II, paragraph 973). Importantly, the manual and appraisers reserved high scores on "Appeal" for homes in White neighborhoods, not Black or Latinx neighborhoods. Thus, when they appraised home value, appraisers checked the surrounding area for "similar"—that is, White—residents because they assumed the default homeowner and home buyer were White and would prefer to live near other White families.

Interpreting appeal in this way was related to the third key carryover component: The FHA, its *Underwriting Manual,* and appraisers assumed that potential home buyers would match the racial and class characteristics of the neighborhood in which individual homes were located. According to the FHA (1938), prospective buyers were grouped by the "income group or the social class which constitutes the market for properties near the location under consideration" (part II, paragraph 973). The FHA presumed that homes were "competitive" with, or comparable to, each other if they were located in race- and class-similar areas and if buyers' race and class characteristics matched the "market" of other home buyers who would purchase homes in these areas. In this way, the FHA required appraisers to *imagine* buyers and determine whether or not they would desire to live in particular neighborhoods. Appraisers were to gauge this desire or demand by considering buyers' racial or social similarity to others already living in the area. This practice reinforced the idea that individuals of distinct races and classes comprised fundamentally distinct markets that corresponded with distinct home values.

Each of these three components of appraisal logic shaped how appraisers assessed home value through the 1960s and into the 1970s. In particular, this logic guided how they selected the main data used for valuation: previous comparable home sales, or "comps," from within the for-sale home's neighborhood. Appraisers used comp sale prices to calculate and adjust the value of the for-sale, or subject, home (Stuart 2003). To select comps, appraisers examined previous home sales from within the same (uniform) neighborhood. Or, if such comps were not available, appraisers selected comps from other similarly uniform neighborhoods. Again, because of the logic outlined and systematized by the FHA, appraisers understood uniformity as racial and class similarity as well as homogeneous architectural style. In its *Underwriting Manual* (1938: part III, paragraph 1405, italics in original), the FHA outlined how appraisers should assess home value through selecting comps:

An estimate of the value of the land is made by comparison in accordance with the instructions in Section 13. . . . A judgment is formed with respect to the *available market price* of the subject property.... This requires consideration of sales data relating to improved properties of similar type and characteristics in the same or in competing neighborhoods.... The derived capital value is compared with the estimates of available market price and replacement cost of property in new condition. This comparison leads to the determination of the *estimate of value*. The latter figure is the Valuator's final total valuation.

In setting out this method, the FHA made its racist and classist appraisal logic concrete. That is, in defining the sales comparison approach in this way, matching a method to this approach, and systematizing the approach as the most common way to appraise home value, the FHA ensured that individual home value was deeply entwined with neighborhood racial and class composition and imagined "markets" of prospective buyers.

The sales comparison approach is not merely a relic of the past; it did not expire with the passage of fair housing laws. Rather, the appraisal industry continued to espouse such explicitly racist logic and methods—upholding the theory and associated practices that "the most desirable urban structure was one in which people were separated by race and class" (Stuart 2003:66)—even after the passage of fair housing legislation. In 1976, the Justice Department brought a lawsuit against the American Institute of Real Estate Appraisers (AIREA), the Society of Real Estate Appraisers, and two other defendants for allegedly continuing to use race and national origin as determinants of lower home value in neighborhoods of color. Ultimately, the case was not resolved through litigation; instead, the parties entered a settlement agreement in which the AIREA agreed to adopt three policy statements negating the importance of race and national origin for property or neighborhood valuation and to incorporate these policy statements in its training and instructional materials.[5] Accordingly, the AIREA removed explicit references to neighborhood racial characteristics and racial homogeneity. But more than eighty years after its initial emergence, the sales comparison approach remains the most common approach used for residential appraisals today.

Even absent explicit guidance tying home values to neighborhood racial composition, the federal government and appraisal organizations continue to perpetuate the logic of neighborhood uniformity and imagined home buyer (sub)markets, which guides how appraisers select comps. In the contemporary housing market, mortgages are often purchased or guaranteed by the

Federal National Mortgage Association, commonly known as Fannie Mae.[6] In its *Selling Guide*, Fannie Mae (2020: section B4-1.3-03) states that "an analysis of the subject property's neighborhood is a key element in the appraisal process" and assumes that "varying conditions . . . characterize different types of neighborhoods." These statements elevate the neighborhood as the key factor shaping subject home value and assume that there are readily recognizable "types" of neighborhoods. Although Fannie Mae emphasizes that its "appraisal report forms and guidelines do not require the appraiser to rate or judge the neighborhood," it nevertheless directs "the appraiser to perform an objective neighborhood analysis by identifying neighborhood boundaries, neighborhood characteristics, and the factors that affect the value and marketability of properties in the neighborhood" (section B4-1.3-03).

In defining the "factors that affect the value and marketability of properties in the neighborhood," Fannie Mae (2020: section B4-1.3-03) explains, "These can be addressed by such things as the proximity of the property to employment and amenities, employment stability, appeal to the market, changes in land use, access to public transportation, and adverse environmental influences." These six criteria are strikingly similar to the eight criteria used in the FHA's (1938) *Underwriting Manual*: relative economic stability; protection from adverse influences; freedom from special hazards; adequacy of civic, social, and commercial centers; adequacy of transportation; sufficiency of utilities and conveniences; level of taxes and special assessments; and appeal (see Figure 5.1).

Moreover, as with the FHA's (1938) emphasis on buyers who could be grouped into "markets," Fannie Mae (2020: section B4-1.3-03) requires appraisers to account for "typical buyers" in determining neighborhood comparability. Appraisers' judgments about "typical buyers" for an area then determine the area(s) from which appraisers can acceptably choose comps:

> An appraiser must perform a neighborhood analysis in order to identify the area that is subject to the same influences as the property being appraised, based on the actions of typical buyers. The results of a neighborhood analysis enable the appraiser not only to identify the factors that influence the value of properties in the neighborhood, but also to define the area from which to select the market data needed to perform a sales comparison analysis.

By instructing appraisers to account for "the actions of typical buyers," federal appraisal guidelines prime appraisers to envision a home buyer reference group that would either want to live in or avoid a particular "type" of neighborhood.

Professional appraisal associations and training materials also continue to emphasize neighborhood homogeneity and the desirability of different neighborhoods to different buyer markets. In the most recent iteration of its *The Appraisal of Real Estate* (2013:165) handbook, the Appraisal Institute states that neighborhood boundaries "may coincide with observable changes in land use or demographic characteristics." Furthermore, it directs appraisers to draw preliminary neighborhood boundaries because "the boundaries of market areas, neighborhoods, and districts identify the areas that influence a subject property's value" (p. 165). Then, it instructs appraisers to check their preliminary boundaries against the demographic characteristics of those who live inside these boundaries. Through this training, the Appraisal Institute reinforces the idea that social difference is between neighborhoods, not within them.

The Appraisal Institute (2013) also assumes that these neighborhoods, or market areas, are "divided into categories based on property types and their appeal to different market participants" (p. 163). Moreover, "focusing on the demographic characteristics that tend to influence property values most in a community" (pp. 166–167) is a necessary aspect of the appraisal process. "Of course," the manual continues, "comparing price levels in one market with prices in competing areas serves as an indication of the overall desirability of the areas" (p. 167). The Appraisal Institute goes on to detail several social, economic, governmental, and environmental influences that it states are necessary for defining neighborhoods and assessing the value of homes within them through selecting comps. These factors include educational characteristics, household size, extent of crime, mean and median household income levels, property value levels and trends, amount of development and construction, quality of public services (e.g., schools), general maintenance, and effective ages of properties, among many others. Like current federal guidelines and rules, these training materials rely on the logic of neighborhood uniformity and "typical buyer" markets as well as the methods to implement such logic in appraisal practice. In doing so, these training guidelines stipulate evaluative criteria that produce higher valuations for White neighborhoods through reference to systemic racial inequality (e.g., mean and median household income levels, property value levels and trends, and amount of development and construction; see Chapter 2) or that produce higher valuations for White neighborhoods through appraisers' *perceptions* of neighborhood characteristics (discussed later).

The federal government and professional appraisal associations have removed all explicit rules about assessing home value through a racialized lens from their official forms and training materials. But their emphasis on neighborhood uniformity, factors affecting value, and "typical buyers" as key to appraisal logic and methods rehash the same ideas about neighborhood difference and social incompatibility as those in the FHA's *Underwriting Manual*, written 80 years prior. These criteria set the stage for how home value inequality and racial segregation continue to be produced by justifying and underwriting appraisers' use of racialized logic in the contemporary valuation process. Such logic infused the narratives and methodological practices of appraisers in my study.

How Much Is a Home Worth?

The appraisers in my study viewed home values as inevitably—even inherently—tied to the neighborhoods in which individual homes were located. They also associated particular markets of prospective buyers with certain neighborhoods. In doing so, appraisers repeatedly relied on several assumptions, including neighborhood uniformity, differences in neighborhood demand resulting in differences in home value, and home buyer markets that matched (or did not match) and demanded (or avoided) homes in particular neighborhoods. Moreover, appraisers showed that they understood neighborhood uniformity in terms of home style as well as neighborhood race and class characteristics. They also imagined competing markets in terms of buyers' race and class characteristics. In this way, the explicitly racist logic characterizing official appraisal standards until 1976 was carried forward in unofficial yet widespread contemporary appraisal practices.

For example, Allan, a White appraiser, began telling me about the appraisal process by describing neighborhoods as key to determining subject home value, especially when it came to his perceptions of neighborhood "charm" and architectural style. As he explained it,

What I've found is that the neighborhood makes a significant difference [for home values]. Like, I'm looking at a townhouse on the [north] side of [Interstate (I-)] 610 right now off of Shepherd. I found a townhouse that was just on the [south] side of [I-]610 within, kind of, the general Heights neighborhood. And the price is about $50,000 more. And it's no nicer, it's just . . . I think the neighborhood south of [I-]610 in the Heights area, the homes are more architecturally interesting. They're older. The construction quality and design—it feels different. *So the houses may look the same on paper, but if you drive around the neighborhood, you can see that the charm goes down a little bit in terms of the construction of the homes.* [Italics added]

Allan emphasized that individual homes could be exactly the same, but the "feel" or "nice-ness" of the neighborhood in which each individual home was located was the overriding factor determining the home's value.

Later in his interview, Allan again elevated the neighborhood as the key logical underpinning of appraising. When I asked him about the relationship between schools and home values, he invoked neighborhood uniformity, indicating that neighborhood demographics were involved in his approach. "And so," Allan continued,

it's important to kind of stay in that neighborhood. It's always best to try and find things that are most similar within your neighborhood. [The re- lationship between schools and home values] kind of depends on—like in Oak Forest. They have one of the best elementary schools in Houston, so if you can get zoned to Oak Forest Elementary. That's really driven the prices up over there in Garden Oaks—it's that elementary school. So, [schools are] important to maybe 10 or 20 percent [of the home's value], but still, I take that into consideration. It really is neighborhood-driven, based on the demographics and the sales price driving the income of homeowners.[7]

I decided to probe further to unpack what Allan meant. I presented him with social scientific evidence that home values in White neighborhoods are systematically higher than home values in neighborhoods of color, and I then asked him to explain what he thought was happening. He replied,

It's kind of generalizing, but it seems to me that neighborhoods where I go to [appraise] where there are pockets where they're very strictly one ethnicity—it just seems like they're generally lower priced, and overall the properties aren't as well-kept.

Allan first ignored that White neighborhoods tend to be predominantly one "ethnicity." Then, he explained that he believed home values were lower in neighborhoods of color, or what he calls "pockets where they're very strictly one ethnicity," because they were uniformly poorly maintained;

simultaneously, he assumed that neighborhoods of color were uniformly low income. Such logic is not new (e.g., see Helper 1969; Taylor 2019). However, it is important to note that this appraiser, interviewed in 2015, still carried this racist logic into his everyday appraisal work.

Like Allan, Eddie, a Hispanic appraiser, subscribed to the principle of neighborhood uniformity and its connection to schools. Initially, Eddie explained differences in property value across different neighborhoods as due to "different ZIP codes." When I showed him a Houston map and pointed to a ZIP code that encompassed an area I knew was understood locally as two distinct neighborhoods, Eddie clarified:

> This is Woodland Heights. Even though it's the same ZIP code, I would never go across [I-]45 for a comp. The first thing you want to do is stay within a ZIP code. And I'm surprised that this is 77009 over here. But we all know—all appraisers know you don't go—especially in Woodland Heights. You certainly don't go across [I-]45 to Fulton Street for comps. They're going to be different schools, for one thing. And different predominant values. I guarantee right now, predominant value is significantly lower over here [in Near Northside]. Everything else the same—same house, same square footage, same quality.

Eddie explained that these two neighborhoods were internally uniform, but differences *across* these neighborhoods made them incomparable. That is, Eddie believed that within each of these neighborhoods, schools were similar. But, because he believed that schools and "predominant values," or the most common home prices (or price ranges), were fundamentally distinct between the two areas, he would never select comps for individual homes across these neighborhood boundaries. Thus, even if he assessed a home in one neighborhood and found a remarkably similar previously sold home in the other neighborhood—one virtually identical in terms of construction quality, size, and so on—he would not select it as a comp.

Another White appraiser, Larry, emphasized "the market" for individual neighborhoods over their presumed inherent characteristics. I interviewed Larry outside a restaurant in Cypress, Texas—a northwest Houston suburb—in November 2015 because the location was convenient for his work that day. Although the muted roar of traffic on U.S. Highway 290 behind us made the setting less than ideal, Larry described his understanding of appraisal logic clearly and plainly:

And then you have to identify the property you're appraising. What are the features and characteristics about it that make it desirable? The competitive part. What are buyers in that market interested in? And once you identify the property, then you can start researching the market. You define what the neighborhood is. What's a similar neighborhood, what would other buyers consider part of that neighborhood.

Larry later went on to explain that he believed neighborhood racial dynamics and demand were associated with neighborhood uniformity, desirability, and home values. He stated that an "influx of minorities" to a neighborhood would be perceived by White homeowners as having a "negative impact" on the area. In turn, White homeowners would leave. He believed this racial change would lower home values in the area in three ways: A heterogeneous (as opposed to uniform) neighborhood would be by definition less desirable; this decreased desirability would lower demand; and, over time, the increasing proportions of homeowners of color would lower the socioeconomic status of the area. Larry thought each of these dynamics, as they unfolded sequentially, would contribute to lower home values in the area.

Each of Larry's beliefs rested on racist assumptions. The first, that a heterogeneous neighborhood is a less desirable neighborhood, assumed that a neighborhood must be uniformly White to be desirable to White homeowners. The second, that less desirability means lower demand, assumed that Whites' perceptions of desirability are the most important factor in determining "demand." Finally, the third, that increasing proportions of homeowning residents of color would lower the socioeconomic status of an area, assumed that individuals of color are low income and that low-income neighbors of color are a harm to home values. Through these assumptions, Larry illustrated one of the implied tenets of the "typical buyer" logic: Appraisers perceived the neighborhoods where White consumers demand homes as more desirable—and thus more valuable—than those where consumers of color demand homes.

Similarly, Diego, a middle-aged Mexican American appraiser, entwined neighborhood uniformity, "typical" buyers (constituting what he called "market groups"), and desirability in his understanding of appraisal logic:

So if a person is going to be interested in buying in Fifth Ward, would that same person go to Denver Harbor to buy? Would that person go to Second Ward to buy? Would they go to Kashmere Gardens? I think that ethnicity has something to do with it. So a person who's buying for that market group is buying in Second Ward, they probably aren't going to go to Fifth Ward and buy a house. Ultimately, I think what's important to look at is your quality of buyer. So the same quality buyer is going to buy in Lindale, and the same buyer is going to buy in midtown. Then they want midtown; they're professional, young, urban, double-income type—you know. They want to buy close to downtown, so that's that market segment.

All of the neighborhoods Diego mentioned were distinguished by distinct racial dynamics. Moreover, in Diego's view, the race of the "typical buyer," or market, for homes in these neighborhoods would match each area. In other words, because of the principles of uniformity and "typical buyers," Diego assumed that buyers' racial identity would lead them to desire and purchase homes in areas that reflected that identity. In his opinion, regardless of the characteristics of individual homes, homes in Latinx neighborhoods (Denver Harbor and Second Ward) and Black neighborhoods (Fifth Ward and Kashmere Gardens) were not directly comparable. Diego believed that Latinx buyers would not consider purchasing homes in Kashmere Gardens or Fifth Ward, and Black buyers would not consider purchasing homes in Second Ward or Denver Harbor.

The "typical buyer" aspect of appraisal logic also emerged during Carl's interview, held at his office in suburban Houston. Carl, a White appraiser and owner of an appraisal management company, explained how he imagined prospective White buyers would react if they thought a home they were interested in purchasing was being sold by a Black homeowner:

> I don't know if when White people are out looking and they go into a home, and sometimes you can walk in and go, "Oh, it's obviously a Black person that lives here." I don't know if White people are saying "I'm not buying this house." I did [appraise] a house one time over in Riverstone. And you walked inside and it was purple, it was Black. I guess he was very ethnic to his race. I thought when I walked in—because [the homeowner wasn't] home—but I thought right away when I walked in, this is a Black guy. I think people want to be near their own kind. And I feel 100 percent about that. And I think it's factual when you look at the racial makeup of neighborhoods.

Carl believed that prospective White buyers would not want to purchase a home owned by a Black person—perhaps because it served as a signal that there were other Black residents nearby—and that they wanted to live near other White individuals. Carl and the other appraisers I studied used the neighborhood uniformity and typical buyer logics to guide their valuation methods.

Finding Comps

Appraisers, like real estate agents, rely heavily on Multiple Listing Service (MLS) or other home sale data and software (e.g., CoreLogic). In order to appraise residential property in Texas, appraisers must be licensed by the Texas Appraiser Licensing & Certification Board.[8] Licensed appraisers use information in the MLS or other databases as a primary resource in carrying out the sales comparison approach to appraising. Just as they did prior to fair housing law, appraisers select comps—previously sold, comparable homes in the vicinity of the for-sale property—and use comp sale prices to determine the appraised value of the for-sale home. Appraisers determine what is "comparable"—it could be similar building and lot square footage, number of bedrooms, number of bathrooms, quality of construction (interior and exterior), the condition of the home, or other features—as well as what is "in the vicinity." Then, they can adjust the appraised value of the for-sale home up or down depending on how it varies from the comp homes.

Appraisers exercise discretion in selecting comps (Howell and Korver-Glenn 2018; Korver-Glenn 2018b); for the appraisers in my study, this discretion was guided by the logic of neighborhood uniformity and "typical buyers," or markets. For example, after Larry explained his understanding of appraisal theory (discussed previously), he described how his logic affected the process of selecting comps:

> So the three biggest things in real estate are location, location, location. If you're able to stay not only within the same subdivision but often times within the same section. Most of the homes that I appraise are in planned developments, which are different from what you do inside the Loop. But in most planned developments, pricing is based on the lot width. And they may have different deed restrictions depending on the different sections. They have different features. So oftentimes I see other appraisers that will just grab comparables from any section as long as it's relatively similar in size. I think, if you can, stay within the same section so you're truly looking at something comparable. I think staying within—so location is the main thing.

For Larry, the logic of uniformity drove his method of choosing comps to the point that, if possible, he would select homes from the same *section* of a subdivision. Larry deemed irrelevant the possibility that homes in other neighborhoods might also be similar in terms of style and deed restrictions. Thus, Larry did not pull comps from different neighborhoods because he believed homes located elsewhere precluded them from consideration.

Other appraisers entwined neighborhood uniformity with their understandings of "typical buyers" when they selected comps. This was particularly clear when they described what they thought were distinct markets that matched each neighborhood. Appraisers' explicit and implicit racist logic and appeals to the racist market rubric were most evident in these instances. Here, I quote Allan at length because he exemplified these dynamics in his explanation of how he selected comps:

ALLAN: The nicer the neighborhood, the more expensive the dirt is.

EKG: Okay. So how do you quantify the demand for land values when you're appraising?

ALLAN: Okay. Well, what we do is we appraise the whole component. We don't break out the land. And so in theory, you're looking for the same building, or the same property, or similar, in that neighborhood. So ideally, you would find either, you know, that same builder or a comparable builder that's in the same pocket that has the same demand. And you have schools, close proximity to universities, employment, freeways, recreation [that drive demand]. So, you know, Montrose is where *everyone wants to be*—it's close to the schools, it's close to downtown, the [medical] center and all the recreation stuff. So the builder down there can charge a . . . $300,000 premium, because that's *where everybody wants to live*. And then up here [north of Montrose] *it's getting better because of all the Mexican people moving out*, but still *no one really wants to live* down by where they tore down the Astrodome,[9] because that's kind of no-man's land. So, again, once you start jumping freeways and going to other neighborhoods, you're gonna have to have a subjective adjustment of what's the land value, and *the demand or the appeal of that neighborhood there*. [Italics added]

Allan did not have all buyers in mind when he described how "nice" he believed a neighborhood was or its level of demand. Instead, Allan used White buyers' racist prejudice as the standard for determining how nice or in demand a neighborhood was when he stated that a neighborhood was getting "better because of all the Mexican people moving out." By contrast, he emphasized that "no one"—meaning no White people—wanted to live near the old Astrodome area, which is proximate to both Black and Asian neighborhoods. In other words, Allan selected comps by referring to *White* buyers' understandings of appeal and desirability. In turn, Allan's comp choices shaped land and property values for current and future residents (just as previous appraisers' choices had shaped the data he was using).

Similarly, Jeremy, another White appraiser, explained that he chose comps based on whether he believed neighborhoods were desirable to the market of White buyers he had in mind:

JEREMY: I think what happens is, *you start at a place that's good, or that's perceived by the market to be good. Alright? Desirable.* And then you work out from there, regardless. I think the highways are a sort of, almost a psychological barrier more than a real—There's not much difference in the houses in Lindale Park, although they're newer than the older part of the Heights. They're fifteen, twenty years newer. But Lindale Park is about the same value as Brooke Smith, which is right on the border of [I-]45. Just on the other side of [I-]45. So I think what happens is, *people wanna live there* [in the Heights], but now that land and the central part of the Heights is $60 a foot, and it used to be $35 not too long ago. Well okay, now that that's $550,000, *that's not really working for me, so what's the next closest place?* So I think right now that's Lindale Park. Here's another thing to think about: If you go north of the freeway, into Independence Heights— Do you know where that is?

EKG: Yes. Yeah.

JEREMY: Okay. *That's terrible up there.* And that's closer to the heart of the Heights than Lindale Park, really. It's literally just on the other side of the [I-610] freeway. [Italics added]

Independence Heights is a predominantly Black Houston neighborhood just north of I-610 and west of I-45. It is located just north of the broader Heights area, across I-610. Although the Independence Heights neighborhood was closer to the Heights than Lindale Park, Jeremy explained he would not choose comps from Independence Heights—an area he described as "terrible"—when appraising a Heights home. The area was geographically closer, but it did not match where "people"—that is, White buyers—wanted to live as much as did Lindale Park, a predominantly Latinx, middle-class neighborhood.

Jeremy continued by explaining that he also chose comps based on land value and age of the home. According to him, land value was higher in more desirable locations and lower in less desirable locations. "People don't necessarily wanna live amongst all that, you know, junk," he asserted, "They'd rather live in a nice, homogeneous sort of area." Like Allan, Jeremy was not referring to *all* prospective buyers when he judged an area's desirability. Rather, he had a particular group of people in mind when describing the desirability of different neighborhoods. These buyers, he assumed, would also think that the Independent Heights neighborhood was "terrible" and that the Heights area, the (increasingly White but still White and Latinx) Brooke Smith neighborhood, and Lindale Park were more desirable than Independence Heights. For Jeremy, White buyers were the "typical buyers" who would find White neighborhoods more desirable. In turn, Jeremy chose comps from other White, increasingly White, or even Latinx areas because he assumed these areas were a better match for the typical White buyer than a Black neighborhood such as Independence Heights.

Carl also compared Lindale Park and the Heights area, but he explained he would not choose comps for a Heights home from Lindale Park. As a reminder, Lindale Park is a largely middle-class, deed-restricted Latinx neighborhood near downtown Houston. The Heights area, west of Lindale Park across I-45, is equally close to downtown Houston and is a largely deed-restricted middle- and upper-middle-class White community (for photographs of Lindale Park and Heights homes, see Figure 5.2). In terms of house size and quality, Lindale Park has comparable housing stock to homes in the Heights. In fact, lot sizes tend to be larger in Lindale Park than in the Heights and, as Jeremy noted, Lindale Park homes tend to be newer than Heights homes. Given its geographic, socioeconomic, and housing stock comparability to some areas of the Heights, it would be reasonable for an appraiser to choose comps across these neighborhood boundaries, as Jeremy noted previously. Yet Carl believed that the Latinx status of Lindale Park meant low housing quality and crime, so he would not choose comps across these areas.

Instead, Carl compared Lindale Park to Quail Valley, a subdivision in a Houston suburb approximately 30 miles away. He believed that because Lindale Park and Quail Valley had similar racial demographics, they were more likely to be comparable than similar properties in a neighboring community with different demographics. Similarly, he compared

(a)

(b)

(c)

(d)

(e)

(f)

Figure 5.2 Comparing Lindale Park and Heights neighborhood housing stock. (A–C) Various scenes from Lindale Park. (D–F) Various scenes from the Heights.

Source: All photographs by Elizabeth Korver-Glenn.

the Heights area to West University Place, or "West U," a small munici-
pality completely encircled by the City of Houston that, like the Heights, is
predominantly White:

> As an appraiser, we run into stuff as far as racial stuff. Lindale Park, being
> on the east side [of I-45]—I'll just use Quail Valley as an example. The west
> part of Quail Valley, they're very nice homes, the highest homes over there
> get to be about $400[000], but you go to Quail Valley east, and they're all the
> one-story, it's a largely Black and Hispanic population, lot of rental houses,
> the homes are not maintained, and so they suffer. It's the same thing with
> Lindale Park. The Heights has always been great, because it's the Heights.
> It's like, "Oh, I'm living in West U." You know, and Lindale Park, it's like, "I'm
> over there in the ghetto." It's kinda scary, 'cause if I go by to appraise a house
> over there, um, I'm kinda looking around. As for the Heights, I'm driving
> right up to the house, I have no worries.

Carl assumed that neighborhoods of color had poorly maintained homes,
and he expressed feeling fear when he appraised homes in these areas.
Moreover, Carl believed that homes in communities of color were comparable or similar despite numerous objective differences—including house
size and quality, neighborhood socioeconomic status, location centrality,
and so on—indicating otherwise. Because Carl assumed neighborhoods of
color were uniformly low quality, low value, high crime, and overall undesirable, he would choose comps for homes in these areas only from other communities of color. Similarly, he would not choose comps for homes in White
neighborhoods from communities of color.

Derek, another White appraiser, also explained how the neighborhood
uniformity and typical buyer logics guided which comps he chose, providing
numerous examples of local neighborhoods and subdivisions to show how
this played out in his everyday work. One such area, Fairfield, was located in
northwest Houston next to a smaller subdivision:

> Fairfield is way up northwest. Big tract homes. And there's some cool
> custom homes up there. And I'm doing one [appraisal] right next to it. Just
> to the east is a three-road subdivision, basically one big road with a couple
> little small little cul-de-sacs. And they're all 3½ acres. They're all giant
> custom homes. You can have horses and stuff. Well people are going to buy
> there for what? Acreage, large custom home, and horses. And you're telling

me the same people that are buying in there [in the three-road subdivision] are buying in Fairfield and vice versa? No. *That is a pocket neighborhood. You don't go out of it. You don't.* But you can. You can go ten miles away, but you'll go two or three school districts out. Not doing that. *I'm in the buyer's head. I am the buyer.* The buyer sets a value, right? Seller is asking the buyer's terms about it. *I am in the buyer's head. What would the typical buyer in the market pay? And we use that term a lot, typical buyer in the market. This home competes directly with the typical buyer in the market.* Whether it's in the neighborhood or not. [Italics added]

Derek repeatedly emphasized that he had to "be the buyer" or get "in the buyer's head" to determine which homes would be comparable and, ultimately, which homes to select as comps. Doing so required making assumptions about what the buyer wanted in a home. In this case, such assumptions included "acreage, large custom home[s], and horses."

But assumptions about what buyers wanted did not end with home or lot characteristics. In an account strikingly similar to that of Carl, Derek went on to describe a White neighborhood (Inwood Forest) and a Black neighborhood (Acres Homes). These neighborhoods bordered each other, but Derek believed they were completely incompatible, especially before Whites began moving out of Inwood Forest. He perceived Acres Homes as crime-ridden and dangerous, which he said was the source of its perceived incompatibility with Inwood Forest. Derek then expressed discomfort appraising homes in Acres Homes—the neighborhood where current Houston Mayor Sylvester Turner grew up and now lives:

So you had a neighborhood on the northwest side, Inwood Forest. Great example of White flight. And they had a great golf course. They had a great club house. It was a good golf course. . . It wasn't championship. It wasn't Memorial Park. And it wasn't Royal Oaks. It was in good shape. The mortgage industry used to have golf tournaments there *all* the time. I mean, it was happening. Next door, Acres Homes. Cops everywhere. Now there is no golf course, there is no club house. You have meadows. It's gone. You're a bike ride away from crime, and people like to be safe, even in this Second Amendment county that we live in. It's pitiful. I do some stuff in Acres Homes, and quite frankly, I don't like going in there in my Tahoe. I get some looks. The older people—when I stop and I kind of stand there, I say, "Hi, I'm [Derek]. I'm just doing an appraisal here." They're all pretty nice. But you get the young kids, you know, they should be working.

As in the previous examples, when Derek mentioned "people" liking safety, he meant the White people who used to live in Inwood Forest and prospective White buyers, not the Black residents who live in Acres Homes or other prospective buyers who would want to live in Acres Homes. Derek's understanding of neighborhood uniformity and the "typical buyer" was supported by racist logics that deem White buyers and White neighborhoods as desirable and comparable and buyers and neighborhoods of color as undesirable and comparable. Specifically, he assumed Acres Homes was crime-ridden and emphasized that Black "young kids" in the area "should be working"—a racist statement that pulls on notions of Black individuals as unenterprising or lazy and simultaneously treats Black children as adults. He then connected these racist ideas to his housing market perceptions and behaviors—illustrating how the racist market rubric works. Derek, like the other appraisers in my study, viewed White buyers and neighborhoods as not comparable to buyers and neighborhoods of color. Thus, they rarely chose comps across White–Latinx neighborhoods and never described choosing comps across White–Black neighborhoods.

A final example of how neighborhood uniformity and "typical buyer" logics affected appraisers' comp choices emerged during Diego's interview. Diego explained,

> So if [neighborhoods] don't directly compete, I don't think they should be used as comparable data. The market value is based on the principle of substitution. If I didn't buy this house in Fifth Ward today, what else am I going to go to buy? Well, so, the demographics are going to dictate that I'm probably going to go to Kashmere Gardens. I'm probably going to go maybe even a little north of [I-]610. Am I going to [choose] maybe even Pleasantville? But am I going to go to Second Ward? The demographics are completely different, and I don't think that they directly compete because of that.

Diego viewed Fifth Ward as comparable to Kashmere Gardens and Pleasantville, two other Black Houston neighborhoods. But he believed that Fifth Ward was not comparable to Second Ward, a nearby Latinx neighborhood. He explained that he would not choose comps for a Fifth Ward home from the Second Ward because these areas had distinct demographics that "dictate" distinct buyer markets. In this way, Diego and the other appraisers I interviewed and observed used race as a major category in determining neighborhood uniformity and "typical buyers," comparability and their individual comp choices, and, ultimately, home values. In particular, they used the racist market rubric to define White areas and buyers as desirable and neighborhoods and buyers of color as relatively undesirable and incompatible with White areas and buyers.

The appraisers I interviewed represent appraisal companies from throughout the Houston metropolitan area, including three appraisers who owned appraisal management companies and oversaw dozens of individual appraisers. As such, these interview data paint a dire picture of how racist ideas form the logical and methodological basis for contemporary appraisal practices. But the appraisers in my sample were not randomly selected, and their views may represent appraisal extremes. To better understand the extent to which race matters in assessing home values, I now turn to a quantitative analysis of appraisal data.

Neighborhood Racial Composition and Appraised Value

Because the appraisers in my study repeatedly referred to (their perceptions of) neighborhood racial composition when describing their appraisal logic and methods, I wanted to understand the extent to which neighborhood racial composition independently predicted home values. Together with sociologist Junia Howell, I obtained a census of all 2015 tax-appraised single-family homes in Harris County, Texas, from the Harris County Appraisal District. (Recall that Harris County is largely coterminous with the City of Houston.) Although the process of appraising property for the purpose of calculating property taxes varies dramatically in cities and states throughout the country, in Houston, as in Chicago, Dallas, and New York, tax authorities rely on property sales data to assess home values. This means that, at least in these localities, the tax-appraised value is a reasonable proxy for the market-appraised value.[10] This census included 879,372 single-family homes with a mean housing value of $233,221.

With these data in hand, we layered in multiple indicators that could be influencing home values, as appraisers had suggested. We included data on a variety of individual home characteristics, including square footage of the home and lot; whether the home had at least one fireplace, garage, patio/porch/deck, or swimming pool/tennis court; date of construction or last major renovation; construction quality; and physical condition. We also included data on several potentially key neighborhood characteristics, including neighborhood owner-occupancy, poverty, and unemployment rates; average condition of homes in the neighborhood (e.g., median number of rooms per housing unit, median year of home construction, and vacancy rate); and neighborhood amenities, such as measures of school quality, violent crime rates, distance from each home to the nearest park, and mean commute times. We also measured demand for housing in each neighborhood. Finally, we measured the proportion of each neighborhood that was Black, Latinx, and White.

With these data, we then estimated a statistical, fixed effects model that predicted appraised values while accounting for each of these individual home and neighborhood characteristics. Once individual home and neighborhood characteristics were accounted for, the proportion of the neighborhood that was Black or Latinx had a significant, negative impact on appraised values. Our model predicted that an average home in an average White neighborhood was valued at $289,000. By contrast, the value of that same home in an otherwise comparable Black neighborhood was $127,000 and, in an otherwise comparable Latinx neighborhood, it was $120,000 (Figure 5.3). In other words, comparable homes in otherwise comparable neighborhoods were worth approximately twice as much in White communities as they were in Black and Latinx communities. This finding, which again describes all of the single-family homes in Harris County, Texas, suggests that the appraisers in my sample were not outliers. Rather, home values in Houston are extremely unequal—and this inequality goes far beyond any individual home and neighborhood socioeconomic, crime, or amenity characteristics.

Yet this model was unable to disentangle the effect that historical appraisals have on home values—those conducted underneath the explicitly racist approach prevalent until the 1970s—from the effect that contemporary appraisals have on home values. That is, although fair housing legislation prohibited explicitly racist redlining, the sales comparison approach remained the most common method of appraising before and after such legislation was passed. This continuity meant that appraisers who assessed home value during the 1970s were selecting comps from homes that had been evaluated under explicitly racist appraisal techniques (Taylor 2019). Such continuity then ensured that the explicitly racist valuations of homes became embedded in the appraisal process even if appraisers no longer used racist logic and methods in their work (a hypothetical that my data do not support).

To disentangle historical and contemporary appraisal practices, we used U.S. census data to run a statistical model called a dynamic panel model to

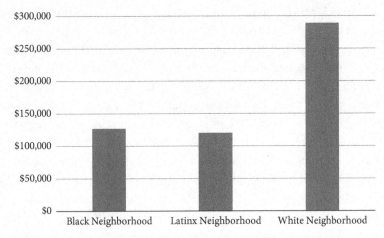

Figure 5.3 Predicted value of homes controlling for individual and neighborhood characteristics.

Source: Harris County Appraisal District data; figure created by Junia Howell and Elizabeth Korver-Glenn.

examine changes in neighborhood home values over time, from 1980 to 2015. This model, which included Houston and 106 other U.S. metropolitan areas, allowed us to differentiate historical appraised values from contemporary racial composition and to estimate the extent to which contemporary appraising practices contribute to contemporary appraisal value inequality.[11] In short, we found that even after accounting for historical appraisals, contemporary neighborhood racial composition continues to influence current appraisals—and the effect of neighborhood racial composition on contemporary appraisals is growing. We used predicted appraisal values for two hypothetical neighborhoods to help visualize this dynamic (Howell and Korver-Glenn, forthcoming:17):

> Both neighborhoods have average housing and socioeconomic status characteristics, are located in average metropolitan cities, and 50 percent of their residents are Black and/or Latinx in 1980. Yet, one community's Black and/or Latinx population is increasing by one percent a year and the other community's Black and/or Latinx population is decreasing by one percent per year. Despite starting with the same average appraisal value, values in the increasingly Black and/or Latinx communities fall by over 22,000 dollars (in 2015 dollars) while those in the community with a decreasing

proportion of Black and/or Latinx residents rise by 73,000 dollars. As the racial composition of these neighborhoods changes, their values sharply diverge, *creating a nearly 100,000 dollar difference in the average home appraisal.* [Italics added]

Although this analysis was not focused on Houston alone, it indicates that the data I collected from Houston-area appraisers are not a departure from the norm. Instead, the analysis provides further evidence that contemporary appraisers' racist appraisal logic and methods—in Houston and throughout the United States—continue to shape neighborhood home value inequality, preserving the highest values for White neighborhoods and the lowest values for Black and Latinx neighborhoods.

Filling in the Racist Blanks

Although the federal government and professional appraisal associations deleted the explicit requirements to assess neighborhood race from official appraisal forms, they still guide appraisers to prioritize neighborhood demographic and other characteristics as part of the appraisal process. In practice, this means that contemporary appraisers still rely on the same racist logic and methods that their predecessors used prior to 1976. Appraisers' racist perceptions of neighborhoods and buyer characteristics continue to provide the logical base for the sales comparison appraisal method. The appraisers in my study believed that neighborhoods with different racial compositions were fundamentally incomparable; that home values in neighborhoods of color were lower than values in White neighborhoods because they housed poor residents, had poorly maintained homes, were dangerous, or had low demand; and that buyers who match a given neighborhood's racial characteristics would likely purchase homes there. In particular, appraisers assumed that White buyers were the standard for determining an area's desirability, with White areas meeting this standard and receiving the highest values and non-White areas falling below the standard. Appraisers then used the neighborhood uniformity and "typical buyer" logics to guide their comp choices, or the actual method they used for determining a for-sale home's value. They chose comps from within the same (micro-)neighborhood or from a separate neighborhood with the same racial composition (but not necessarily the same class composition).

Although my interview data do not allow me to directly measure the extent to which racist appraisal logic and methods directly shape home values, my quantitative analyses with sociologist Junia Howell demonstrated that neighborhood racial composition was a strong predictor of home value in Houston in 2015 (Howell and Korver-Glenn 2018) and that neighborhood racial composition has had an *increasing* effect on contemporary appraisals of home value throughout the United States between 1980 and 2015 (Howell and Korver-Glenn, forthcoming). This substantial and growing inequality in contemporary appraisals of home value has enormous implications for other forms of inequality, such as wealth accumulation and funding for local infrastructure (e.g., streets and sidewalks) and local schools. In Houston, as in many cities throughout the country, both infrastructure and public schools are funded by property taxes, which are assessed as a percentage of home value (Lareau and Goyette 2014).

Together, these data illuminate how contemporary appraisers still rely on appraisal logic and methods that remain essentially unchanged from their racist roots, even as official trainings and forms have turned color-blind. Contemporary appraisers assessed home value through their racialized perceptions of neighborhoods and how desirable they believed neighborhood residents were to "typical"—that is, White—buyers. They reserved the highest values for White neighborhoods and lower values for Black and Latinx neighborhoods, which they thought were also only comparable with other racially similar areas. They use the existing structure of racial segregation in their work and, in so doing, reify that structure. In short, appraisers continue to animate the housing market and reproduce racial housing inequality "around a scaffolding of racial knowledge that presume[s] insight into the speculative elements of 'good housing' and 'good neighborhoods,' which [can] then be actualized through ascending property values" (Taylor 2019:9).

These findings, together with those from the previous three chapters, have significant implications for housing inequality and racial segregation. Housing developers, real estate agents, mortgage bankers, and appraisers all perform their professional work in ways that reinforce and even exacerbate the existing, racially unequal urban landscape. Importantly, these findings also point to concrete policy interventions that can interrupt housing market professionals' reliance on racist ideas to determine everyday action.

6

Fair Housing

As the housing developers, real estate agents, mortgage bankers, and appraisers in my study demonstrated, racial segregation and neighborhood inequality are active processes animated by racism. This process hinges on the work of housing market professionals, who control knowledge, social connections, and other resources that are key for building, purchasing, selling, and evaluating homes and neighborhoods. By regularly acting out racialized organizational routines and interpreting ostensibly neutral routines through the lens of racist ideas comprising the racist market rubric, these real estate professionals separate people and neighborhoods by race. In doing so, these race and racism brokers ensure that the most housing market opportunities and resources are reserved for White individuals and neighborhoods. Their actions exclude individuals and neighborhoods of color from such opportunities.

Yet several housing market professionals in my study—particularly some housing developers and real estate agents of color—adopted the people-oriented market rubric and alternate routines that emphasized the worth of people and neighborhoods of color. In doing so, these professionals—including Pablo (Chapters 2 and 4), Ramon (Chapters 2 and 3), Kevin and Candace (Chapter 3), and Tony, Janice, and Melissa (Chapter 4)—asserted agency in defining what race means and critiqued and denaturalized racist assumptions about people and places.[1] They also applied these subversive ideas to their work, showing that there are other ways to work successfully in real estate—ways that do not perpetuate a hierarchical racial–economic neighborhood order. These professionals were race brokers and racism *breakers*. They illuminated pathways toward a more equitable housing market and an urban future in which residents of color can experience fewer barriers in finding and securing a place to live.

In this chapter, I propose several policy recommendations that build on racism breakers' alternate routines and that interrupt racism brokers' racialized routines. Grouped under the three main categories of monitoring, legal approaches, and direct intervention, these policy recommendations

Race Brokers. Elizabeth Korver-Glenn, Oxford University Press (2021). © Oxford University Press.
DOI: 10.1093/oso/9780190063863.003.0007

will be most effective in furthering fair housing if American governmental entities (e.g., the federal government and state licensing boards), fair housing lawyers and advocates, and industry organizations (e.g., real estate boards) implement them in concert (see Reskin 2012). Given the fifty-year track record of U.S. governmental and housing market professionals ignoring, downplaying, and, in some cases, abandoning fair housing concerns (Massey 2015), the chances of a coordinated effort to implement all of these policy recommendations appears small. Nevertheless, implementing even a small number of them would chip away at the cornerstone of systemic racial inequality in the United States.

Monitoring Housing Market Professionals

Of all the housing market industries I examined in my research, only the mortgage lending industry is comprehensively monitored by the federal government with the express purpose of detecting patterns of racial, ethnic, or sex inequality. Through the data collected via Form 1003 (the Uniform Residential Loan Application) and by the mandate of the Home Mortgage Disclosure Act, mortgage lenders provide detailed data about mortgage loan and mortgage borrower characteristics to the federal government. Researchers have used these data extensively to document various forms of systematic racial inequality in the mortgage lending industry, leading in part to major complaints and lawsuits against lenders such as Wells Fargo as well as settlements providing compensation to thousands of borrowers of color who were discriminated against by these lenders. On a much smaller scale, the federal government monitors the real estate brokerage industry through audit studies by the U.S. Department of Housing and Urban Development (HUD). However, the entrenched use of racial stereotypes and the overt and coded forms of racial discrimination I observed across the housing development, real estate brokerage, mortgage lending, and appraisal industries suggest that all of these industries merit more systematic, federal- and state-level monitoring for various forms of discrimination.[2] Comprehensive governmental monitoring would be a helpful first step in determining when and how racist ideas continue to shape housing exchange and, consequently, the scale of interventions necessary to prevent this from continuing. Such monitoring could take several forms.

Let us begin with housing developers. One of the most notable ways that this group of housing market professionals differs from the others in my study is that housing developers do not need a government-administered license to do their work. That is, developers are not required to take any real estate-related training—including fair housing training—or examinations. Instead, developers and builders are subject to tight controls related to permitting and inspections regarding the physical structure of the homes they are building. On several occasions, the developers in my study took me to the City of Houston permitting office downtown and showed me how they navigated the paperwork, multiple lines and waiting areas, and interactions with permitting staff. This process takes so much time that they usually hire a staff member (also called a "runner") to visit the permitting office on their behalf. I also spent hours with developers on site as they waited for city inspectors who had to provide approval of the developers' projects at various stages on their way to completion. Inspectors were examining the physical integrity of homes and even the impact of the new homes on the nearby sewage and water systems, but not how the properties came to be developed or who would likely benefit from their construction.

In addition to monitoring construction permits and the physical integrity of the homes developers construct, federal and state government entities should bring housing developers under fair housing oversight. They could do this by first requiring a professional licensing process for housing developers as part of efforts to better track who developers are and what they do. Current real estate commissions that oversee licensure for real estate agents and brokers, including the Texas Real Estate Commission (TREC), have fair housing training that is minimal and inadequate (discussed later). But if such training were improved and required as part of a separate developer licensing process, developers would be aware of their ethical and legal fair housing obligations. Professional licensure would also provide a means for auditing or testing developer practices and holding them accountable. Second, municipalities or other regulatory entities could also require developers to submit an analysis of the social impacts of their planned developments along with their construction plans and environmental impact analyses. A social impact analysis would require developers to identify and describe the neighborhood characteristics, such as racial composition, household income, and current home values, of the areas in which they plan to build. Developers would also estimate the effects of their new development on future home values. Such an analysis would enable those monitoring developers to document the extent to which developers make planning and construction decisions in racially unequal ways (similar to the purpose of Form 1003 in mortgage lending). It would also provide at least one metric to determine the extent to which housing developers' decisions create disparate opportunities for White neighborhoods and neighborhoods of color.

Bringing housing developers under some type of fair housing oversight would not be an entirely new enterprise. For example, fair housing advocacy organizations have monitored developers' use of federal low-income housing tax credits, which they use to build housing intended for low-income or mixed-income populations. Recently, the U.S. Supreme Court ruled in favor of one such fair housing organization. Specifically, in *Texas Department of Housing and Community Affairs v. Inclusive Communities Project, Inc.* (2015), the Supreme Court ruled that the Texas Department of Housing and Community Affairs had used federal low-income housing tax credits to disproportionately concentrate low-income housing in neighborhoods of color in Dallas. The court found that this constituted disparate impact discrimination—that is, disproportionately negative effects for members of a protected class without demonstrable discriminatory intent.

The sort of monitoring I am proposing would additionally examine where developers concentrate middle- and upper-income housing, thus disproportionately contributing to higher home values and the presence of amenities in these areas. Such monitoring would direct our attention not only to the relative lack of housing opportunities and concentrated poverty in neighborhoods of color but also to the disproportionate abundance of opportunities in White neighborhoods. Developers who disproportionately concentrate new housing developments in (increasingly) White areas— piggybacking on local, publicly funded infrastructures (Feagin 1988)—are also creating disparate impacts by reinforcing the distance between housing stock, housing values, and local infrastructures in White neighborhoods and neighborhoods of color.

My findings also point to ways to improve the monitoring of real estate agents and brokers. The National Association of Realtors (NAR) board of directors recently passed a rule (the "clear cooperation" rule) that requires its affiliate Multiple Listing Service (MLS) members to list homes for sale publicly within 24 hours of marketing them in any other way (e.g., through email or social media) (Lerner 2019; Schuetz 2019). Yet it remains to be determined whether and how local real estate boards will implement the new rule. State regulatory entities should require local real estate boards and brokerages to publicly report the number of pocket listings their agents engage; this would help ensure that agents comply with the new NAR rule. In addition, real estate brokerages, like mortgage lending organizations, should be required to report information on their clients, such as their race and ethnicity, and detail the services their clients receive as well as the outcomes of the real estate agent–client relationship (e.g., offer made to seller; offer accepted by seller). Such information could be used to document whether patterns of differential treatment exist beyond what current audit studies capture.

Mortgage lenders are monitored more comprehensively than housing developers, real estate agents, or appraisers. But *how* monitoring is implemented matters for racial segregation, too. By requiring lenders whose mortgage loans it is or will be purchasing or guaranteeing to collect race/ethnicity and sex information on the front of Form 1003, the federal government ensures that it can examine the extent to which lenders disproportionately loan or deny loans to different groups. However, this information is not concealed for underwriter review, which means borrowers' identifying information can be used (even if unintentionally) as part of underwriters' discretionary evaluations of mortgage loan applicants. One way to fix this unintended consequence of Form 1003 is to implement a loan application review system not unlike a peer review process in which the author and reviewer do not know who each other are: Neither the mortgage applicant nor the underwriter knows the other's identity, including their race/ethnicity or sex. Such an approach would decrease the racialized discretion involved in evaluating loans and the segregated housing opportunities that emerge as a result (Reskin 2012; Williams et al. 2005).

Transparent, consistent monitoring of the appraisal industry has not occurred to date. Market appraisal data are simply not available—at least for researcher use. But these data do exist because lending organizations require homes being purchased through a mortgage loan to be appraised. Moreover, lending organizations monitor the perceived risk of appraisals through various software applications, including Collateral Underwriter, produced by Fannie Mae, and CoreLogic, produced by a private firm. These data should be made available to researchers and should be systematically analyzed by the federal government. Researchers and analysts should examine the comparables (comps) that appraisers select and the conditions under which home appraisals are associated with mortgage outcomes (loan approval or denial).

Governmental entities, such as HUD, and private fair housing organizations should also audit appraisers. These audits would examine how appraisers assess homes that are similar along key axes (e.g., individual size and quality, and neighborhood amenity and housing characteristics) but different in terms of neighborhood racial composition. Such audits would provide further information on the extent to which appraisers assess otherwise similar homes in otherwise comparable neighborhoods at different values depending on neighborhood racial composition. Finally, to better understand appraisers' perceptions and valuation practices as well as their relationships to other housing market professionals, such as mortgage bankers, appraisal boards and fair housing advocacy groups should conduct appraisal field studies.

Collectively, these examinations would deepen our understanding of how and when racism persists across multiple housing market industries. They would also better equip lawyers and other relevant stakeholders to litigate fair housing claims and policymakers to intervene in more relevant, substantive ways.

Legal Approaches to Fair Housing

The Fair Housing Act of 1968, later strengthened by the Fair Housing Amendment Act of 1988, is an expansive civil rights tool that has been interpreted broadly by the courts.[3] The act has also been supported by Obama-era executive actions, such as the 2013 Implementation of the Fair Housing Act's Discriminatory Effects Standard rule and the 2015 Affirmatively Furthering Fair Housing (AFFH) rule. The Discriminatory Effects, or disparate impact, rule attempted to formalize and standardize a "three-part burden shifting test" (HUD 2013:11460) for establishing discriminatory effects in housing matters. The AFFH rule was the Obama administration's attempt to fulfill the Fair Housing Act's mandate to "affirmatively further"—that is, foster—fair housing in addition to penalizing unfair housing (HUD 2015:42272).

Yet the federal government has yet to systematically, consistently enforce existing fair housing law or penalize professionals who engage in discrimination and, thus, violations of the law. This lack of systematic enforcement and penalization contributes to the racist interactions and transactions that continue to flourish in behind-the-scenes, all-White housing market settings, such as those described in this book. Even governmental entities that have been tasked with fulfilling the Fair Housing Act's mandates, such as HUD, have inconsistently and unevenly enforced this and other related legislation (Krysan and Crowder 2017; Massey 2015; U.S. Government Accountability Office 2010). More recently, officials in President Trump's HUD pushed back the deadline for the AFFH rule to take effect (Capps 2018). Then, under the leadership of Secretary Ben Carson, HUD eliminated the rule altogether in 2020 (HUD 2020). Despite multiple tools to pursue legal action and prosecute instances of housing discrimination using existing laws and rules, the public will to implement the law and make it effective has been weak (Hannah-Jones 2015).

Despite federal, state, and local governments' lack of commitment to, or even undermining of, fair housing enforcement, many dozens of private U.S. fair housing organizations continue to use testing, or auditing, to uncover the extent to which housing discrimination occurs (Abedin et al. 2018). My data indicate that fair housing advocates and governmental entities should continue and expand such testing for discrimination[4] and then pursue litigation if ample evidence is procured. Testing should focus on all four types of housing market professionals I studied. For example, I found that housing developers purchased and developed land using racist interpretations of neighborhoods. Furthermore, they used racist interpretations of current homeowners to identify and purchase specific plots of land (see Chapter 2 on reverse blockbusting). Real estate agents regularly told me that they "couldn't say" explicit racial categories (referring to either individuals or neighborhoods) when assisting their clients. But these same agents cooperated with and anticipated their clients' explicit and coded racist prejudices and drew on explicit or coded racial stereotypes when interacting with others or choosing some strategies over others.[5] White real estate agents also used pocket listings—that is, listings that they distribute only through their White networks. In doing so, they interfere with the ostensibly free housing market by limiting the buyer pool to a predominantly White clientele. (By contrast, agents of color almost never used pocket listings.)[6] White mortgage bankers used racially segregated and discriminatory interindustry networking strategies to seek out what they thought were low-risk, high-profit borrowers (i.e., White borrowers) via White real estate agents.[7] And, appraisers assessed home value by using racist interpretations of neighborhoods and buyers. Creative strategies to test how and under what conditions housing market professionals engage in these and other forms of racism could help fair housing lawyers successfully litigate housing discrimination in America's courts.

Yet testing would not address some of the most problematic practices I observed during my research, which occurred in the context of *familiar* relationships. By necessity, testing brings housing market professionals into contact with people whom they have never previously met. But my data suggest that professionals behave differently—and more cautiously—around people with whom they are not familiar. In Chapter 3, for instance, Grady described how he would respond to a question about schools differently if it were asked by someone he knew as opposed to someone with whom he had little to no prior interaction. Because developers, real estate agents, mortgage bankers, and appraisers are all accustomed to working with other professionals and, to greater and lesser extents, with housing consumers whom they already know, testing would not capture the racism and discrimination that characterize many of these familiar relationships.

Given the prevalence of such discrimination, it will take the power of federal, state, and local governmental entities, including the U.S. Department of Justice (DOJ) and HUD, to test for, prosecute, and penalize housing discrimination at a more systemic level. Only when there is serious enforcement of fair housing law at the highest levels of governance will housing market professionals take fair housing law more seriously, even in the context of their familiar relationships. Unfortunately, the DOJ and HUD—which is specifically tasked with enforcing fair housing law—have done very little on these matters to date (Hannah-Jones 2015). These failures are no accident; rather, they reflect the broader White public's satisfaction with racism and its relationship to racial segregation.

Although the federal government has failed to adequately enforce fair housing law, eschewing many opportunities to interrupt and penalize housing discrimination and challenge the system of racial segregation, my research suggests several ways that federal, state, and local governments, fair housing organizations, legal experts, and lawyers can use existing fair housing law by expanding testing strategies and pursuing litigation. Moreover, the government has many opportunities to penalize housing discrimination—and do so in meaningful ways that will de-incentivize racism whether professionals are interacting with familiar or unfamiliar others. By continuing to litigate multiple forms of housing discrimination and by adopting consistent, serious penalties at a systemic level for such discriminatory practices, these individuals and entities can support equal housing opportunity and hold housing market professionals liable for the role they play in brokering racism.

Intervening in Racialized Housing Market Routines

Many of the racialized routines in which housing market professionals today actively participate—for example, cultivating networks of value, racist and racially segregated interindustry networking, and racialized appraisal logic and methods—were legal and expected ways of doing housing business decades ago. Enacting these routines allowed White housing market professionals and White-dominated governmental entities to entrench racial segregation and control access to housing and other resources (Helper 1969; Jackson 1985; Massey and Denton 1993; Stuart 2003; Taylor 2019). Although explicitly racist housing market routines are nowadays illegal, White housing market professionals still contribute to racial segregation through explicitly racist behaviors in behind-the-scenes settings and in less obvious ways across a wide spectrum of contexts. They do so by acting out professional routines in ways that prioritize White consumers and neighborhoods and denigrate consumers and neighborhoods of color. Because it would be a fool's errand to try to change professionals' racist ideas from the top down, this section focuses on intervening in the routines that encourage or even require professionals to rely on these ideas in their everyday work.

Prohibit and Penalize Reverse Blockbusting

In 1968, the Fair Housing Act outlawed blockbusting, a common practice in which real estate agents targeted White homeowners and got them to sell at low prices by preying on their racial prejudices and fears (see section 3604(e) of the Fair Housing Act), and then agents would sell those same houses to Black home buyers at inflated prices. Today, a close cousin to blockbusting—reverse blockbusting—persists. Housing developers enact this routine by making racist assumptions about homeowners of color and then targeting these homeowners in attempts to purchase the land at unfairly low prices. Among other ramifications, reverse blockbusting interferes in open housing exchange by limiting competition for homes and dampening homeowners' profits on the sale of their home. Once they have purchased the land, developers then either tear down the existing property and build a new home or completely renovate and expand the existing property. They then sell these new properties at significantly higher prices, often to White families. This practice seems a likely mechanism for gentrification or neighborhood "Whitening"—a discriminatory one.

Although my data do not allow me to determine the extent to which such reverse blockbusting behavior occurs in Houston or other cities, they do suggest a predatory housing practice that has yet to receive much attention from scholars, regulatory entities, or fair housing organizations. Like blockbusting, reverse blockbusting must be outlawed, and there must be legal and professional consequences for developers and land speculators who target homeowners of color in this way. To prohibit reverse blockbusting and penalize developers who engage in it, state governments and regulatory boards or commissions should first bring developers under their oversight (discussed previously). In doing so, developers would be bound to the same legal and professional standards as their real estate agent and other professional counterparts. Such oversight could de-incentivize this predatory behavior because developers could be held liable and lose their professional licenses for purchasing land in this way.

Penalize Pocket Listings

Pocket listings are exemplary of real estate agent routines that are not necessarily an intentionally racist practice but have significant implications for racial segregation. Real estate agents typically build their businesses by networking with family and friends, and these networks tend to be racially segregated. Brokering real estate through segregated networks means that even if consumers and agents do not engage in explicitly racist or discriminatory behavior, they still contribute to racial segregation (see Korver-Glenn 2018b; Krysan and Crowder 2017). Yet agents who engage pocket listings go one step further in imprinting their racially segregated networks on urban landscapes by excluding most of the general public from accessing for-sale homes and disproportionately excluding those not represented in agents' networks. (For White agents—those who engaged pocket listings most frequently in my study—this meant disproportionately excluding buyers of color.)

As described previously, NAR recently took the step of requiring its member agents and brokers to publicly list for-sale homes on the MLS within

24 hours of marketing the home in any way. But the new clear cooperation rule does not indicate how real estate boards, brokerages, or agents would be penalized for engaging pocket listings. Rather than relying on private, for-profit organizations to monitor, prohibit, and penalize such practices, state and local regulatory boards should implement penalties for brokerages whose agents continue to use pocket listings because of their exclusionary ramifications.

Improve and Require Ongoing Fair Housing Education

Regulatory agencies (e.g., the Appraisal Foundation), real estate commissions (e.g., TREC), boards (e.g., the Texas Appraiser Licensing & Certification Board; the Houston Association of Realtors), and brokerages should improve and standardize fair housing education and training materials and require real estate agents, mortgage bankers or loan officers, appraisers, and other licensed real estate professionals to take this training regularly (e.g., every two years).[8] Such training would provide professionals with concrete, real-life examples of the kinds of explicit and coded racism that agents are likely to encounter and demonstrate how to respond to these situations appropriately. Trainings should also remind agents of what their commitments to fiduciary responsibility and client confidentiality do and do not entail. Maintaining client confidentiality in real estate, for example, does not override agents' legal and ethical obligations to fair housing law. Along with such training, real estate brokerage firms should incentivize agents to sever professional ties with consumers who express coded or explicit racial prejudice or who engage in discriminatory behavior. Brokerages should also penalize agents who maintain ties with such consumers and fire agents who express and behave in racist ways as well.

Since conducting this research, I have participated in multiple events and meetings in which real estate boards and brokerages have engaged these more substantive, concrete approaches to fair housing training. Yet given how pervasive both coded and explicit racism were in behind-the-scenes, White settings, this kind of organizational intervention would require a concerted effort on the part of many real estate brokerage firms. If only a small number of brokerages implemented a firm, zero-tolerance policy for racist consumers or agents, individual White agents could easily leave and join a different brokerage without these sanctions, taking their clients with them. Although I am skeptical of the extent to which educational reform can mitigate racial discrimination in real estate,[9] implementing and requiring regular fair housing training is the very least real estate organizations should do to interrupt professionals' racist contributions to racial segregation.

Abandon Market Area Maps and Neighborhood-Oriented Data

Real estate brokerage organizations also sometimes require agents to enact racialized routines that are not immediately obvious. For example, the Houston Association of Realtors (HAR) requires agents to list homes using a market area map that both reflects racial segregation and treats White areas and neighborhoods of color in unequal ways (see Chapter 3).[10] Moreover, through its public website HAR.com, HAR reinforces neighborhood racial distinctions in other ways. For example, when consumers browse HAR.com, they see not only information about individual homes but also information about the local area. This information includes the elementary, middle, and high schools to which the individual home is zoned. In addition, HAR provides links to these schools' demographic data, including the student body's racial/ethnic composition, the proportion of students who receive free or reduced-price lunches, and students' standardized test scores. At the time I conducted my research, other information included with home listings fell under the headings of "Local Happenings" and "Explore Around [Neighborhood Name]." The latter category included links to restaurants, religious organizations, entertainment, and transportation that were located within the HAR-determined market area as well as consumers' reviews of these places.

If a consumer or housing market professional were not already familiar with a local area, they could easily click on any of these links to find dozens of other individuals—often identifiable through profile photos and names—writing about these areas. In addition to visual and linguistic cues, the links to these places provide other racial cues, including the content of the reviews, which are sometimes written in local Black, Latinx, or White vernaculars to describe an experience with a business. For example, when reviewing J&J Lounge in Fifth Ward (which HAR locates in its "Denver Harbor" market area), "Machel Churchman" wrote the following:

Oh the atmosphere is just loving. You feel the love as you talk with the employees. The owner Redd cooks off the chain. The food is just delicious once you try them there no going anywhere else. The prices meet the qualifications to the food. Just a feeling of family being there. 3303 Lee st. That's the nickel[11] baby. . . .

Another example, from "Hailey Loveday's" review of Andy's Hawg Wild Bar-B-Que in Pasadena, just across the highway from the Golden Acres neighborhood, describes the restaurant as follows:

First time eating here! I love this place. It has such a sweet family vibe and I immediately felt welcome. My brisket is literally falling apart. Cole slaw is soooo creamy and my potato salad is to die for. I want seconds! Staff were attentive and friendly. Definitely will be stopping by offen.

Such cues can prime consumers and professionals away from or toward particular areas before they even view a single home in person. Together with school information and neighborhood or market area maps, the local real estate board inscribes the housing exchange process with racial cues and unequal marketing practices, even when professionals or consumers do not wish to draw on the racist market rubric to make housing decisions. HAR and other similar real estate boards should abandon a market area or neighborhood-centric mode of advertising individual homes, which continues to reify neighborhood *racial* distinctions and not just distinctions in style, commute times, and amenities.

Abandon Percentage-Based Commission Fees

For both real estate agents and mortgage bankers, the percentage-based commission fee is the widely shared norm for generating profit. Although I have less data on how mortgage bankers understood and applied the percentage-based commission pay structure to their work, real estate agents' relationships to commission are clear. Although most real estate agents in my study were quick to say that nothing about their pay was "fixed," in practice they staunchly defended and policed the going 6 percent rate to ensure its persistence. And these percentage-based real estate commissions supported real estate agents' racist interpretations of clients. White agents assumed that White individuals were wealthy or would bring them the most profit because they thought these individuals could either pay more for homes or had homes that would sell for higher prices. White agents also viewed White individuals as requiring the least amount of work, with the smallest chance of work-related headaches. These agents then provided more and better service to White consumers relative to consumers of color, whom they assumed were low income, uneducated about the home-buying process, or even posing a threat to their physical safety (see Chapter 3).

My data also suggest that real estate agents' use of the percentage-based commission, combined with these racist assumptions, affects entire neighborhoods. Specifically, when agents provide better housing service to wealthy or White individuals, they are also providing benefits to the neighborhoods where those individuals are located. Consider, for instance, an agent who works hard on behalf of her home-selling client. She pounds the pavement looking for prospective buyers, hosts multiple open houses, and even sends a mailer that includes details about the home. After these efforts, the home ends up selling for higher than its asking price. That price of course benefits both the home seller and the agent. But it also benefits the neighborhood because that home now becomes a comparable sale that will influence the home value and future sales of nearby homes—in this case, in a positive direction (see Chapter 5). Meanwhile, when a home seller of color receives lower quality or lesser service, the amount their home sells for will reflect that lower service. Less or lower quality service will influence what these homeowners make off the sale of their home and will also influence nearby home values by becoming a comparable sale—but this time in a negative direction. These differences in home value across neighborhoods go on to create racialized differences in homeowners' ability to accumulate wealth, as well as racialized differentials in public school funding and educational opportunities. Ultimately, providing different levels of housing service based on clients' (assumed) wealth or race contributes to racial segregation and multiple forms of related inequality.

In theory, real estate agents offer equal service to all of their clients. But the unofficial, yet widespread, use of the percentage-based pay structure incentivizes agents to look for and provide better service to higher value clients, and agents interpret client value through a racialized lens. To change this, brokerages must change their pay structures to incentivize agents to service clients equally. Real estate brokerages and mortgage lenders should adopt a flat-fee model, such as the one used by Ramon (see Chapter 3) and their counterparts in the appraisal industry. A flat-fee structure would encourage professionals to generate as many leads as possible, regardless of the price point of the house or the client. Moreover, because they would get paid the same amount regardless of buyer, seller, or home characteristics, it would help discourage housing market professionals from using racial stereotypes to interpret clients or neighborhoods.

Open Access to Mortgage Lending

To offset the exclusionary and segregationist interindustry networking between White mortgage bankers and real estate agents and to complement the equitable interindustry networking and mortgage banker referral strategies used by Tony, Janice, and others (see Chapter 4), federal and state governmental entities should ensure that housing consumers have equal, open access to mortgage loan products. To facilitate equal access to lenders and information about loan products, for example, state organizations such as the Texas Department of Savings and Mortgage Lending could create open access websites that contain information on all active Nationwide Mortgage Lending System loan officers and originators as well as the types of loan products they offer. Such a website could also flag mortgage companies that have been accused of or held liable for discriminatory lending practices (e.g., Wells Fargo) and provide consumer ratings of these companies to foster transparency. Consumers could sort by the location (e.g., city) of the loan officer and/or the type of loan product (e.g., conventional or U.S. Department of Veterans Affairs-guaranteed loans). In short, because consumers' access to mortgage lenders is shaped by their access to real estate agents and these connections tend to be racially segregated, it is crucial to ensure that consumers know there are lender and loan product options outside of the particular ones to which they have been referred. Moreover, as real estate agents of color in my study emphasized, it is essential for mortgage borrowers to know whether prospective lenders have engaged in (alleged) racial discrimination so that they can avoid these lenders and instead find others who have a track record of excellent service to communities of color.

Alter the Appraisal Structure and Redress Past Racism
in Valuation Processes

Given the racist, neighborhood-oriented logic and methods underpinning contemporary appraisals, the U.S. Congress-authorized Appraisal
Foundation, the Appraisal Institute (the largest professional association of
real estate appraisers in the United States), state appraisal boards, and appraisal management companies should work together to discard and re-
place the neighborhood-centered sales comparison approach or modify it
significantly. At the very least, the sales comparison approach as currently
implemented imprints explicit, historic racism into contemporary valuation processes. It does so by requiring that past sales from nearby areas be
used to evaluate individual home worth. Given the explicitly racist strategies
used over the course of the twentieth century to racially segregate American
neighborhoods, requiring appraisers to use past sales within these racially
segregated neighborhoods ensures that parity in home value across these
areas will never be reached, no matter how nice or desirable appraisers perceive them to be. Worse, the data I collected demonstrate that appraisers
viewed White neighborhoods as the most desirable and thus of highest value.
Appraisers used methods such as choosing comps only from within a White
neighborhood or across other White neighborhoods to ensure that their estimated values reflect their perceptions of higher demand. In short, the sales
comparison approach, founded on explicitly racist ideas about racial mixing
and desirability, continues to reproduce a hierarchy of home value across racially distinct neighborhoods (see Howell and Korver-Glenn, forthcoming;
Taylor 2019). This hierarchy has significant implications for wealth accumulation (or loss) and funding for local infrastructure and public schools,
among other outcomes (Shapiro 2017).

Governmental and industry entities should discard the sales comparison approach and instead consider using a modified cost approach to
appraising. The cost approach entails taking the land value, adding the cost
of home construction, then accounting for home depreciation over time. If
implemented in this way, the cost approach would still result in home value
inequality because of existing land value disparities across racially distinct
neighborhoods. However, among other possibilities, the cost approach could
be modified by incorporating a model that predicts what current land values
would have been if explicitly racist policies (e.g., redlining) had not been
enacted. Because land in Black and Latinx areas has long been devalued, these

projections would most likely result in increases in land value for these communities. The adjusted land value would then be used as the basis for the cost
approach to home value. In addition to leaving land values in White areas
intact, this approach would enable homeowners in Black and Latinx areas to
recoup and gain equity. Local tax assessment bodies could lower current caps
on year-to-year property value changes to ensure that homeowners were
not unduly harmed by the resulting increases in property values and con-
current changes in property taxes (see also Howell and Korver-Glenn 2018).
Implementing such a modified cost approach would help eliminate ongoing
neighborhood inequality and prevent appraisers' racist understandings of
neighborhood desirability, demand, and "typical buyers" from influencing
the valuation process.

Because a complete overhaul of the appraisal industry seems unlikely, another way to intervene in appraisers' routine, racialized logic and methods
is to modify the sales comparison approach. As a first step, appraisal and
related financial entities (e.g., Fannie Mae) should abandon the notion of a
"typical buyer" in their training models. This concept far too easily allows
appraisers to imagine White buyers as the (implicit) default reference group
and White neighborhoods as the most appealing, and thus most valuable,
to this reference group. Second, appraisal organizations should require
appraisers to quantify demand for homes. They could do this by using conventional approaches taken by real estate economists, such as calculating the
average number of days homes are on the market in local areas and what
percentage of homes in a local area take a price cut. (Appraisers in my study
never offered any metric but their own opinions and perceptions of local demand when discussing neighborhood desirability. It is worth noting, however, that according to the measures real estate economists use, Black and
Latinx neighborhoods in Houston had higher rates of demand than White
neighborhoods in 2015 (Howell and Korver-Glenn 2018).) A third step
to modify the sales comparison approach would involve developing and
implementing software that would compare similar homes across the metropolitan area. The software would take into account individual home characteristics (e.g., size and quality) and amenities (e.g., commute time, access
to parks). Then, it would randomly select comparable past sales based on this
individual home data from similar neighborhoods across the entire metropolitan area (see Howell and Korver-Glenn 2018). Without accounting
for the explicitly racist historical inequities in home values, this approach
would preserve relatively higher values in White areas overall. However,

by inhibiting contemporary appraisers' ability to inject racist ideas about neighborhoods into their comp selection, the method may also promote higher home values in Asian, Black, and Latinx neighborhoods. Middle- and upper income communities of color in cities across the United States may especially benefit from an automated comp approach because appraisers appear more likely to devalue homes in these areas than they do in low-income neighborhoods of color (Thomas et al. 2018).

Finally, since fair housing laws have not addressed the historical value inequalities wrought by systematic, federally backed redlining and lenders' and appraisers' devaluation of communities of color through the 1960s and 1970s, lawmakers should account for these historical injustices in future legislation. I join other scholars (e.g., Dantzler and Reynolds 2020) in calling for reparations to address the inequalities produced by past and present racialized housing policy. Moreover, any attempt to rectify historical and contemporary racial injustices in appraisal and valuation processes, including reparations and developing and implementing a cost or modified sales comparison approach or some other appraisal method, should be done in conversation and concert with Indigenous tribes alongside Asian, Black, Latinx, and other communities of color. European settlers devalued and stole Indigenous lands and economies over centuries (e.g., Harris 1993; Kuokkanen 2011; Ramirez 2007), and these injustices have never been adequately redressed. Moreover, although European settlers used genocide as a tool to erase Indigenous people, dramatically decreasing their numbers and attempting to render them invisible,[12] Indigenous people have long cultivated thriving urban communities (Ramirez 2007). And, like their Asian, Black, and Latinx counterparts, Indigenous homeowners and renters continue to be devalued and experience discrimination in housing market and other urban spaces (e.g., Levy et al. 2017). To foster fair housing, appraisal and other regulatory bodies and industry organizations must put a stop to the ongoing devaluation of Asian, Black, Indigenous, Latinx, and other communities of color and rectify historical injustices.

* * *

No one solution or set of solutions can undermine how racism perpetuates racial segregation. I agree with many scholars who advocate for consistent enforcement of existing fair housing law, among other proposed changes (e.g., Krysan and Crowder 2017). At the same time, I propose new, concrete approaches to monitoring, litigating, and intervening in racialized housing market routines to address how racism happens in the contemporary housing market. The ideas that I have proposed in this chapter emerged from understanding how White housing market professionals in particular use racist ideas to interpret the informal, or unofficial, and formal, or official, routines and rules that guide their actions (Ray 2019). My recommendations do not adjudicate on whether racist perceptions and behaviors are conscious or unconscious, intentional or unintentional, or an interplay across these spectrums. Rather, my proposals home in on the routines that prompt or enable racist perceptions and behaviors and make such ideas and actions seem normal, insignificant, or even attractive.

My ideas also provide concrete, plausible alternatives to existing housing market routines and prospects for future fair housing litigation. Implementing these recommendations will not be easy, convenient, or without resistance. Indeed, because White housing market professionals and the organizations that support them appear to reproduce racial prejudice, discrimination, and segregation as a matter of course when they are in all-White settings, resistance is to be expected. But *unfair* housing and the racial segregation that results will persist unless such resistance is overcome by meaningfully addressing the fact that providing housing in America often means brokering racism. Breaking racism among housing market professionals is difficult but doable. Either option—breaking or brokering racism—is a series of active choices that American governmental bodies, housing market industries, real estate organizations, and the people who are a part of them make. We should do everything we can to ensure that they make choices supporting, rather than undermining, equal housing opportunities.

Conclusion

Race brokers are influential individuals who use, transform, or reject ideas about race and connect these ideas to consequential, real-life situations. Such individuals exercise their influence through their power as experts, representatives, or leaders who control access to information and resources. Others look up to and follow these individuals because they trust them or because they believe they must, given their own lack of information or resources.

Housing market professionals are an exemplary case of race brokers.[1] They are trusted experts on whom consumers rely to provide knowledge and resources associated with home buying and selling. What these individuals say or do not say about race and what they do or do not do with race shape consumers' comfort in expressing or acting on racial ideas or racist prejudices. Even if they do not interact directly with consumers, which is often the case for housing developers and appraisers, their attitudes and actions concerning race still have consequences for consumers' options and segregation. Housing market professionals have access to indispensable knowledge and resources—for example, land, social connections, and value. By connecting racist or equitable, people-affirming ideas to such resources, housing market professionals influence whether and how racial segregation and other forms of housing inequality are perpetuated or mitigated.

In my study, I found that housing market professionals tend to broker racist ideas and actions *or* equitable, people-affirming ideas and actions, although some, including Tony (Chapters 2 and 4), went back and forth between the two. White professionals regularly and repeatedly relied on the racist market rubric—they were racism brokers—while professionals of color did so rarely. Within the context of housing market routines that enabled or required professionals to interpret individuals and neighborhoods through the lens of race, these individuals relied heavily on positive assumptions about White individuals' economic and social status. They also relied heavily on racist stereotypes of Asian, Black, Latinx, and, at times, Middle Eastern individuals, which emphasized these groups' perceived economic, moral, and cultural

Race Brokers. Elizabeth Korver-Glenn, Oxford University Press (2021). © Oxford University Press.
DOI: 10.1093/oso/9780190063863.003.0008

deficiencies as relevant to the functioning of the housing market. A much smaller proportion of professionals in my sample, almost all of color, tended to rely on the people-oriented market rubric. Working within the same context of housing market routines as their White counterparts, these individuals interpreted people of color as worthy, welcoming, hard-working, and successful. Also, they connected these perceptions to how they thought the housing market should function. These professionals were racism breakers.

How all of these professionals viewed race shaped how they acted or did not act in everyday housing interactions. Those who interpreted people and neighborhoods through the racist market rubric contributed to the process of unfair housing and related racial segregation. Those who interpreted people and neighborhoods through the people-oriented market rubric helped interfere in this process in some way or at least mitigate its negative effects.

Yet the implications of my research extend beyond the individual people I studied and, indeed, beyond the Houston housing market. *Race Brokers* demonstrates that housing exchange is composed of active, concrete interactions and dynamics that in many ways depend on how people interpret race. It pushes us to de-naturalize what is often portrayed as an abstract, passive, and natural market in many pockets of popular and academic discourse.[2] This means that in addition to being a numeric descriptor of how people are distributed across space, racial segregation is also an actively sustained, racialized process. Those who animate this process and the organizations in which they are embedded must be the focus of serious attempts to dismantle racism's contribution to segregation—attempts that are needed now more than ever.

From Natural and Neutral to Unnatural and Unequal

Race Brokers demonstrates that the housing market is anything but free, neutral, or natural. Through their everyday work, the White housing market professionals in my study—who dominated the Houston housing landscape, as they do throughout the United States—perceived and acted in ways that helped keep housing market racism and related racial segregation in motion. I have chosen to foreground these professionals to highlight the active, biased/partial, *un*natural, and concrete ways racial segregation persists. Yet the story of how these race brokers matter would be incomplete if I did not also bring housing consumers into conversation with the findings portrayed in this book.

Consumers play a key role in the housing market by expressing their racialized residential preferences and expecting that these preferences will be realized, in part through customer service performed by professionals (e.g., Krysan and Crowder 2017). Housing consumers are highly dependent on professionals to provide them with information and access to resources (Besbris 2020), and the consumers I interviewed as part of the larger project were no exception. The home buyers, sellers, and renters I interviewed told me, again and again, that they trusted the professionals with whom they had worked, particularly real estate agents, but also mortgage bankers. They also trusted appraisers' assessments of home value, although they rarely interacted directly with these professionals. Consumers' trust meant that professionals influenced consumers by changing their preferences (making them more racialized); validating their existing racialized preferences; and shaping what options consumers thought were good, even if these options were exploitative.

Consumers trusted real estate agents to the point that agents were able to alter consumers' preferences. Two home buyers, Maddie and her husband Sam, illustrate this dynamic. Maddie, a thirty-something home buyer I met at a neighborhood association meeting, described herself as White and Hispanic.[3] She and her White husband had lived in Texas previously and were moving back after a stint in the Midwest. Maddie explained,

> We actually started renting sight-unseen, and we were looking at a place that was on East [Interstate-]45. And the realtor at that time was very nice; he actually told us, "You don't want this place, I have another place for you." Uh, asked us a lot about ourselves over the phone. And he said, "Well listen, this is where you're gonna be happiest." He's like, "Why don't you rent here for your first introduction to Houston, because otherwise I don't think you'll be happy in that other area." Which, we did drive by that other area once we moved in. That was still a little bit more up-and-coming and a little rougher. A little bit more east of [Near] Northside. Like, closer to that Fifth Ward area. So we actually rented in the Woodland Heights for about a year and a half, maybe two years.

Maddie and Sam trusted their real estate agent when he told them they would not be happy in Fifth Ward. Indeed, they were so swayed by their real estate agent's counsel that they did not even bother going to look at the home they had previously considered renting in Fifth Ward until after they had already rented a place in the Heights neighborhood.[4] Maddie and Sam continued working with their real estate agent when they decided to take the leap into purchasing a home. As before, they trusted their agent and did exactly what he told them to do as they searched for options:

> That's something our realtor told us. He's like, "Go to—before you move into this area," he said, "Why don't—why don't we do this. Why don't you drive to the grocery store you'd go to, drive to the gas station you would go to—just pinpoint all of those places. And re-create your space." So I was just, like, "Oh, okay." [Chuckles] So we did that. But I think that's a big part of it, too. Feeling comfortable.

Maddie and Sam followed their agent's advice and drove around the areas they were considering, re-creating their daily routines in these areas to determine where they would "feel comfortable." They ended up purchasing a home in a White area.

Real estate agents also validated consumers' racialized preferences, or prejudices. Stef and Brett, two home buyers who had retained Michael as their real estate agent, wanted to start a family. They explained as much to Michael during their first meeting when Michael was trying to get to know the pair, who had been referred to him by a mutual acquaintance. Stef and Brett also explained that because of their desire to start a family, schools were important to them. Michael then began to describe homes and prices in the east Sunset Heights area, matching the specifics of square footage and pricing that Stef and Brett had just outlined. Stef quickly asked which schools were "on that side" (east) of Main Street. "Field Elementary," Michael replied,

> [is] a great school. It's very diverse, because of where it is. Everything around it is getting really expensive, and that's obviously going to bring the school up. And you know, even in Memorial, which is a great area, the schools are horrible because there are apartment complexes and the kids from the apartment complexes go to the schools. In all honesty, agents with the most listings drive a lot of the school changing. Within five to seven years, it will turn around. Obviously, I can't guarantee that.

Michael validated Stef's worry about schools by describing it as "very diverse" and comparing it to other schools he perceived as "horrible" in another area of town. Simultaneously, however, he cloaked his real opinion by describing Field Elementary as "great" and expressed confidence (but not a guarantee) that it would "turn around" from its current state. Stef and Brett clearly felt validated in their concern about purchasing a home zoned to a racially diverse school. Immediately after Michael described his perceptions of Field Elementary, they began discussing the possibility of purchasing a home out in the suburbs, near Conroe, Texas, closer to where they had family members and where Brett said they "could get more with better schools."

In contrast to Michael and the real estate agent with whom Maddie and Sam worked, some real estate agents who acted as racism breakers fostered racial diversity in neighborhoods through their equitable approach to inter-industry networking. For example, Sheila, a Black home buyer, worked with Denise, a Black real estate agent at Kevin's brokerage.[5] Sheila purchased one of Pablo's newly developed homes, located in a predominantly Black neighborhood. Then, Denise began working with Pablo more directly. From Sheila's perspective, the relationship between Pablo and Denise was fantastic because Denise began "pipelining" other home buyers who wanted to live in urban Houston to the area. Once Denise, Kevin, and other agents at Kevin's brokerage found out about Pablo and the new homes he was building, they began sending a racially diverse group of Black, Latinx, and White individuals to the predominantly Black area.

Yet professionals also influenced consumers' options in more exploitative ways. Susana, a middle-aged Mexican American woman who had purchased a home in the Near Northside neighborhood, thought that Americans "segregate ourselves." But, she said, this was "with a lot of help from the realtors." Then, she went on to describe how she and her husband had been victims of predatory lending. Their loan officer, a Latinx man who had been a friend of theirs, had offered them the loan. When they realized they were being exploited by Wells Fargo, they returned to ask their friend what had happened. According to Susana,

> But [the loan officer] said that the bankers and the mortgage people were being pushed to do this, in a way. But, for whatever reason, they were offering this [loan product] to the minorities to get them in, even though it was gonna cause trouble later. We didn't know it. I didn't know it. If we don't take the time to research, or we don't take the time to read every single

paper in that stack about two inches thick. Who's gonna learn all of that? Who's gonna read all that? You trust the people that you're working with. In this case, he was a friend. But he's been the victim: "It's my business. If I don't sell, I don't make a living. So, then I had to go with the flow, what is it they're pushing me to do, then if I don't do it, they don't approve this loan, I don't have a sell." So, for whatever reason they did it, it affected us. We didn't know. And that's the deal with minorities. And I heard somebody else mention that, and I said, "Oh, that's funny, that happened to me—what bank were you with?" "Well, I'm with Chase." So, it wasn't just Wells Fargo. It was a lot of banks doing this. So, who can you trust? What do you have to do, as a homeowner? Especially a young person trying to buy their first home, or anybody trying to buy their first home. You think you trust the person, and then you say, the realtor's not working for you, they're working for the one who's selling it. Well, when you hire them, now they're working for you? Not really; they're still working for the one selling it.

Just like Maddie, Stef and Brett, and Sheila and the other buyers working with Denise, Susana and her husband had trusted the housing market professionals with whom they worked. In particular, they trusted their friend, the loan officer. Because they trusted him, they had no reason to expect that the loan would be exploitative. It ultimately cost them thousands of dollars and untold stress from the threat of losing their home.

Americans consider many things when they are searching for a place to live. Among other things, home seekers think about home cost, size, and structural soundness; proximity to work, amenities, and people they know; and their ability to get a mortgage loan. Housing market professionals guide and sometimes change the trajectory of these considerations. In my study, far more often than not, White professionals' influence reinforced or exacerbated White consumers' racism and provided White consumers and consumers of color with unequal options. For consumers of color, these options were frequently in some way "less than" their White peers' options. At times, they were downright predatory (see Chapter 2 and the discussion of reverse blockbusting). By contrast, a small number of professionals, most of them of color, attempted to provide consumers with whom they worked (most of them also of color) equitable housing opportunities. These professionals were swimming against the strong current of housing market racism—a current that continues to pervade "popular culture and real estate acumen in the United States" (Taylor 2019:259) and perpetuate racial segregation.

Racial Segregation as a Racialized Process

Most of the academic research conducted on racial segregation in the United States has focused on the extent to which residents of American cities live in separate places. This research has highlighted three primary explanations for overall segregation patterns (also known as the "big three"): consumers' residential preferences, racial discrimination, and economic inequality. Using a variety of quantitative and qualitative methods, scholars of segregation have attempted to measure each of these three key mechanisms (e.g., Krysan and Crowder 2017; Turner et al. 2013). More recent research has highlighted that such mechanisms exist within a social process of decision-making as home buyers and renters choose where to live (Bruch and Swait 2019; Krysan and Crowder 2017).

Race Brokers builds on the theoretical and empirical contributions of this large body of work. It also pushes research in this vein to grapple with racial segregation as a racialized process—a process that housing market professionals shape in powerful ways at each and every stage of housing exchange. That is, racial segregation and the "big three" are mired in relationships of power between professionals and consumers that unfold dynamically over time and space. Moreover, these relationships do not always fit neatly into any of the "big three" boxes and even call into question how these mechanisms are defined.

Home buyers, for example, have preferences about where they want to live and prejudices against places they do not want to live. Their preferences are shaped by interactions not only with their peers but also with the trusted experts who build homes (i.e., developers) and guide them through the housing search process (i.e., real estate agents). Buyers learn that race matters to these professionals, at which point their own preferences and racism are either affirmed or become more salient. White home sellers also hold and express racist ideas about people to whom they would prefer not to sell (see Chapter 3). The White professionals who typically represent these White consumers accommodate or coach such home buyers and sellers, but they generally do not meaningfully interfere because doing so would violate the relationship of trust. These cases, too, offer instruction because sellers learn from their trusted real estate experts that it is okay to care about the race of the person purchasing their home and to enact such racism in their marketing strategies. Professionals and consumers produce and reproduce their racist ideas about where they "prefer" to live or whom they "prefer" to purchase their home through an iterative, interactive process that shapes the housing options consumers have as well as the options they view as desirable.

It is also clear that White housing market professionals discriminate against consumers of color, treating them negatively relative to their White counterparts. Indeed, the most prominent studies of racial discrimination in housing rely on paired-tester audit methods, which depend on interactions between real estate agents and prospective home buyers of color (e.g., Turner et al. 2013). In reality, White housing market professionals only rarely interact with consumers of color. Instead, they interact primarily with White consumers, often those they know personally. Within these familiar White professional–White consumer relationships, explicit and coded racist ideas and behaviors abound (see Picca and Feagin 2007). In other words, racial discrimination—mistreatment of an individual or group of color—does not require the presence of a person of color. Rather, racial discrimination should be understood as (inter)actions that, over time, preserve the perceived superiority of White individuals and spaces and the perceived inferiority of other individuals and spaces deemed not White (Bobo and Fox 2003).[6] When these myriad behind-the-scenes racist ideas and behaviors are taken into account, it becomes clear that audit studies likely underestimate the extent to which housing market racial discrimination persists.

Scholars have also argued that racial segregation persists because of economic inequality between racial groups. On average, White individuals have the highest incomes and most wealth relative to any other racial group: Indeed, "in 2013, the average white family owned $13 for every $1 owned by a typical black family and $10 for every $1 owned by the average Latino family" (Shapiro 2017:33). In the United States, this differential in wealth has many roots, ranging from White colonists' theft of Indigenous land and exploitation of enslaved Africans who cultivated the land to subsidies from the federal government and explicit housing market policies that excluded people of color in the early and mid-twentieth century (e.g., see Clergé 2019; Harris 1993; Lipsitz 2011; Rothstein 2017). One of the contemporary outcomes of these historical processes is that, on average, White individuals purchase more expensive homes in neighborhoods they perceive as nice and end up living near other White individuals who are more likely to be able to afford these homes, too. Meanwhile, individuals of color are, on average, less likely to be able to afford homes in these areas and so end up purchasing homes near other individuals of color in less expensive areas.

Although economic inequality may contribute to segregation, housing market professionals also *produce* economic inequality as they contribute to the racial segregation process. This becomes apparent in the day-to-day work of professionals. White mortgage bankers, for example, regularly use average economic differences between racial groups (e.g., credit scores and income) as proxies for individual borrower financial risk—a clear example of how the racist market rubric maps racist economic ideas onto market actions, interactions, and transactions. That is, regardless of an individual borrower of color's actual income or credit score, mortgage lenders ascribe low income and low credit scores to them. Going a step further, they frequently align these economic assumptions with other racist stereotypes about borrowers of color in general, such as when they perceive borrowers as lazy and financially irresponsible. White mortgage bankers incorporate these racist assumptions into their approach to finding clients. Specifically, they seek out White real estate agents in the hope of gaining access to agents' White clients, whom they assume have good credit and income as well as the moral and cultural values that they think support this economic status.[7] Then, White mortgage bankers' segregated, exclusionary networking strategies mean that they rarely encounter borrowers of color, and when they do, they interpret these borrowers through a racist lens rather than fairly evaluating their loan applications. As a result of this process, mortgage bankers present borrowers who have similar economic profiles but different racial identities with unequal economic opportunities.

Working in tandem with inequitable mortgage lending processes, appraisers also actively contribute to economic inequality by adopting neighborhood-oriented logic and methods that assume White neighborhoods are more desirable than neighborhoods of color and that White neighborhoods have the highest demand. They then devalue homes in neighborhoods of color, which they view as undesirable and in low demand. Appraisers' assessments of value influence how much, if any, wealth homeowners gain when they sell their homes. In the case of homeowners living in neighborhoods of color, appraisers' valuations may well mean wealth *loss*. In other words, appraisers ensure that there are economic penalties or disincentives for homeowners who purchase or consider purchasing homes in neighborhoods of color—unless these areas are near White neighborhoods and are perceived as becoming more White or gentrified. They also devalue homeowner equity and destroy economic mobility in these areas.

Beyond rethinking the "big three," viewing racial segregation as a racialized process also means grappling with how White professionals and consumers cooperate with and legitimate racism in myriad ways through housing exchange. Here, I refer not to one-off cases of explicit, overtly racist individuals. Instead, I mean racism as a way that White professionals do real estate and as a way White consumers buy and sell real estate—it is their way of life, or at least housing life. Flowing from the organizational and industry contexts in which they are embedded, White professionals in particular weave color-blind and explicit racial prejudice and discrimination into their actions and interactions with White consumers. They broker racism.

Color-blind racism, or the subtle ways through which racial hierarchy is justified or "explained away" in contemporary society, was common among the housing market professionals and consumers I observed. For example, I observed White professionals and consumers minimizing racial inequality and using coded race language on numerous occasions (Bonilla-Silva 2006). Some of the color-blind racism I observed was a form of racial ignorance, when White professionals in particular performed acrobatics to avoid acknowledging racism or simply did not recognize racism even when they had direct encounters with it (Jung 2015; Mueller 2017, 2018).

In addition, I witnessed White professionals and consumers participating in explicit racism, or invoking overt biological, cultural, and moral justifications for racial hierarchy, especially in all-White spaces. In some cases, White professionals actively perpetuated such explicit racism. In other cases, White professionals expressed racial apathy. They acknowledged that explicit racism had occurred but did not view it as important in the grand scheme of things (Forman and Lewis 2006). And, in some cases, White professionals engaged in complicit racism; that is, they actively cooperated with racism while verbally expressing shock, disgust, or dismay at it. In all of these cases, White professionals legitimated and perpetuated racism.

Thus, viewing racial segregation as a racialized process reveals what many professionals and consumers of color in my study already knew to be true: The U.S. housing market is a fundamentally racialized market that White professionals and White-dominated professional organizations maintain and animate, day after day. In doing so, they preserve White space and privilege. In addition, although the White-dominated U.S. federal government no longer explicitly supports a racialized housing market, it has never meaningfully accounted for its role in building the racist foundation of that market.

The Imperative to Interrupt Housing Market Racism

As I write this concluding chapter, it has only been days since a White police officer murdered Atatiana Jefferson in her home, located in a predominantly Black neighborhood in Fort Worth, Texas. She was playing video games with her nephew when the police responded to a "wellness check" call by a neighbor who saw a door slightly ajar and lights on at Atatiana's home. The police officer, Aaron Dean, opened fire on Atatiana from outside the home when she approached the window (Hawkins and Paul 2019). The Jefferson family attorney told reporters that "he believed the fact that Jefferson lived in a predominantly black neighborhood led officers to respond to the call more aggressively than they might have otherwise" (Hawkins and Paul 2019). Social scientific evidence supports the attorney's theory. Studies consistently show that in places with larger numbers of Black and Latinx people and higher levels of racial segregation (and net of actual crime rates), Black and Latinx residents are more likely to be arrested or experience excessive use of force by police, jail and prison populations are likely to be larger, police forces are likely to be bigger, and police are more likely to kill unarmed victims of color than White victims (e.g., Bell 2020a; Holmes et al. 2019; Kent and Carmichael 2014; Mesic et al. 2018; Terrill and Reisig 2003).

Racism-produced racial segregation has a long history in the United States. It is a tool that White people have used to keep their resources for themselves in their neighborhoods. It is also a tool that White people and a White-dominated state have used to monitor and suppress individuals of color to prevent any hint of encroachment into White social, economic, or cultural territory (Bell 2020a). On one level, it is accurate to state that racial segregation means that people live separately. On another truer, deeper level, racial segregation is a process that White people actively maintain in order to maintain their power. Racial segregation means an unequal distribution of power, such that those in power—White people and a White-dominated state—can use and abuse their power with relative ease. Unfortunately, Atatiana's tragic death illustrates the dire consequences of power abused. It also provides yet another unmistakable call for White Americans to loosen their grip on this power.

Racial segregation actively benefits White people, and they are invested in it. Only by changing the racialized routines that endow them with these benefits, by penalizing participation in racism, and by rewarding racially equitable practices will White people begin to divest from the racism brokerage business.

Although *Race Brokers* tells a deeply disturbing story about how White housing market professionals in particular facilitate racial segregation through racist ideas and practices, it also argues that this story can change. Several professionals of color in my study pursued alternate strategies and clung to empowering, antiracist narratives that affirmed people and neighborhoods of color. These strategies at the very least mitigated some of racial segregation's negative effects and, in some cases, seemed to foster racially equitable opportunities within and across neighborhoods. These racism breakers have much to teach their respective industries and their professional White counterparts about fair housing. But first we have to stop construction on the current housing market, which White real estate professionals and organizations continue to build on a racist foundation with racist materials.

Methodological Appendix

When I first proposed the original research study on which *Race Brokers* is based—what was to become my doctoral dissertation—my advisors expressed concern. They wondered whether I would be able to collect the data I thought I could collect, particularly because they (rightly) pointed out that there are legal and professional sanctions for real estate agents and other housing market professionals who talk about race or engage in discriminatory behavior. Ultimately, I convinced them to let me try. For that project, I ended up collecting one year of ethnographic data (hundreds of pages of field notes with thirteen informants, in addition to photographs and brochures) and in-depth interviews with 102 housing market professionals and consumers. After completing my dissertation, I went back to all of these data and re-analyzed them in concert with conducting several supplementary quantitative analyses and consulting archival and historical sources. In the process, I completely retooled my understanding of how the U.S. housing market—a prominent example of what Hirschman and Garbes (forthcoming) call a "racialized market"—works.

In this appendix, I first describe the qualitative research methods I used to gather and analyze my primary data. In addition to reflecting on methodological choices—choices I made as I learned from other scholars calling for more critical sociological approaches to urban ethnography (Auyero 2012; Ray and Tillman 2019; Small 2015)—I also discuss what Hoang (2015b:192) calls the "embodied costs" and benefits of doing ethnography. On the one hand, as a woman and new mother when I first conducted this research, I continually put up with more than I should have had to in trying to collect these data. On the other hand, as a White person, I was able to observe and record the processes I report in this book at least in part because White informants and respondents assumed that my shared skin color was a signal of shared (racist) interests and opinions. Finally, I provide an overview of the quantitative research methods I used for the supplemental analysis presented in Chapter 5 of this book.

Qualitative Methods

The primary data for *Race Brokers* consisted of ethnographic field notes and in-depth interviews. From February 2015 to February 2016, I conducted ethnographic fieldwork with 13 housing developers and real estate agents who were all active in Houston's urban housing market and, in several cases, the greater metropolitan area as well. At the same time, I attended and took field notes at more than fifty open houses and neighborhood association events. I chose to observe developers and agents because prior research on historic and contemporary housing exchange processes suggested that these professionals were key to shaping urban landscapes through decisions about land and gatekeeping (e.g., see Gotham 2014; Jackson 1985). These housing developers and real estate agents comprised a race- and gender-diverse sample. Three were Black, five were Latinx, and five were White; four were women and eight were men. (Given how few women developers and developers of color there were in Houston, I have at times obscured developers' paired gender and race characteristics in the book to avoid revealing informants' identities.) My fieldwork with these 13 individuals and attendance at open houses and neighborhood association events brought me into contact with 222 additional individuals (professionals and consumers), many of whom I went on to encounter several times throughout the year. During the same period, I conducted 102 in-depth interviews with a race-, gender-, and age-diverse sample of housing market professionals and consumers. Professionals included housing developers, real estate agents, mortgage bankers, appraisers, escrow officers, and landlords. These professionals represented not only different industries but also different levels and years of experience and different types of companies. Consumer interviewees included home buyers, home sellers, and renters.

Recruitment

My research participants were not randomly chosen. Instead, I intentionally recruited participants who reflected a number of different social characteristics—race, gender, profession and years of experience, age, and so on—and who were active in a large number of Houston neighborhoods (see Small 2009). I used a variety of strategies to ensure that informants and respondents were not all recruited in the same way, thus ensuring greater reliability. I began my recruitment of study participants by identifying three urban Houston neighborhoods that were racially distinct as a way to foster encounters with a racially diverse sample. I constructed a master list of all single-family homes that were for sale in these three neighborhoods in January 2015. Then, I identified agents with multiple listings and began approaching them about participating in the study as informants. I also used this master list to help recruit real estate agent respondents, but I did not limit this recruitment to those with multiple listings. Another recruitment strategy, which I used for both housing developers and real estate agents, was attending open houses I had seen advertised online. Similarly, I used online "for-rent" advertisements to locate and recruit landlords. Yet another strategy was asking informants and respondents for their recommendations about whom I should speak with or using introductions made during fieldwork as a way to access other professionals, such as mortgage bankers and home buyers. I also used neighborhood association meetings as a way to locate potential participants, including home buyers, home sellers, and renters. Furthermore, I kept notes about the mortgage bankers, escrow officers, and appraisers whom I observed during the course of fieldwork or whom real estate agents used or recommended to their clients. I used these notes to help locate and recruit professionals in the lending, escrow, and appraising industries.

A key part of my overall recruitment strategy included trying to locate as many professionals of color as possible—using websites and open house advertisements, which often contained agents' names and headshots, as well as in-person housing events to identify them. I intentionally focused more time and recruiting energy among professionals of color for three reasons. First, I suspected that White participants would be easier to find because they are overrepresented among housing market professionals compared to the size of the White population in Houston overall.[1] This turned out to be the case. Second, I expected that White informants and respondents would rarely interact with or refer me to professionals or consumers of color. This also turned out to be the case. Third, and most important, I wanted to prioritize understanding how professionals of color do their housing-related work. Particularly as I began to hear and observe increasingly more racism among White participants, I wanted to discover how housing market professionals of color view the realities of racism, denaturalize such racism, and envision a more equitable housing future—how they engage what sociologist W. E. B. Du Bois (1986 [1903]:364) calls "second-sight."

Using all of these techniques to locate and recruit potential informants and respondents was key in cultivating a sample of housing market professionals who represented many different social and professional characteristics as well as the urban Houston housing market. In total, across the year of data collection, I conducted fieldwork or interviews in twenty-five Houston-area ZIP codes.

Data Collection

The research I conducted received Institutional Review Board (IRB) approval from Rice University, my graduate institution. I openly told potential participants that I was researching the housing market and "ethnic identity," but I remained vague on the details. (I made this discursive choice to avoid alarming White individuals, who often put up their guard when others they do not know use the word "race.") I also explained and provided them with an IRB-approved consent form, which described voluntary participation, confidentiality, and compensation. Informants were offered a $100 gift card (only one of them accepted it). Respondents were offered a $25 gift card (most of them accepted it).

When conducting fieldwork, I did not use an audio recorder. Instead, I took notes by hand as unobtrusively as possible and then typed these notes as soon as I could after leaving the field. I also paid attention to the kinds of interactions and settings I was observing and, whenever possible, attempted to observe informants across numerous types of situations throughout the year of research in order to deepen my understanding of how they went about their work (Tavory and Timmermans 2013). I ended up observing informants as they hosted broker and public open houses as well as client appreciation events; checked on construction sites; attended home-sale closings; ran staff meetings; prospected for land; met with past, current, and prospective clients; met with investors; and other situations. In addition to writing field notes, I also wrote memos about emergent observations or surprises. When conducting interviews, I used an audio recorder and participants knew that I was doing so. I used an IRB-approved interview guide that consisted of two main batteries of questions. The first part of the interview asked respondents general questions about their experiences in, views of, and, for professionals, work in the housing market. The second set of questions asked professionals and consumers explicitly about their experiences and views of race in the housing market. Then, I used two professional transcription agencies (again with IRB approval) to transcribe these interviews. I also took context notes for interviews, in which I jotted down notes about where and how I met the respondent and things of note that happened during the interview. What I learned during interviews informed what I looked for and asked about during fieldwork and vice versa. Overall, I approached data collection and analysis using an iterative, abductive approach (see Timmermans and Tavory 2012).

Analysis

In addition to ongoing memo writing and ongoing analyses, I merged all field notes, memos, and transcribed interviews into a single document after data collection was complete. I then coded the data as a whole using ATLAS.ti qualitative software, remaining aware of the knowledge I carried with me into the project while paying attention to how my data seemed surprising or different from prior research. I did my first complete analysis in 2016 and wrote three stand-alone papers that I combined for my doctoral dissertation. Small portions of two of these papers, which were published in the *American Sociological Review* and *Social Currents*, appear in Chapters 3–5 of this book. I also wrote a co-authored paper, published in *Sociology of Race and Ethnicity*, that used some of these data. A small portion of that article appears in Chapter 5, and the description of quantitative methods is provided later.

Before writing this book, I went back to my data again in 2018 and re-analyzed them with an eye for big-picture themes and new revelations. As a result, almost all of the writing here reflects my own evolving understanding of how people produce race and racism and how racism underwrites the process of racial segregation.

Qualitative Research as a White*Woman*Mother

I collected these qualitative data from a particular social position that meant participants understood and interacted with me in ways that both reinforced power distinctions between them and me (particularly in terms of gender, parental status, and sexual performativity) and assumed power distinctions between "us" White people and "them" (people of color). I embodied many costs during this research (Hoang 2015b). I was also able to collect much of these data, particularly from White participants, because of my symbolic status as a White person (see Gonzalez Van Cleve (2016) and Royster (2003), who discuss being perceived as White and accessing White-dominated spaces to collect data on criminal justice system and employment processes, respectively).

I am a cisgender, heterosexual, married woman. I am also a parent. In fact, my son was four months old when I began collecting the data for this research project. To maximize my ability to collect ethnographic data, I performed gender submissiveness around most of the male informants in my sample. I did nothing to display what they could have read as "assertive" or "difficult" feminine behavior. Rather, if I had a question about what they were doing, I asked it in ways that played to their egos. I also put up with one who engaged in sexual flirtation, which he persisted in doing despite knowing I was in a committed long-term relationship. Fieldwork with this participant regularly involved being in close quarters and acting as though his verbal comments about my body and his sexually charged body language did not bother me.

It was also an intentional choice on my part to hide my parental status from almost all of my informants—especially the men—because I feared it would lead them to treat me less respectfully or even disparage me (one of the male informants told me he "hated kids" outright). As part of hiding my status, I never tried to bring my son with me when doing fieldwork except for on one occasion when I met one of the female informants in the field on a day that I did not have access to other childcare options. (I could only afford two days of childcare a week when I first began the project, so I worked those two days, both weekend days, and every naptime and evening.) I also had to find a way to manage the embodied aspects of being a new mother with a newborn. In particular, because I was breastfeeding my son, I had to adjust when, where, and how long I pumped breast milk to accommodate my participants' schedules. Making my body conform to participants' schedules meant that I often found myself sitting in the back seat of my vehicle and pumping breast milk with a battery-operated pump, trying desperately to cover myself with a cardigan or blanket to protect my privacy. I changed the times that I pumped and for how long I pumped based on when my participants were available. Breastfeeding for the first time was an extremely difficult endeavor for me, even before imposing these external constraints onto my body. With these constraints, which I persisted through for four months of fieldwork, breastfeeding became a dreaded chore and more difficult to manage. My milk supply changed and was more difficult to predict. In the end, I stopped breastfeeding my son a few months earlier than I had planned in large part because of how these fieldwork constraints wore my body down.

But my body was also interpreted as a form of symbolic racial capital by many of my participants, particularly White participants. As the many examples of explicit and coded racism in this book demonstrate, White informants and respondents did not appear to hide or change what they were doing when I was around. Instead of fearing any social repercussions that could result from exposing their views and behaviors around me, they seemed to take it for granted that I was a "safe" interloper. I was able to witness backstage racism in all-White spaces because I am White. I have tried to use this benefit of racialized embodiment to expose the pervasiveness of racism in the contemporary housing market—a market that has, at least with respect to race, changed very little in the more than fifty years since the passage of the Fair Housing Act. By exposing the pervasiveness of racism and the continuities with the publicly, explicitly racialized housing market of the early to mid-twentieth century, I have also aimed to convey the necessity of dismantling the existing housing market organizational and cultural infrastructure.

Finally, to envision a more equitable way of doing professional housing market work, I have relied heavily on the many individuals of color who also invited me into their professional lives. These individuals trusted me with their stories and shared how racism had shaped their professional choices and options. In some cases, perhaps fearing that I would discount their experiences or even become defensive, professionals of color couched their comments by trying to "soften the blow" their comments could have when they first met me. For example, the first time I met Melissa, a Black real estate agent informant, she became animated as she discussed her views on race and the housing market. When I asked her a clarifying question, she responded, "Am I going to offend you?" "No," I replied. She continued her narrative and finished her thought, stating that

> But I do think that most White folks—most Whites feel superior . . . the world has always revolved around them. So but that's changing. Things are changing. I'm not quite sure they're ready for that, but things are definitely changing. Have I offended you?

I quickly replied to assure her I was not offended: "No, not at all," I said, "I happen to fully agree with you." After that, Melissa did not appear to try to "soften the blow" of her honest evaluations of race and the housing market during our interactions. That several professionals of color believed they needed to accommodate me like this when they first met me speaks volumes to how their past interactions with other White individuals and White-dominated organizations have gone. They not only have experienced the bite of systemic, organizational, and interpersonal racism but also have been required or felt the need to do the emotional work of accommodating White feelings.

Doing fieldwork and collecting interview data entail making choices about how to collect data, embody social location, and relate to those one is researching. Moreover, qualitative research, as with all research, involves making choices about how to interpret data—and social location shapes these decisions, sometimes without our knowledge. It is thus imperative to excavate these relational, methodological, and hermeneutic choices to make the unknown or ignored known because the results of these decisions are never neutral. Instead, they come with costs and benefits, both to the researched and to the researcher. For urban ethnography and, I believe, other forms of qualitative and quantitative research to have "radical potential" (Ray and Tillman 2019:5), researchers have a responsibility to critically evaluate research decisions at every step, from research questions to research design, sampling, data collection, coding, analysis, writing, and presenting. Research must "do justice" (Ray and Tillman 2019:5).

Quantitative Methods

Appraising in Houston

The tax appraisal data[2] in this study comes from Harris County Appraisal District (HCAD) public records. For our analysis, Junia Howell and I (Howell and Korver-Glenn 2018) used a census, not a sample, of *all* single-family tax-appraised residences in Harris County, Texas, in 2015.

This census consisted of 879,372 single-family homes with a mean housing value of \$233,221.[3] In addition to the tax appraisal value, these data also included information on house characteristics and quality. In our models, we operationalized house characteristics as square footage of the home and lot as well as dichotomous indicators of whether the home has at least one fireplace, garage, patio/porch/deck, and swimming pool/tennis court.[4] To adjust for the positive skew in home values, square footage, and lot size, we logged these three variables in our models. In addition, to measure home quality, we used date of construction or last major renovation, construction quality, and physical condition. Construction quality was determined by the appraisers using letter grades. We quantified and centered this scale such that the poorest quality construction is assigned a −7 and the highest quality is given a 10. Likewise, physical condition was determined using a categorical scale. We quantified and centered this scale such that it ranges from −3 to 4.

To answer our question regarding the relationship between neighborhood racial composition and tax appraisal value, we linked HCAD's GIS shape file of properties to census tracts.[5] Using the 2011–2015 American Community Survey (ACS), we calculated the proportion of the neighborhood that identified as non-Hispanic Black (Black, hereafter), Hispanic/Latinx, non-Hispanic Other (Other, hereafter), or non-Hispanic White (White, hereafter). In our models, we include the neighborhood's Black proportion, the neighborhood's Latinx proportion, and the proportion of the neighborhood that is of another race. Consequently, our reference group was the neighborhood's White proportion. To account for additional neighborhood factors that could explain the relationship between neighborhood racial composition and housing values, we included a series of additional neighborhood control variables.

Neighborhood Housing Stock

Even if a specific home is of high quality, appraisers assign lower home values to houses in neighborhoods with small, unkempt, or vacant properties. To operationalize the quality of the neighborhood housing stock, we used ACS estimates of census tract median number of rooms per housing unit, median year of home construction, and vacancy rate.

Community Socioeconomic Attributes

Likewise, we used the ACS estimates of census tract owner occupancy rate, poverty rate, and unemployment rate to control for community socioeconomic characteristics. Previous research indicates that higher owner occupancy rates, lower poverty rates, and lower unemployment rates correlate with higher home appraisals.

Neighborhood Amenities

We operationalized neighborhood amenities as school quality, violent crime rate, park accessibility, and location convenience. Using the GIS files made available by the School Attendance Boundary Information System, each house was linked to its corresponding elementary school. School quality was measured as the proportion of students who passed the state standardized tests in 2014 according to the Texas Education Agency.[6] Violent crime rate was operationalized as the number of violent crimes per capita in the census tract. Using the latitude and longitude coordinates of all crimes reported to the Houston Police Department and the Harris County Sheriff's Office from January 1, 2014, to December 31, 2014, we compiled the total number of violent crimes[7] in each census tract and divided this by the total population. Park accessibility was operationalized as the distance from each home in the dataset to the nearest park (in feet). This variable was calculated using a GIS shape file made available by the City of Houston. Given that the more rural sections of the county are farther from parks, this variable had a positive skew and was thus logged in all models. Finally, location convenience was measured as access to employment opportunities—specifically, the census tract's mean commute time in minutes. Theoretically, higher commute time corresponds with inconvenience and thus lower home values.

Consumer Housing Demand

Following real estate and economics conventions, we measured consumer housing demand as the mean number of days houses remain on the market and the percentage of houses for sale that decrease their asking prices. Areas where houses sell quickly and prices are not reduced are considered high-demand areas. We obtained consumer housing demand data from the Houston Association of Realtors (HAR) Multiple Listing Service (MLS) and Zillow. From the HAR MLS, we obtained the average number of days houses remained on the market in each ZIP code for each month (January 2015– December 2015) and then averaged across the year. From Zillow, we gathered the percentage of homes on the market in each ZIP code that experienced a price cut for each month (January 2014–December 2014) and then averaged across the year. Despite their different sources, these two variables were highly correlated, building our confidence in measurement validity.[8]

Modeling

To examine the influence of neighborhood racial composition on 2015 tax appraisals, we estimated multilevel models to address the clustering of multiple houses in each census tract. All models were run in Stata using the xtreg command.[9] Table A.1 shows the results of our four models.

Table A.1 Coefficients from Multilevel Regressions Predicting 2015 Logged Housing Appraisal Value

	Model 1	Model 2	Model 3	Model 4
Neighborhood race				
Black proportion	−2.11 (0.10)	−1.28 (0.09)	−0.86 (0.09)	−0.82 (0.10)
Latinx proportion	−2.00 (0.10)	−0.93 (0.09)	−0.91 (0.09)	−0.88 (0.08)
Other proportion	1.15 (0.31)	0.33 (0.24)	0.27 (0.18)	0.37 (0.19)
House characteristics				
House area, logged		0.60 (0.01)	0.60 (0.01)	0.60 (0.01)
Land area, logged		0.20 (0.01)	0.20 (0.01)	0.20 (0.01)
Fireplace		0.01 (0.01)	0.01 (0.01)	0.01 (0.01)
Garage		0.08 (0.01)	0.08 (0.01)	0.08 (0.01)
Patio, porch, or deck		0.07 (0.01)	0.07 (0.01)	0.07 (0.01)
Pool or tennis court		0.05 (0.00)	0.05 (0.00)	0.05 (0.00)
House quality				
Year improved		0.04 (0.00)	0.04 (0.00)	0.04 (0.00)
Construction quality		0.08 (0.00)	0.07 (0.00)	0.07 (0.00)
Physical condition		0.10 (0.00)	0.10 (0.00)	0.10 (0.00)
Neighborhood housing stock				
Median number of rooms			0.03 (0.02)	0.03 (0.03)
Median year built			−0.01 (0.01)	−0.01 (0.00)
Vacancy rate			−0.15 (0.22)	−0.13 (0.22)
Community socioeconomic attributes				
Owner occupancy rate			−0.70 (0.13)	−0.68 (0.13)
Poverty proportion			0.14 (0.18)	0.13 (0.18)
Unemployment rate			−2.36 (0.36)	−2.34 (0.36)
Neighborhood amenities				
Proportion of students passing state test			0.46 (0.09)	0.45 (0.09)
Violent crimes per capita			−3.31 (1.80)	−2.95 (1.83)
Feet to nearest park, logged			0.01 (0.01)	0.01 (0.01)
Mean commute time			−0.04 (0.00)	−0.04 (0.00)
Consumer housing demand				
Average days on the market				0.01 (0.04)
Percentage of homes with price cut				0.79 (0.72)
Constant	13.08 (0.08)	−2.27 (0.65)	13.82 (2.40)	13.64 (2.40)
R^2 overall	0.5003	0.7243	0.8095	0.8091
Number of houses	879,372	879,372	879,372	879,372
Number of tracts	708	708	708	708

Note: P values are not displayed because our data are a census, not a sample. Hence, we do not need to use probability to estimate the likelihood of our sample mean being the population mean because presented data are the mean of the population.

Source: Harris County Appraisal District (n.d.).

Notes

Introduction

1. Former U.S. Senator and current President Joe Biden, for example, opposed school busing (a policy intended to reduce racial segregation between schools) because he believed it would cause his children to grow up in a "racial jungle" (Herndon and Stolberg 2019)—thus upending their all-White environment. For recent examples of contemporary home buyers' takes on racial segregation, see Krysan and Crowder (2017).

2. I use the term "Latinx" instead of "Hispanic" or "Latino" in my own descriptions of neighborhoods and groups to avoid some of the problems associated with the latter terms. "Hispanic," for example, is linked to Spain/Spanish identity and, for many, to colonization, conquest, and genocide. "Latino" signals masculine identity, but "Latinx" avoids gender specificity. (See also sociologist Cristina Mora's book *Making Hispanics* (2014) as well as her recent interview with Schelenz and Freeling (2019) on this topic, found here: https://www.universityofcalifornia.edu/news/whats-in-a-name-how-concepts-hispanic-and-latino-identity-emerged). When I refer to specific individual participants who were part of my research, however, I typically use the ethnic labels they claimed for themselves (e.g., Mexican American) unless doing so would reveal their identity and compromise confidentiality.

3. Fields and Fields (2014:17) define racism as "the theory and the practice of applying a social, civic, or legal double standard based on ancestry, and to the ideology surrounding such a double standard. . . . *Racism* is first and foremost a social practice, which means that it is an action and a rationale for action, or both at once" [italics in original].

4. For other work that highlights how people of color have formed, circulated, and advanced such ideas, specifically as they relate to housing and space, see: Clergé (2019); Connolly (2014); De León (2001); Hunter and Robinson (2018); Lipsitz (2011); Pattillo (2007); and San Miguel (2001).

5. Rothstein (2017:45) documents that the following cities had such racial zoning ordinances in the first two decades of the twentieth century: Atlanta, Baltimore, Birmingham, Charleston, Charlotte, Dade County (Miami), Dallas, Louisville, New Orleans, Oklahoma City, Richmond (Virginia), and St. Louis, among others.

6. Rugh et al. (2015) estimated that in Baltimore alone, individual Black home buyers who borrowed between 2000 and 2008 would pay excess costs of approximately $15,000 across a thirty-year mortgage loan; individual Black borrowers living in Black neighborhoods would pay excess costs of approximately $16,000 over a thirty-year loan. They estimated that the Black Baltimore borrowers in their sample

experienced a total excess loss of approximately $2.1 million through foreclosure and repossession by the end of 2012. Although their data include information on individuals borrowing from multiple lending institutions, Wells Fargo was a major source of mortgage loans for borrowers in Baltimore and throughout the United States. Wells Fargo has had to pay millions of dollars to settle class-action lawsuits emerging from such discriminatory practices (see, for example, Rothacker and Ingram 2012), and borrowers continue to file lawsuits against Wells Fargo for such practices (Egan 2018).

7. Feagin (2013:3) defines the White racial frame as "an overarching white worldview that encompasses a *broad and persisting set of racial stereotypes, prejudices, ideologies, images, interpretations and narratives, emotions, and reactions to language accents, as well as racialized inclinations to discriminate*" (italics in original).

8. The racist ideas conveyed in the racist market rubric emerged during ethnographic fieldwork and interviews with housing market professionals. These ideas were a specific iteration of the White racial frame and were used to impose White dominance and privilege in the housing market (Feagin 2013). These racist ideas largely overlapped with what other contemporary researchers on racism and stereotyping in criminal justice, employment, educational, and housing spheres have found (see, for example, Chavez 2013; Collins 2000; Gonzalez Van Cleve 2016; Lewis and Diamond 2015; Moss and Tilly 2001; Taylor 2019; Treitler 2013; Wortham et al. 2009).

9. Note that real estate professionals could pick and choose from the rubric to suit a given situation. For example, they may have affirmed the financial stability of Latinx individuals or neighborhoods in one setting while questioning these individuals' financial knowledge. In a different setting, they may have stereotyped Latinx individuals or neighborhoods as financially unstable as well as not having knowledge necessary for navigating American financial institutions.

10. The people-oriented market rubric draws its name from Dr. Martin Luther King, Jr.'s speech at Riverside Church in New York City on April 4, 1967: "I am convinced that if we are to get on the right side of the world revolution, we as a nation must undergo a radical revolution of values. We must rapidly begin the shift from a 'thing-oriented' society to a 'person-oriented' society. When machines and computers, profit motives and property rights are considered more important than people, the giant triplets of racism, materialism, and militarism are incapable of being conquered. A true revolution of values will soon cause us to question the fairness and justice of many of our past and present policies. On the one hand we are called to play the Good Samaritan on life's roadside; but that will be only an initial act. One day we must come to see that the whole Jericho Road must be transformed so that men and women will not be constantly beaten and robbed as they make their journey on Life's highway" (King 2015:214). There is an inherent tension within this name: As long as housing is a commodity exchanged within a fundamentally racialized market (Pattillo 2013; Taylor 2019), professionals who draw on equitable, people-affirming ideas will be limited in the extent to which they can pursue just or redistributive housing possibilities (see also Dantzler and Reynolds 2020).

11. The equitable, people-affirming ideas conveyed in the people-oriented market rubric also emerged during ethnographic fieldwork and interviews with housing market professionals, especially those of color.

12. In other spheres such as the labor market, scholars have studied brokerage processes, or how social exchange vis-à-vis brokers happens. They have also studied brokers' structural position in social networks, or to whom brokers are connected. In this literature, there is broad agreement that brokers are people who bridge gaps in the social structure, either by channeling information or other resources between two otherwise disconnected parties or by connecting parties so that they may exchange information directly (Halevy et al. 2019; Obstfelt et al. 2014; Stovel and Shaw 2012). Although my understanding of race brokers encompasses people who make these types of social connections, thus fitting these classic definitions, it also includes people who connect individuals directly to other resources, such as land and capital.

13. I am indebted to Dan Hirschman for pointing me to this concept, which echoes the "complicit masculinity" construct in gender studies (Buschmeyer and Lengersdorf 2016; Connell 2005).

14. *Race Brokers* foregrounds housing market professionals. But I also interviewed thirty housing consumers for this project, including three Asian, eight Black, seven Latinx, and twelve White home buyers, home sellers, and renters. During interviews, consumers shared their perspectives on the housing market and experiences with real estate professionals (particularly real estate agents). Although consumers do not feature prominently in this book, they do inform my analysis of housing market professionals by corroborating my findings about and prompting me to ask new questions of professionals.

15. Three of these developers were also licensed real estate agents.

16. Other research has shown that White individuals more openly share their racist thoughts with other White individuals (Picca and Feagin 2007; see also Royster 2003). I am a White woman, and I suspect that the White informants and respondents represented in this book granted me access because they assumed I was a "safe" interloper. Moreover, although I grew up in a family in which cash was usually scarce, I learned how to pass as middle class in middle- and upper-class contexts through interactions with wealthier White friends and acquaintances. This cultural capital also likely helped with the data collection process because all of the professionals I observed and interviewed were middle or upper class.

17. As mentioned previously, three of the developers I observed were also licensed real estate agents. I do not count them twice here, but I do examine how they occupy both of their professional roles and include them in both Chapters 2 and 3.

18. Despite many attempts throughout the year, I had difficulty locating additional mortgage professionals of color to interview, and even when I did, the contact information I found or was given often appeared to be incorrect or insufficient. Of the ten mortgage bankers I interviewed, one was also a licensed real estate agent.

19. Reflecting broader patterns of representation in the appraisal industry (e.g., Hobby Center for Public Policy 2015), I did not encounter any Asian or Black appraisers during my fieldwork, nor I was able to find Asian or Black appraisers to interview.

One White appraiser who owned an appraisal management company and had been active in the business for decades told me that during all his years in the business, he had only encountered one Black appraiser.

20. Despite my best attempts to recruit more escrow/title officers to interview, I was only able to secure interviews with six of these professionals, all of whom were White and one of whom was also a licensed real estate agent (I encountered and observed an additional seven escrow/title officers during fieldwork; all but one of these were White). In contrast to my developer, real estate agent, mortgage banker, and appraiser samples, there were no consistent themes present within these interviews, which is why I do not devote a chapter to them in this book. Future research should continue to explore how this group of understudied professionals affects processes of individual and neighborhood racial housing inequality.

Chapter 1

1. See, for example, Pager et al.'s (2009) work on employers' racialization of prospective male employees in New York City; Gonzalez Van Cleve's (2016) research on how judges, lawyers, and police officers racialize individuals accused of crimes in Chicago; and Rosen's (2014) work on landlords' racially determined geographic sorting of renters in Baltimore.

2. The Akokisa were part of the Western Atakapa band of the Atakapa Ishak people. As of this writing, the Atakapa Ishak Nation is seeking federal recognition for their tribe (see Atakapa Ishak Nation, "Register for Roll," retrieved December 9, 2020, from http://www.atakapa-ishak.org/register-for-roll/).

3. Union General Gordon Granger and many hundreds of federal troops arrived at Galveston Island, located to the southeast of Houston's urban core, on June 19, 1865. Their proclamation of emancipation was the first news enslaved Texans had received of Robert E. Lee's surrender two months previously. Emancipated Black Texans then birthed the Juneteenth holiday. In subsequent years, Black Houstonians celebrated Juneteenth at Emancipation Park after White Houstonians used the power of Jim Crow to forbid them from participating in city-sponsored Fourth of July festivities (Steptoe 2016).

4. On the significance of *Shelley v. Kraemer* for Black residential mobility, see Kucheva and Sander (2014).

5. Prior to declaring its independence from Mexico in 1836 and its subsequent annexation by the United States in 1845, Texas was part of Mexico. Many local Mexican Americans with ancestral ties to the area say, "We didn't cross the border; the border crossed us."

6. Of these four cities, note that Chicago's housing values have only recently recovered to pre-crash (2000) levels.

7. Specifically, the formula for dissimilarity (D) gives us a statistic that indicates what proportion of either of the two groups would have to move to mirror the distribution of the other population.

8. In Houston, these changes in segregation levels are in part a function of the relative and absolute increase in the number of Latinx individuals and the relative and absolute decrease in the number of White individuals (Emerson et al. 2012).

9. Other methods include measuring segregation vis-à-vis road distance relative to straight line distance (Roberto 2018), accounting for the presence and even distribution of multiple groups across space (rather than only two groups at a time) (Howell and Emerson 2018), and examining changes or stability in neighborhood racial composition over time (Krysan and Crowder 2017). Logan and Parman (2017) derived a new measure of segregation by using the complete manuscript pages of the 1880 and 1940 U.S. federal censuses. They "use the location of households in adjacent units in census enumeration to measure the degree of integration or segregation in a community" (Logan and Parman 2017:134).

10. This measure has been used by other researchers to examine group over- or underrepresentation in occupations (e.g., Logan et al. 2003).

11. Source: Texas A&M Real Estate Center, n.d., "Housing Activity for Harris County," retrieved March 27, 2019, from https://www.recenter.tamu.edu/data/housing-activity/#!/activity/County/Harris_County. This is comparable to, for example, Cook County (Chicago), where during roughly the same period (March 2018 to February 2019), 61,233 homes were sold, or 1 out of every 13 owner-occupied homes (Source: Mainstreet Organization of Realtors, n.d., September Closed Sales," retrieved March 27, 2019, from https://mred.stats.10kresearch.com/infoserv/s-v1/jbPO-dFK).

12. See Houston Association of Realtors, n.d. (d), "MLS Press Release," retrieved April 30, 2020, from https://www.har.com/content/mls/?m=04&y=20.

13. March 2010 is the earliest date for which Zillow data on Houston are available. Author's own calculations using Zillow data (Zillow, n.d., "Home Values," retrieved January 15, 2018, from https://www.zillow.com/research/data).

14. The name Crisol comes from the word *creosote*, "a brownish oily liquid used to preserve railroad ties" (Steptoe 2016:80).

15. Houston Heights Association, n.d., "Deed Restrictions," retrieved April 1, 2019, from http://www.houstonheights.org/deed-restrictions.

16. These districts—Houston Heights West, East, and South—roughly correspond to Ashland Street on the west, Sixteenth Street on the north, and Eleventh Street on the south (Houston Heights West); Oxford Street on the east, Twentieth Street on the north, and Eleventh Street on the south (Houston Heights East); and Heights Boulevard on the west, Fourth Street on the south, and Oxford Street on the east (Houston Heights South).

Chapter 2

1. Specifically, developers and builders constructed 31,226,000 new one-unit single-family homes between 1974 and 2018. This number is four times higher than the number of contractor-built single-family homes (when private landowners hire a contractor to build a home on land they have purchased) and more than five

times higher than the number of owner-built homes (when private landowners build a home themselves). Source: U.S. Census Bureau, n.d., "Historical Data: New Residential Construction," retrieved August 22, 2019, from https://www.census.gov/construction/nrc/historical_data/index.html.

2. Metrostudy News, 2016b, "Houston Housing 4Q15: Rising Affordability Issues Challenge the Top Single-Family Market in the Country," retrieved April 1, 2019, from https://www.metrostudy.com/houston-housing-4q15-rising-affordability-issues-challenge-the-top-single-family-market-in-the-country.

3. According to McConnell and Wiley (2012:7), the "broadest and most common definition for infill is development that occurs in underutilized parcels in already developed, urbanized areas."

4. I am not the first to use the phrase "reverse blockbusting." However, I could find only a handful of academic references that use the phrase, most of which refer to a general, somewhat abstract process by which older, run-down homes in lower income neighborhoods of color are purchased and eventually "flipped" and then occupied by comparatively well-to-do newcomers. Only one older reference used the phrase "reverse blockbusting" to specify a group of people doing the blockbusting: "In a kind of reverse blockbusting, speculators comb neighborhoods on foot and by telephone just ahead of the restoration movement, making attractive cash offers to owners" (Bryant and McGee 1983:66). One recent piece draws from a small number of interviews with real estate agents, developers, and homeowners in North Nashville, Tennessee, to theorize a *racialized* reverse blockbusting process (Hightower and Fraser 2020). My definition builds on Hightower and Fraser's work in that it specifies particular actions taken by housing developers to explicitly target homeowners of color in developers' predatory efforts to acquire land for redevelopment.

5. Note that even though Jesse could have drawn attention to Fifth Ward's lower income status (relative to other areas such as Lindale Park and the Heights), he did not do so. Instead, he specifically oriented his where-to-build decision around the neighborhood's racial composition.

6. Because the number of developers active in this particular neighborhood is so small, I have obscured its name to avoid identifying the developer. In addition, there are several other instances in this chapter in which I obscured potentially identifying details about the developer and/or neighborhood because the number of developers active in some areas (especially neighborhoods of color) is so small.

7. I calculated the violent crime rate for the neighborhood and for the City of Houston using public Houston Police Department data. When I conducted this study in 2015 and 2016, the most recent year for which full crime data were available was 2014.

8. Again, all names used in the text are pseudonyms to protect research participant confidentiality.

9. Internalized racism is also defined as "the 'subjection' of the victims of racism to the mystifications of the very racist ideologies which imprison and define them" (Hall 1986:27).

Chapter 3

1. This number is seasonally adjusted. Source: National Association of Realtors, 2019, "Summary of July 2019 Existing Home Sales Statistics," retrieved August 29, 2019, from https://www.nar.realtor/sites/default/files/documents/ehs-07-2019-summary-2019-08-21.pdf.

2. Author's calculations using Houston Association of Realtors' Multiple Listing Service monthly press releases (retrieved August 29, 2019, from https://www.har.com/content/mls).

3. NAR's name has changed at various points throughout its history. Initially founded as the National Association of Real Estate Exchanges in 1908, it became the National Association of Real Estate Boards (NAREB) in 1916 and then the National Association of Realtors in 1972. (See http://nar.realtor/about-nar/history, retrieved May 14, 2020.) NAREB ensured its White real estate agents towed the racist line by heavily penalizing those who dared transgress the organization's explicitly racist policy of upholding racial segregation (Taylor 2019).

4. See Besbris (2020) for a thorough discussion of how real estate agents, as key housing market intermediaries, shape home-buying and neighborhood inequality.

5. National Association of Realtors, n.d. (b), "Farming & Prospecting," retrieved January 14, 2019, from https://www.nar.realtor/farming-prospecting.

6. From p. 12 of a brochure titled "How to Get Started in Real Estate" (Greene, n.d., retrieved December 15, 2016, from http://home.garygreene.com/downloads/career_opportunities_current.pdf).

7. In its 2017 survey of members, NAR found that 31 percent of surveyed agents' business comes from referrals or repeat clients (National Association of Realtors, n.d. (c), "2017 Member Profile," retrieved January 14, 2019, from https://www.nar.realtor/sites/default/files/reports/2017/2017-member-profile-highlights-05-11-2017.pdf). In its 2018 profile of home buyers and sellers, NAR reported that 53 percent of housing consumers found their agents through referrals or relied on an agent with whom they had worked in the past (National Association of Realtors, n.d. (d), "Highlights from the Profile of Home Buyers and Sellers," retrieved January 14, 2019, from https://www.nar.realtor/research-and-statistics/research-reports/highlights-from-the-profile-of-home-buyers-and-sellers).

8. See, for example, *United States v. National Association of Real Estate Boards, et al.*, 339 U.S. 485 (1950), which found this type of practice to be in violation of the Sherman Act.

9. Michael, like the other real estate agent informants in my study, listed or sold properties across a wide price spectrum during my fieldwork (between May 2015 and February 2016 inclusive, his range was approximately $215,000 to $1,425,000). However, perhaps because he was keener to have me join him at the higher priced properties, my field notes about go-alongs with Michael contained more information about these more expensive properties.

10. Social networking in the real estate brokerage industry reproduces racially segregated networks, which then reinforce racially segregated neighborhoods (Korver-Glenn

2018a; Krysan 2008; see also Royster 2003). For example, White real estate agents—who have lived experiences and community knowledge largely circumscribed by White space—typically have clients who are also White (Korver-Glenn 2018a; Krysan 2008). White agents then funnel White home buyers, who also have lived experiences and community knowledge of White spaces, into White neighborhoods (see Krysan and Crowder 2017). Relying on social networks for housing opportunities can reproduce racial segregation without any observable racial stereotyping or overt discrimination.

11. Some White agents I studied at times provided a 1 percent discount to their repeat White clients in order to encourage loyalty.

12. I was not audio-recording this portion of our conversation. Instead, I took detailed field notes about this part of our conversation immediately after Amanda and I parted ways.

13. HAR was the second largest local real estate association/board in the United States as of this writing. See Houston Association of Realtors, n.d. (a), "Join HAR," retrieved September 4, 2019, from https://www.har.com/content/page/har_inside.

14. Four years after conducting this research and during the final drafting of this book manuscript, NAR passed a resolution that essentially forbids its member agents and brokers to engage pocket listings. Whether and how local real estate boards implement this resolution remain open questions.

15. Due to copyright restrictions, I could not reproduce the HAR market area map in this book. As of November 12, 2019, the map was available online at http://web.har.com/mlsareamap.html (Houston Association of Realtors, n.d. (c)).

16. National Association of Realtors, n.d. (a), "Safety," retrieved January 20, 2018, from https://www.nar.realtor/safety.

17. In Texas, real estate agents must take 30 hours of continuing education coursework the first time they renew their real estate license. Thereafter, they must take 18 hours of continuing education coursework every two years as part of renewing their license.

18. HAR.com Training Finder. Houston Association of Realtors, n.d. (b), "Open Houses, Open Doors," retrieved January 19, 2019, from https://www.har.com/education/course_detail/5/931.

19. ChampionsSchool.com, n.d., "Elective CE Course Topics," retrieved January 19, 2019, from https://www.championsschool.com/real-estate/tx/ce/#ce-courses.

20. Perry Homes is one of the largest housing development companies in the Houston area.

21. After my study ended, HAR published a blog post in 2018 titled "Home Sellers Should Understand the 'Off-MLS' or 'Pocket' Listing." This post was a reprint of an opinion piece written by real estate agent Chaille Ralph in 2014 and published in the *Houston Chronicle* online (https://www.chron.com/news/article/Realtor-View-Understand-an-off-MLS-or-pocket-5798828.php, retrieved May 3, 2020). The post is addressed to home sellers and does not function as an HAR policy permitting or prohibiting pocket listings among its agents. Along with other "downsides," the post notes that "if your home isn't on the MLS, you may well be leaving money on the table." (The post

was published July 10, 2018; retrieved May 3, 2020, from https://www.har.com//ri/152/home-sellers-should-understand-the-off-mls-or-pocket-listing.)

22. Contemporary real estate organizations illustrate what sociologist Victor Ray (2019:42) calls "racialized decoupling"—that is, when "racialized organizations . . . decouple formal commitments to equity, access, and inclusion from policies and practices that reinforce, or at least do not challenge, existing racial hierarchies."

Chapter 4

1. In 2017, 54.1 percent of all owner-occupied homes had a regular and/or home equity mortgage. This is a conservative estimate of mortgage activity because presumably some portion of those who owned their homes free and clear had previously paid off a mortgage. (To estimate the percent of owner-occupied homes with a mortgage, I used the U.S. Census Bureau's American Housing Survey Table Creator, publicly available at https://www.census.gov/programs-surveys/ahs/data/interactive/ahstablecreator.html; retrieved September 12, 2019.)

2. See the American Housing Survey Table Creator at https://www.census.gov/programs-surveys/ahs/data/interactive/ahstablecreator.html (retrieved September 12, 2019).

3. Mortgage lenders are the financial entities that fund the mortgage loan. Mortgage brokers typically work for the home buyer as independent consultants who try to match the buyer to a loan product. They are not attached to a specific mortgage lender. Mortgage bankers work for a specific lender and assist home buyers who purchase loans through that institution. Both mortgage brokers and mortgage bankers are classified as loan officers by the federal Bureau of Labor Statistics. (For a brief, plain-English overview, see Haring, n.d., "Difference Between a Mortgage Banker vs. a Mortgage Broker," *Houston Chronicle*, retrieved November 14, 2019, from https://work.chron.com/difference-between-mortgage-banker-vs-mortgage-broker-1281.html.) All of the individuals I interviewed were mortgage bankers who worked for a specific lender. I refer to them as mortgage bankers or loan officers throughout the chapter.

4. As Stuart (2003:22) notes, "apart from mortgage loans that remain in the portfolio of a financial institution without government insurance, any loan originated in the United States must directly comply with either Fannie Mae, Freddie Mac, FHA [Federal Housing Administration], or VA [Veterans Administration] underwriting rules. I say directly because these institutions' influence extends beyond their direct activities. Even if a lender keeps its loans in portfolio it may want to be able to sell them at some time in the future. For it to do so, the loans would have to be in compliance with the rules of Fannie Mae or Freddie Mac." In practice, this means that virtually all mortgage borrowers who plan to purchase a single-family home complete Fannie Mae's Uniform Residential Loan Application (Form 1003).

5. For more on racialized discretion in 'traditional' banking, see Faber and Friedline (2020). See Haney-López (2000) and Gonzalez Van Cleve (2016) for examples of how racialized discretion occurs in U.S. court systems.

6. Specifically, Asian, Black, and Latinx loan applicants were 4.1, 9.4, and 5.1 percent less likely, respectively, to be approved than their White counterparts. Black and Latinx loan applicants were 2.8 and 5.2 percent more likely, respectively, to receive a high-cost loan than their White counterparts. Faber (2018) demonstrates that these patterns of unequal loan outcomes held even when controlling for individual applicant, loan, and spatial characteristics.

7. This strategy is not new among mortgage bankers, but it has received scant attention. One notable exception is Stuart's (2003) work on mortgage lending in Chicago. He interviewed forty-five real estate brokers in two neighborhoods in Chicago, one Black and one White and Latinx. He found that twenty-six out of twenty-nine brokers in the Black neighborhood listed three specific lending institutions they worked with and said they referred 65 percent of their clients to these three lenders on average. He also found that twelve out of sixteen brokers in the White and Latinx neighborhood listed three lending institutions and referred 87 percent of their clients to these on average. Stuart also highlights training material from Fannie Mae that noted 80 percent of home buyers choose one lender over another because of a recommendation from a real estate agent. Recent work by Steil et al. (2018) shows that mortgage lending professionals networked with others besides real estate agents as well. They found that these individuals networked with nonprofit and church leaders in neighborhoods of color to build a market for their predatory, subprime loans.

8. Here, Dave is indicating their preference for either a two-bedroom, two-bathroom or a two-bedroom, one-and-a-half-bathroom home.

9. Although getting preapproved for a mortgage loan may make them more attractive to home sellers, buyers do not have to get preapproved prior to putting an offer on a house. Michael misled Dave and Shanna in this instance, using his professional status as the "expert" as a tool to direct them toward specific mortgage bankers with whom he had relationships.

10. My interviews with real estate agents reinforced findings from my fieldwork. After only a handful of interviews, I realized that agents were referring their home-buying clients to mortgage bankers they knew. I therefore began asking agents to tell me the specific mortgage bankers to whom they referred their clients. During the remaining interviews, real estate agents provided a total of twenty-five unique mortgage bankers to whom they referred their buying clients (some mortgage bankers were referred more than once; I do not count these repeat mentions). Of these, 64 percent were White ($n = 16$), 12 percent were Black ($n = 3$), 8 percent were Latinx ($n = 2$), 4 percent were Asian ($n = 1$), and 8 percent were of unknown race ($n = 2$). These numbers overrepresent White mortgage bankers and underrepresent mortgage bankers of color in Harris County (see the Appendix, Endnote 1). Furthermore, interviewed White agents said they referred their (typically White) clients to specific mortgage bankers of color (one Asian and one Black) only two times throughout all interviews.

11. I formally interviewed a total of ten mortgage bankers in addition to ethnographic observation of seven mortgage bankers. Despite repeated attempts to find and formally interview multiple mortgage bankers of color, my final interview sample included only one Black mortgage banker and nine White mortgage bankers. I had much more luck encountering mortgage bankers of color during fieldwork with agents and developers, as descriptions in the chapter illustrate. The difficulty in locating mortgage bankers as well as appraisers of color to interview (see Chapter 5) reflects the paucity of professionals of color within these industries.

12. At the time of my study, all but one of the dozen-plus agents in Jane's brokerage were White.

13. I have not disclosed the name of the neighborhood to protect Mateo's confidentiality; very few Latinx agents and developers work in Houston's White neighborhoods.

14. See Bonam et al. (2020:42) for their discussion of intersectional invisibility, a "phenomenon [that] occurs when targets with nonprototypical intersecting identities elicit perceptions that fail to align with each constituent identity. . . . To elaborate, a strong psychological link between two social categories (e.g., Black space with lower-class or Black person with male) inhibits accurate categorization and facilitates downstream stereotyping of nonprototypical category intersections (e.g., Black space with middle-class or Black person with female)."

15. Mortgage lenders typically do not require home inspections, but home buyers often order home inspections on their own dime. In my research, buyers tended to hire inspectors referred to them by real estate agents.

16. See Federal Deposit Insurance Corporation, 2005, "Frequently Asked Questions on Residential Tract Lending," retrieved November 14, 2019, from https://www.fdic.gov/news/news/financial/2005/fil9005a.html.

Chapter 5

1. Appraisals are not necessary for homes purchased with cash.

2. Specifically, the Appraisal Subcommittee (comprised of individuals from federal finance-related entities, including the Federal Housing Finance Agency and the Federal Deposit Insurance Corp., among others) oversees state licensing boards and the Appraisal Foundation, which sets appraiser qualifications and appraisal standards (Appraisal Foundation, n.d., "The Appraiser Regulatory System in the United States," retrieved December 8, 2020, from https://www.appraisalfoundation.org/imis/TAF/About_Us/Appraiser_Regulatory_System/TAF/Regulatory_Structure.aspx).

3. Buyers can also challenge the appraised value and request a second appraisal; however, the lender does not have to grant their request.

4. For Federal Housing Administration (FHA) and other federally backed mortgage loans (e.g., Veterans Administration loans), appraisers must also consider an additional battery of items to help determine property risk. If the appraiser identifies any issues with the property based on the FHA's requirements, for example, the seller must fix or address the issues or the sale will fall through.

5. *United States v. American Institute of Real Estate Appraisers of the National Association of Realtors, the Society of Real Estate Appraisers, the United States League of Savings Associations, and the Mortgage Bankers Association* 442 F. Supp. 1072 (1977). In this case, the Society of Real Estate Appraisers also tried (unsuccessfully) to argue that appraisers were not covered by the Fair Housing Act. Also note that private appraisal associations continued to use explicitly racist language in their training materials at least until 1977 (see Gotham 2000).

6. In 2019 alone, for example, Fannie Mae purchased more than 2 million single-family home mortgages. Source: Fannie Mae, 2019, "Annual Housing Activities Report, Annual Mortgage Report 2019," retrieved December 8, 2020, from https://www.fanniemae.com/media/33501/display.

7. Allan then told me that he got his information on schools and school quality from local friends: "To be honest with you, like, in my neighborhood, I wasn't real familiar with the elementary schools, and so when I started looking, I had friends who'd lived here... that had young kids.... Mothers are [chuckles] a great source of information." Thus, when Allan referred to "everyone" wanting their kids to go to "one of the best elementary schools," it is reasonable to conclude that his reference point was his set of White friends (White women who are mothers in particular) who provided him their opinions. Allan did not use another form of measuring school quality or demand when calculating the effect of schools on home value.

8. The U.S. federal government began to monitor appraisers more closely after the recent housing crash (U.S. Government Accountability Office 2012), in part by collecting appraisal data and compiling them into the Uniform Appraisal Dataset. As of this writing, there is no clear way for nongovernmental, academic, or independent researchers to access these data.

9. Note that as of this writing, the Astrodome has not yet been demolished.

10. When studying contemporary appraisals, an immediate problem is the lack of available data on residential market appraisals—that is, appraisals conducted by individual, for-profit appraisers on behalf of mortgage lending agencies. These data, unlike mortgage lending data, simply are not yet available for research purposes. However, property tax appraisal data are public and thus more easily analyzed. See the Appendix for more details on the data and methods we used for our analysis of these appraisal data.

11. See Howell and Korver-Glenn (forthcoming) for more details. We used U.S. Census data in our analysis, which consisted of running a series of distinct models that allowed us to examine four hypothesized mechanisms contributing to contemporary appraisal inequality: historical segregation, socioeconomic inequality, real estate demand, and contemporary appraisal practices. See Allison et al. (2017) for more information about dynamic panel models.

Chapter 6

1. Note that I did not encounter or interview any appraisers who adopted the people-oriented market rubric (see Chapter 5).

2. Multiple private fair housing organizations use testing to monitor the extent to which housing discrimination occurs, and private fair housing organizations receive the vast majority of all housing discrimination complaints filed in the United States (Abedin et al. 2018). But although these organizations can use testing and reporting to file suit in court, they do not have the power to enforce fair housing legislation or penalize those who engage in housing discrimination.

3. See, for example, *Trafficante v. Metropolitan Life Insurance Company*, 409 U.S. 205 (1972); *Havens Realty Corp. v. Coleman*, 455 U.S. 363 (1982); *Gladstone Realtors v. Village of Bellwood*, 441 U.S. 91 (1979); and *Texas Department of Housing and Community Affairs v. Inclusive Communities Project, Inc.*, 135 S. Ct. 2507 (2015).

4. Current fair housing law and opinions define discrimination as (intentional) disparate, or discriminatory, treatment and (unintentional) disparate impact, or discriminatory effects. Disparate treatment discrimination refers to the instances in which someone treats an individual differently because of the biases they have about that individual (e.g., with respect to their race). As fair housing advocates and legal scholars have noted, proving intent to discriminate in a court of law is possible but difficult. Part of the difficulty lies in the more covert, coded forms of racial expression that characterize publicly acceptable interactions in twenty-first-century America (Daniel 2011). Is it really about race, skeptics ask, if an explicit racial epithet or category was not used when interacting with that individual?

   More recently, scholars have expanded conceptualization of disparate treatment discrimination to include implicit or automatic bias, in which individuals with implicit bias against some group unwittingly yet no less potently treat members of that group differently than they do their own. However, although they may do so in the future, the courts have not advanced this conceptualization, instead repeatedly falling back on "intent to discriminate." This places a difficult burden of proof on claimants seeking to prosecute what they believe is unfair treatment based on a protected class characteristic (Daniel 2011; Girvan 2015).

   Disparate impact discrimination refers to the ostensibly equal treatment of people that, due to the rules or policies surrounding such treatment, may nonetheless produce unequal results—in particular, disproportionately negative effects for members of a protected class (Galster 1992; Pager and Shepherd 2008; Reskin 2012).

5. For a recent example of testing among real estate agents, see *Newsday*'s investigation of racism among real estate agents in Long Island, New York ("Long Island Divided," 2019, https://projects.newsday.com/long-island/real-estate-agents-investigation; retrieved November 17, 2019).

6. Although Houston's real estate board and the local brokerages I studied did not publicly discourage agents from using pocket listings during my research, pocket listings have come under scrutiny in some areas throughout the United States. Indeed, as mentioned previously, NAR has adopted a rule that essentially aims to eliminate its

members' use of pocket listings except in very rare cases. Others, including the senior legal counsel for the California Association of Realtors, have noted the disparate impact implications of pocket listings. They have also cautioned their agents to avoid pocket listings because these listings may not have the home sellers' best economic interests in mind (theoretically, they decrease competition for the home) and because they "may have an alleged discriminatory effect (i.e. reinforcing segregated housing patterns) even when there is no intent to discriminate" (Miller-Bougdanos and Bailey 2013:15). The potential for disparate impact consequences, they explain, comes from "limit[ing] their listing exposure to only certain sectors of the market" (Miller-Bougdanos and Bailey 2013:15). My research indicates that pocket listings limit exposure for "certain" home buyers—that is, buyers of color—because White real estate agents have predominantly White client networks and distribute information about these for-sale homes only to their White networks.

7. See Helper (1969) for an explanation of how this kind of networking happened in the pre-fair housing era.

8. In presenting this research to hundreds of real estate agents throughout the United States, many have explained that the only fair housing education they were required to receive was when they first took a course to obtain their real estate license.

9. On its own, education about racism has not meaningfully altered White Americans' racist beliefs or practices. Writing around the same time the U.S. federal government and real estate industries were institutionalizing explicitly racist practices such as redlining, Du Bois noted (1935:266): "For many years it was the theory of most Negro leaders that this attitude was the insensibility of ignorance and inexperience, that white America did not know of or realize the continuing plight of the Negro. Accordingly, for the last two decades, we have striven by book and periodical, by speech and appeal, by various dramatic methods of agitation, to put the essential facts before the American people. Today there can be no doubt that Americans know the facts; and yet they remain for the most part indifferent and unmoved." I am particularly skeptical about the supposed promise of educational reform in housing market professional contexts. My skepticism is partially founded on ethnographic observation I conducted of a fair housing continuing education course. Although the person who led the training, an influential representative from the U.S. Department of Housing and Urban Development, did not make any overtly racist comments (at least at this specific training), he admitted that he had not planned for the event and made several jokes about the sexual harassment and disability discrimination claims that come across his desk.

10. Large and small real estate boards throughout the United States use similar maps, including the Beverly Hills/Greater Los Angeles Association of Realtors (n.d.) (https://geocoding.themls.com/index.html; retrieved April 3, 2019), the Real Estate New York Group in Albany, New York (Real Estate New York Group, n.d., http://reny.net/Albany-County-Sub-Areas.htm; retrieved April 3, 2019), and the Taos County Association of Realtors in Taos, New Mexico (Taos County Association of Realtors, n.d., https://taoscountyassociationofrealtors.com/mls-areas-map; retrieved April 3, 2019).

11. "The Nickel" is a local nickname for Fifth Ward.
12. Among many other consequences, this has meant that Indigenous people generally comprise a very small percentage of city populations relative to Asian, Black, Latinx, and White people. Likewise, there are relatively few Indigenous people in real estate professions: For instance, I did not encounter any Indigenous real estate professionals during my research in Houston. (However, I did encounter one White developer and real estate agent, Brad, who falsely claimed a "Native American" identity on an application form in an attempt to gain access to federal disaster relief money.)

Conclusion

1. Examples of race brokers in other social spheres may include teachers and school administrators (Lewis 2003; Lewis and Diamond 2015); doctors, nurses, and health-care professionals (McLemore et al. 2018); government officials and representatives (Flores 2018); and business owners and employers (Pager et al. 2009), among others.
2. This discourse carries to the highest judicial body in the land. In writing the majority opinion for the 2015 *Texas Department of Housing and Community Affairs v. Inclusive Communities Project, Inc.*, U.S. Supreme Court Justice Anthony Kennedy (576 U.S. 10 (2015); italics added) stated, "Disparate-impact liability must be limited so employers and other regulated entities are able to make the practical business choices and profit-related decisions that sustain a *vibrant and dynamic free-enterprise system.*"
3. Maddie told me that she was White and Hispanic but did not know her ancestors' country of origin. She explained that her self-identification as Hispanic was "because of how I look, and my parents' first language is Spanish. Four years ago when my dad died, I asked my aunts and uncles more about their history, but they would just change the subject. I just don't know. But now that I think about it, I know my parents were hit in school if they spoke Spanish, so maybe that's why they didn't talk about it."
4. As a reminder, Fifth Ward is predominantly Black and the Heights is predominantly White. In between these two neighborhoods is the predominantly Latinx Near Northside community.
5. Recall that Kevin was a Black real estate agent I observed during my year of fieldwork.
6. According to this definition of racial discrimination, (inter)actions that preserve the perceived superiority of Whites and White spaces in relation to other individuals and spaces perceived as not White can be undertaken by individuals of color. However, when such (inter)actions do occur, as Harris (1993), Hoang (2015a), and others remind us, they occur against a backdrop of White supremacy: Individuals of color pursue strategies they view as necessary for their well-being, but if systems of White dominance birthed these strategies, they can reproduce White privilege.
7. Steil et al. (2018) found that lending professionals used economic-racist assumptions to seek out leaders or real estate agents of color to gain access to borrowers of color, whom they then targeted with subprime, high-risk loans.

Methodological Appendix

1. In 2010, 60 percent of real estate agents and brokers, 52 percent of credit counselors and loan officers, and 79 percent of appraisers who worked in Harris County (Houston) were White (U.S. Census Bureau 2010). As a reminder, Harris County (Houston) is about 33 percent White. In contrast to the extreme overrepresentation of Whites in housing market professions, Black and Latinx individuals are severely underrepresented in almost every housing market profession. In 2010, 13 percent of real estate agents and brokers, 19.1 percent of credit counselors and loan officers, and seven percent of appraisers who worked in Harris County were Black. Latinx professionals were also underrepresented. In 2010, about 21 percent of real estate agents and brokers, 18 percent of credit counselors and loan officers, and five percent of appraisers who worked in Harris County were Latinx (U.S. Census Bureau 2010). Recall that Harris County is about 41 percent Latinx and 20 percent Black.

2. To be sure, tax appraisers do not often have access to the inside of homes, so their assessments are often based on initial measurements of the home's size and quality of construction (obtained when the home was first built), observable exterior characteristics, and information they receive from home buyer and seller surveys. To estimate whether tax appraised values differed systematically from market appraised values, we examined the correlations between the tax appraised value and mortgage loan amounts (via Home Mortgage Disclosure Act data, which provide the mortgage loan amount and act as a proxy for appraised value) and tax appraised value and Zillow's estimates of home value. These data are all strongly correlated ($r=.96$ for tax appraisal/ HMDA data and $r=.99$ for tax appraisal/Zillow data), giving us confidence that the tax appraised values are a close approximation of market appraised value.

3. Because the original data had 13 lots that exceeded one million square feet, we triangulated the data to ensure its accuracy and then ran models with and without these cases. Model results were identical with or without these cases. We chose to exclude these extreme cases in the presented results.

4. Supplemental models were run operationalizing the exact number of fireplaces, swimming pools, and tennis courts, as well as the square footage of the garage, patio, porch, and deck. Results were comparable, so we use the dichotomous variables for simplicity. Additionally, other home characteristics were considered, including the number of bedrooms, bathrooms, total rooms, and carports, as well as the type of foundation, exterior wall material, central heating and air conditioning, basement, and attic square footage. As expected, more amenities increased home value; however, none of these additional controls changed any substantive results. Thus, we chose the home characteristics that were theoretically compelling and explained the most variation in home value.

5. Census tracts were utilized instead of smaller geographic areas such as block groups because we surmised that evaluations of place are influenced by specific blocks and their surrounding areas (Crowder and South 2008). Since census tracts are generally more racially diverse than census blocks, we presume our results are conservative estimates.

6. We used the 3rd grade school attendance zone boundaries and measure school quality for all public schools in each zone that teach 3rd grade.

7. In both police departments, violent crimes include assault, murder, and rape, while non-violent crimes include burglary and drug charges, among others. Models were run using the total number of crimes per capita, violent crimes per capita, and non-violent crimes per capita. Results were comparable but correlations were strongest for violent crime.

8. In addition to using these two scores as a construct validity test, we also conducted supplemental tests with national data. As expected, zip codes with the highest demand (fewest price cuts) were in San Francisco, San Jose, and New York City. Conversely, the three zip codes with the lowest demand were on the outskirts of Philadelphia. On a metropolitan level, the metros with the highest demand were San Francisco, Honolulu, and Seattle while the metros with the lowest demand were Phoenix, Albuquerque, and Philadelphia.

9. The Stata xtreg command can be used for multilevel or longitudinal data as both utilize the same estimation equations. Random effects are required to estimate the census tract level coefficients.

References

Aaronson, Daniel, Daniel Hartley, and Bhashkar Mazumder. 2017. *The Effects of the 1930s HOLC "Redlining" Map*. Chicago: Federal Reserve Bank of Chicago.

Abedin, Shanti, Cathy Cloud, Alia Fierro, Debby Goldberg, Jorge Andres Soto, and Morgan Williams. 2018. *Making Every Neighborhood a Place of Opportunity: 2018 Fair Housing Trends Report*. The National Fair Housing Alliance. Retrieved October 29, 2019, from https://nationalfairhousing.org/wp-content/uploads/2018/04/NFHA-2018-Fair-Housing-Trends-Report.pdf.

Allison, Paul D., Richard Williams, and Enrique Moral-Benito. 2017. "Maximum Likelihood for Cross-Lagged Panel Models with Fixed Effects." *Socius* 3:1–17.

American Community Survey. 2010. "5-Year Estimates." Retrieved July 30, 2019, from http://factfinder2.census.gov.

American Community Survey. 2014. "5-Year Estimates." Retrieved October 30, 2016, from http://factfinder2.census.gov.

American Community Survey. 2015. "5-Year Estimates." Retrieved July 30, 2019, from http://factfinder2.census.gov.

American Community Survey. 2017. "5-Year Estimates." Retrieved July 30, 2019, from http://factfinder2.census.gov.

Anderson, Elijah. 2015. "'The White Space.'" *Sociology of Race and Ethnicity* 1(1):10–21.

Appraisal Foundation. n.d. "The Appraiser Regulatory System in the United States." Retrieved December 8, 2020, from https://www.appraisalfoundation.org/imis/TAF/About_Us/Appraiser_Regulatory_System/TAF/Regulatory_Structure.aspx.

Appraisal Institute. 2013. *The Appraisal of Real Estate*. 14th ed. Chicago: Appraisal Institute.

Atakapa Ishak Nation. n.d. "Register for Roll." Retrieved December 9, 2020, from http://www.atakapa-ishak.org/register-for-roll/.

Auyero, Javier. 2012. *Patients of the State: The Politics of Waiting in Argentina*. Durham, NC: Duke University Press.

Bader, Michael and Siri Warkentien. 2016. "The Fragmented Evolution of Racial Integration Since the Civil Rights Movement." *Sociological Science* 3:135–64.

Bell, Monica. 2020a. "Anti-Segregation Policing." *N.Y.U. Law Review* 95(3):650–765.

Bell, Monica. 2020b. "Located Institutions: Neighborhood Frames, Residential Preferences, and the Case of Policing." *American Journal of Sociology* 125(4):917–73.

Besbris, Max. 2016. "Romancing the Home: Emotions and the Interactional Creation of Demand in the Housing Market." *Socio-Economic Review* 14(3):461–82.

Besbris, Max. 2020. *Upsold: Real Estate Agents, Prices, and Neighborhood Inequality*. Chicago: University of Chicago Press.

Besbris, Max and Jacob William Faber. 2017. "Investigating the Relationship Between Real Estate Agents, Segregation, and House Prices: Steering and Upselling in New York State." *Sociological Forum* 32(4):850–73.

Beverly Hills/Greater Los Angeles Association of Realtors. n.d. "Beta 2012 MLS/CLAW Google Area Maps Reference." Retrieved April 3, 2019, from https://geocoding.themls.com/index.html.

Blumer, Herbert. 1958. "Race Prejudice as a Sense of Group Position." *Pacific Sociological Review* 1(1):3–7.

Bobo, Lawrence D. and Cybelle Fox. 2003. "Race, Racism, and Discrimination: Bridging Problems, Methods, and Theory in Social Psychological Research." *Social Psychology Quarterly* 66(4):319.

Bonam, Courtney M., Valerie J. Taylor, and Caitlyn Yantis. 2017. "Racialized Physical Space as Cultural Product." *Social and Personality Psychology Compass* 11(9):e12340.

Bonam, Courtney, Caitlyn Yantis, and Valerie Jones Taylor. 2020. "Invisible Middle-Class Black Space: Asymmetrical Person and Space Stereotyping at the Race–Class Nexus." *Group Processes & Intergroup Relations* 23(1):24–47.

Bonilla-Silva, Eduardo. 2006. *Racism Without Racists: Color-Blind Racism and the Persistence of Racial Inequality in the United States.* New York: Rowman & Littlefield.

Bruch, Elizabeth and Joffre Swait. 2019. "Choice Set Formation in Residential Mobility and Its Implications for Segregation Dynamics." *Demography* 56(5):1665–92.

Bryant, Donald C., Jr., and Henry W. McGee, Jr. 1983. "Gentrification and the Law: Combating Urban Displacement." *Washington University Journal of Urban and Contemporary Law* 25:43–144.

Bullard, Robert D. 1987. *Invisible Houston: The Black Experience in Boom and Bust.* College Station, TX: Texas A&M University Press.

Buschmeyer, Anna and Diana Lengersdorf. 2016. "The Differentiation of Masculinity as a Challenge for the Concept of Hegemonic Masculinity." *NORMA* 11(3):190–207.

Campen, James T. 1998. "Neighborhoods, Banks, and Capital Flows: The Transformation of the U.S. Financial System and the Community Reinvestment Movement." *Review of Radical Political Economics* 30(4):29–59.

Capps, Kriston. 2018. "Trump's HUD Just Suspended an Obama-Era Fair Housing Rule." CityLab. Retrieved October 10, 2019, from https://www.citylab.com/equity/2018/01/the-trump-administration-derailed-a-key-obama-rule-on-housing-segregation/549746.

Champions School of Real Estate. n.d. "Elective CE Course Topics." Retrieved January 19, 2019, from https://www.championsschool.com/real-estate/tx/ce/#ce-courses.

Chavez, Leo. 2013. *The Latino Threat: Constructing Immigrants, Citizens, and the Nation.* 2nd ed. Palo Alto, CA: Stanford University Press.

Clergé, Orly. 2019. *The New Noir: Race, Identity, and Diaspora in Black Suburbia.* Oakland, CA: University of California Press.

Collins, Patricia Hill. 2000. *Black Feminist Thought: Knowledge, Consciousness, and the Politics of Empowerment.* New York: Routledge.

Connell, R. W. 2005. *Masculinities.* 2nd ed. Cambridge, UK: Polity Press.

Connolly, N. D. B. 2014. *A World More Concrete: Real Estate and the Remaking of Jim Crow South Florida.* Chicago: University of Chicago Press.

Crowder, Kyle and Scott J. South. 2008. "Spatial Dynamics of White Flight: The Effects of Local and Extralocal Racial Conditions on Neighborhood Out-Migration." *American Sociological Review* 73(5):792–812.

Daniel, Audrey. 2011. "The Intent Doctrine and CERD: How the United States Fails to Meet Its International Obligations in Racial Discrimination Jurisprudence." *DePaul Journal for Social Justice* 4(2):263–312.

Dantzler, Prentiss A. and Aja D. Reynolds. 2020. "Making Our Way Home: Housing Policy, Racial Capitalism, and Reparations." *Journal of World-Systems Research* 26(2):155–67.

Davies, David Martin. 2014. "Pasadena Sued over Latino Voting Rights." Texas Public Radio. Retrieved December 3, 2019, from https://www.tpr.org/post/pasadena-sued-over-latino-voting-rights.

De León, Arnoldo. 2001. *Ethnicity in the Sunbelt: Mexican Americans in Houston*. College Station, TX: Texas A&M University Press.

Du Bois, W. E. B. 1935. "A Negro Nation within the Nation." *Current History* 42(3):265–69.

Du Bois, W. E. B. 1986 [1903]. *The Souls of Black Folk*. Pp. 375–548 in *Du Bois: Writings*, edited by Nathan Huggins. New York: Library of America.

Egan, Matt. 2018. "Wells Fargo Accused of Preying on Black and Latino Homebuyers in California." *CNN Business*. Retrieved November 10, 2019, from https://money.cnn.com/2018/02/27/investing/wells-fargo-sacramento-lawsuit-discriminatory-lending/index.html.

Emerson, Michael O., Jenifer Bratter, Junia Howell, P. Wilner Jeanty, and Mike Cline. 2012. "Houston Region Grows More Racially/Ethnically Diverse, with Small Declines in Segregation." Report prepared for the Kinder Institute for Urban Research.

Emerson, Michael Oluf and Kevin T. Smiley. 2018. *Market Cities, People Cities: The Shape of Our Urban Future*. New York: New York University Press.

Esparza, Jesus Jesse. 2011. "La Colonia Mexicana: A History of Mexican Americans in Houston." *Houston History* 9(1):2–8.

Faber, Jacob William. 2018. "Segregation and the Geography of Creditworthiness: Racial Inequality in a Recovered Mortgage Market." *Housing Policy Debate* 28(2):215–47.

Faber, Jacob William. 2020. "We Built This: Consequences of New Deal Era Intervention in America's Racial Geography." *American Sociological Review* 85(5):739–75.

Faber, Jacob and Terri Friedline. 2020. "The Racialized Costs of 'Traditional' Banking: Evidence from Entry-Level Checking Accounts." *Race and Social Problems* 12:344–61.

Fannie Mae. 2020. "Selling Guide." Retrieved December 8, 2020, from https://selling-guide.fanniemae.com/.

Fannie Mae. 2019. "Annual Housing Activities Report, Annual Mortgage Report 2019." Retrieved December 8, 2020, from https://www.fanniemae.com/media/33501/display.

Feagin, Joe R. 1988. *Free Enterprise City: Houston in Political and Economic Perspective*. New Brunswick, NJ: Rutgers University Press.

Feagin, Joe R. 2013. *The White Racial Frame: Centuries of Racial Framing and Counter-Framing*. 2nd ed. New York: Routledge.

Federal Deposit Insurance Corporation. 2005. "Frequently Asked Questions on Residential Tract Lending." Retrieved November 14, 2019, from https://www.fdic.gov/news/news/financial/2005/fil9005a.html.

Federal Housing Administration. 1936. *Underwriting Manual: Underwriting and Valuation Procedure Under Title II of the National Housing Act*. Washington, D.C.: U.S. Government Printing Office.

Federal Housing Administration. 1938. *Underwriting Manual: Underwriting and Valuation Procedure Under Title II of the National Housing Act*. Washington, D.C.: U.S. Government Printing Office.

Feldman, Martha S. and Brian T. Pentland. 2003. "Reconceptualizing Organizational Routines as a Source of Flexibility and Change." *Administrative Science Quarterly* 48(1):94.

Fields, Karen E. and Barbara Jeanne Fields. 2014. *Racecraft: The Soul of Inequality in American Life*. New York: Verso Books.

Fisher, Robert. 1989. "Urban Policy in Houston, Texas." *Urban Studies* 26(1):144–54.

Flippen, Chenoa. 2004. "Unequal Returns to Housing Investments? A Study of Real Housing Appreciation among Black, White, and Hispanic Households." *Social Forces* 82(4):1523–51.

Flores, René D. 2018. "Can Elites Shape Public Attitudes Toward Immigrants? Evidence from the 2016 US Presidential Election." *Social Forces* 96(4):1649–90.

Forman, Tyrone A. and Amanda E. Lewis. 2006. "Racial Apathy and Hurricane Katrina: The Social Anatomy of Prejudice in the Post-Civil Rights Era." *Du Bois Review: Social Science Research on Race* 3(1):175–202.

Foster, Thomas B. and Rachel Garshick Kleit. 2015. "The Changing Relationship Between Housing and Inequality, 1980–2010." *Housing Policy Debate* 25(1):16–40.

Frey, William H. 2010a. "Largest Metros (Total Population of 500,000 or More): Black–White Segregation Indices Sorted by 2010 Segregation." Retrieved June 15, 2019, from https://www.psc.isr.umich.edu/dis/census/segregation2010.html.

Frey, William H. 2010b. "Largest Metros (Total Population of 500,000 or More): Hispanic–White Segregation Indices Sorted by 2010 Segregation." Retrieved June 15, 2019, from https://www.psc.isr.umich.edu/dis/census/segregation2010.html.

Galster, George. 1992. "Research on Discrimination in Housing and Mortgage Markets: Assessment and Future Directions." *Housing Policy Debate* 3(2):639–83.

Garb, M. 2006. "Drawing the 'Color Line': Race and Real Estate in Early Twentieth-Century Chicago." *Journal of Urban History* 32(5):773–87.

Girvan, Erik J. 2015. "On Using the Psychological Science of Implicit Bias to Advance Anti-Discrimination Law." *George Mason University Civil Rights Law Journal* 26(1):1–86.

Gladstone Realtors v. Village of Bellwood, 441 U.S. 91 (1979).

Goldberg, Michael A. 1974. "Residential Developer Behavior: Some Empirical Findings." *Land Economics* 50(1):85–89.

Gonzalez Van Cleve, Nicole. 2016. *Crook County: Racism and Injustice in America's Largest Criminal Court*. Palo Alto, CA: Stanford University Press.

Gotham, Kevin Fox. 2000. "Urban Space, Restrictive Covenants and the Origins of Racial Residential Segregation in a US City, 1900–50." *International Journal of Urban and Regional Research* 24(3):616–33.

Gotham, Kevin Fox. 2014. *Race, Real Estate, and Uneven Development, Second Edition: The Kansas City Experience, 1900–2010*. Albany, NY: State University of New York Press.

Greene, Gary. n.d. "How to Get Started in Real Estate." Better Homes and Gardens Real Estate. Retrieved December 15, 2016, from http://home.garygreene.com/downloads/career_opportunities_current.pdf.

Halevy, Nir, Eliran Halali, and Julian J. Zlatev. 2019. "Brokerage and Brokering: An Integrative Review and Organizing Framework for Third Party Influence." *Academy of Management Annals* 13(1):215–39.

Hall, Stuart. 1986. "Gramsci's Relevance for the Study of Race and Ethnicity." *Journal of Communication Inquiry* 10(2):5–27.

Haney-López, Ian F. 2000. "Institutional Racism: Judicial Conduct and a New Theory of Racial Discrimination." *The Yale Law Journal* 109(8):1717–884.

Hannah-Jones, Nikole. 2015. "Living Apart: How the Government Betrayed a Landmark Civil Rights Law." *ProPublica*, June 25.

Haring, Bob. n.d. "Difference Between a Mortgage Banker vs. a Mortgage Broker." *Houston Chronicle.* Retrieved November 14, 2019, from https://work.chron.com/difference-between-mortgage-banker-vs-mortgage-broker-1281.html.

Harris, Cheryl I. 1993. "Whiteness as Property." *Harvard Law Review* 106(8):1707–91.

Harris County Appraisal District. n.d. "Public Data." Retrieved November 30, 2015, from https://pdata.hcad.org.

Haupert, Tyler. 2019. "Racial Patterns in Mortgage Lending Outcomes During and After the Subprime Boom." *Housing Policy Debate* 29(6):947–76.

Havens Realty Corp. v. Coleman, 455 U.S. 363 (1982).

Hawkins, Derek and Deanna Paul. 2019. "Fort Worth Officer Who Fatally Shot Woman in Her Home Has Been Charged with Murder, Police Say." *The Washington Post.* Retrieved October 20, 2019, from https://www.washingtonpost.com/nation/2019/10/14/fort-worth-police-shooting-atatiana-jefferson-investigation.

Helper, Rose. 1969. *Racial Policies and Practices of Real Estate Brokers.* Minneapolis, MN: University of Minnesota Press.

Herndon, Astead W. and Sheryl Gay Stolberg. 2019. "How Joe Biden Became the Democrats' Anti-Busing Crusader." *The New York Times*, July 15. Retrieved November 1, 2019, from https://www.nytimes.com/2019/07/15/us/politics/biden-busing.html.

Hightower, Cameron and James C. Fraser. 2020. "The Raced-Space of Gentrification: 'Reverse Blockbusting,' Home Selling, and Neighborhood Remake in North Nashville." *City & Community* 19(1):223–44.

Hirschman, Daniel and Laura Garbes. Forthcoming. "Toward an Economic Sociology of Race." *Socio-Economic Review.*

Hoang, Kimberly Kay. 2015a. "Nailing Race and Labor Relations: Vietnamese Nail Salons in Majority-Minority Neighborhoods." *Journal of Asian American Studies* 18(2):113–39.

Hoang, Kimberly Kay. 2015b. *Dealing in Desire: Asian Ascendancy, Western Decline, and the Hidden Currencies of Global Sex Work.* Berkeley, CA: University of California Press.

Hobby Center for Public Policy. 2015. "The Texas Appraisers and Appraisal Management Company Survey, 2015." University of Houston Hobby Center for Public Policy and Texas A&M University Real Estate Center. Retrieved November 1, 2015, from https://www.talcb.texas.gov/sites/default/files/uploaded-files/texas_appraiser_amc_survey_report_2015.pdf.

Holme, Jennifer Jellison. 2002. "Buying Homes, Buying Schools: School Choice and the Social Construction of School Quality." *Harvard Educational Review* 72(2):177–206.

Holmes, Malcolm D., Matthew A. Painter, and Brad W. Smith. 2019. "Race, Place, and Police-Caused Homicide in U.S. Municipalities." *Justice Quarterly* 36(5):751–86.

Houston Association of Realtors. n.d. (a). "Join HAR." Retrieved September 4, 2019, from https://www.har.com/content/page/har_inside.

Houston Association of Realtors. n.d. (b). "Open Houses, Open Doors." Retrieved January 19, 2019, from https://www.har.com/education/course_detail/5/931.

Houston Association of Realtors. n.d. (c). "Real Estate Market Areas in Greater Houston." Retrieved January 14, 2019, from http://web.har.com/mlsareamap.html.

Houston Association of Realtors, n.d. (d). "MLS Press Release." Retrieved April 30, 2020, from https://www.har.com/content/mls/?m=04&y=20.

Houston Heights Association. n.d. "Deed Restrictions." Retrieved April 1, 2019, from http://www.houstonheights.org/deed-restrictions.

Howell, Junia and Michael O. Emerson. 2018. "Preserving Racial Hierarchy Amidst Changing Racial Demographics: How Neighbourhood Racial Preferences Are Changing While Maintaining Segregation." *Ethnic and Racial Studies* 41(15):2770–89.

Howell, Junia and Elizabeth Korver-Glenn. 2018. "Neighborhoods, Race, and the Twenty-First-Century Housing Appraisal Industry." *Sociology of Race and Ethnicity* 4(4):473–90.

Howell, Junia and Elizabeth Korver-Glenn. Forthcoming. "The Increasing Effect of Neighborhood Racial Composition on Housing Values, 1980–2015." *Social Problems.* https://doi.org/10.1093/socpro/spaa033

Hunter, Marcus Anthony and Zandria Robinson. 2018. *Chocolate Cities: The Black Map of American Life.* Oakland, CA: University of California Press.

Itzigsohn, José and Karida Brown. 2015. "Sociology and the Theory of Double Consciousness: W. E. B. Du Bois's Phenomenology of Racialized Subjectivity." *Du Bois Review: Social Science Research on Race* 12(2):231–48.

Jackson, Kenneth T. 1985. *Crabgrass Frontier: The Suburbanization of the United States.* New York: Oxford University Press.

Jan, Tracy. 2018. "The Senate Rolls Back Rules Meant to Root out Discrimination by Mortgage Lenders." *The Washington Post.* Retrieved October 10, 2019, from https://www.washingtonpost.com/news/wonk/wp/2018/03/14/the-senate-rolls-back-rules-meant-to-root-out-discrimination-by-mortgage-lenders.

Jung, Moon-Kie. 2015. *Beneath the Surface of White Supremacy: Denaturalizing U.S. Racisms Past and Present.* Palo Alto, CA: Stanford University Press.

Kaplan, Barry J. 1981. "Race, Income, and Ethnicity: Residential Change in a Houston Community, 1920–1970." *The Houston Review* 3(1):178–202.

Kent, Stephanie L. and Jason T. Carmichael. 2014. "Racial Residential Segregation and Social Control: A Panel Study of the Variation in Police Strength Across U.S. Cities, 1980–2010." *American Journal of Criminal Justice* 39(2):228–49.

Kimelberg, Shelley McDonough. 2011. "Inside the Growth Machine: Real Estate Professionals on the Perceived Challenges of Urban Development." *City & Community* 10(1):76–99.

King, Martin Luther, Jr. 2015. *The Radical King.* Boston, MA: Beacon Press.

Kleiner, Diana J. 2010. "Fifth Ward, Houston." Texas State Historical Association. Retrieved April 19, 2019, from https://tshaonline.org/handbook/online/articles/hpfhk.

Koopman, Colin. 2019. *How We Became Our Data: A Genealogy of the Informational Person.* Chicago: University of Chicago Press.

Korver-Glenn, Elizabeth. 2014. "Middle-Class Mexican Americans, Neighborhood Affect, and Redevelopment in Houston's Northside Barrio." *City & Community* 13(4):381–402.

Korver-Glenn, Elizabeth. 2015. "(Collective) Memory of Racial Violence and the Social Construction of the Hispanic Category Among Houston Hispanics." *Sociology of Race and Ethnicity* 1(3):424–38.

Korver-Glenn, Elizabeth. 2018a. "Brokering Ties and Inequality: How White Real Estate Agents Recreate Advantage and Exclusion in Urban Housing Markets." *Social Currents* 5(4):350–68.

Korver-Glenn, Elizabeth. 2018b. "Compounding Inequalities: How Racial Stereotypes and Discrimination Accumulate Across the Stages of Housing Exchange." *American Sociological Review* 83(4):627–56.

Korver-Glenn, Elizabeth and James R. Elliott. 2016. "Urban Churning: The Formation of Black, Latino, and White Enclaves in Houston, 1960–2010." Paper presented at the 2016 meeting of the American Sociological Association, Seattle, WA, August 20–23.

Krysan, Maria. 2008. "Does Race Matter in the Search for Housing? An Exploratory Study of Search Strategies, Experiences, and Locations." *Social Science Research* 37(2):581–603.

Krysan, Maria and Kyle Crowder. 2017. *Cycle of Segregation: Social Processes and Residential Stratification.* New York: Russell Sage Foundation.

Kucheva, Yana and Richard Sander. 2014. "The Misunderstood Consequences of *Shelley v. Kraemer.*" *Social Science Research* 48:212–33.

Kummerow, Max and Joëlle Chan Lun. 2005. "Information and Communication Technology in the Real Estate Industry: Productivity, Industry Structure and Market Efficiency." *Telecommunications Policy* 29(2):173–90.

Kuokkanen, Rauna. 2011. "Indigenous Economies, Theories of Subsistence, and Women: Exploring the Social Economy Model for Indigenous Governance." *American Indian Quarterly* 35(2):215–40.

Kusenbach, Margarethe. 2003. "Street Phenomenology the Go-Along as Ethnographic Research Tool." *Ethnography* 4(3):455–85.

Lareau, Annette and Kimberly Goyette. 2014. *Choosing Homes, Choosing Schools.* New York: Russell Sage Foundation.

Lerner, Michele. 2019. "A Real Estate Association Is Cracking down on 'Off- Market' Properties. Here's What That Means for Buyers." *The Washington Post.* Retrieved November 12, 2019, from https://www.washingtonpost.com/realestate/a-real-estate-association-is-cracking-down-on-off-market-properties-heres-what-that-means-for-buyers/2019/11/11/e391c3ae-0013-11ea-8bab-0fc209e065a8_story.html.

Levy, Diane K., Jennifer Biess, Abby Baum, Nancy Pindus, and Brittany Murray. 2017. *Housing Needs of American Indians and Alaska Natives Living in Urban Areas.* Washington, DC: U.S. Department of Housing and Urban Development.

Lewis, Amanda E. 2003. *Race in the Schoolyard: Negotiating the Color Line in Classrooms and Communities.* New Brunswick, NJ: Rutgers University Press.

Lewis, Amanda E., and John B. Diamond. 2015. *Despite the Best Intentions: How Racial Inequality Thrives in Good Schools.* New York: Oxford University Press.

Lin, Jan. 1995. "Ethnic Places, Postmodernism, and Urban Change in Houston." *Sociological Quarterly* 36(4):629–47.

Lipsitz, George. 2011. *How Racism Takes Place.* Philadelphia, PA: Temple University Press.

Lipsky, Michael. 2010. *Street-Level Bureaucracy, 30th Anniversary Edition: Dilemmas of the Individual in Public Service.* New York: Russell Sage Foundation.

Logan, John R., Richard D. Alba, and Brian J. Stults. 2003. "Enclaves and Entrepreneurs: Assessing the Payoff for Immigrants and Minorities." *International Migration Review* 37(2):344–88.

Logan, John R. and Harvey Luskin Molotch. 1987. *Urban Fortunes: The Political Economy of Place.* Berkeley, CA: University of California Press.

Logan, Trevor D. and John M. Parman. 2017. "The National Rise in Residential Segregation." *Journal of Economic History* 77(1):127–70.

"Long Island Divided." 2019. *Newsday.* Retrieved November 17, 2019, from https://projects.newsday.com/long-island/real-estate-agents-investigation.

Mainstreet Organization of Realtors. n.d. "September Closed Sales." Retrieved March 27, 2019, from https://mred.stats.10kresearch.com/infoserv/s-v1/jbPO-dFK.

Massey, Douglas S. 2015. "The Legacy of the 1968 Fair Housing Act." *Sociological Forum* 30:571–88.

Massey, Douglas S. and Nancy A. Denton. 1993. *American Apartheid: Segregation and the Making of the Underclass.* Cambridge, MA: Harvard University Press.

Massey, Douglas S., Jacob S. Rugh, Justin P. Steil, and Len Albright. 2016. "Riding the Stagecoach to Hell: A Qualitative Analysis of Racial Discrimination in Mortgage Lending." *City & Community* 15(2):118–36.

Mayorga-Gallo, Sarah. 2019. "The White-Centering Logic of Diversity Ideology." *American Behavioral Scientist* 63(13):1789–1809.

McCabe, Brian J. 2016. *No Place Like Home: Wealth, Community, and the Politics of Homeownership.* New York: Oxford University Press.

McCabe, Brian J. 2018. "Why Buy a Home? Race, Ethnicity, and Homeownership Preferences in the United States." *Sociology of Race and Ethnicity* 4(4):452–72.

McConnell, Virginia and Keith Wiley. 2012. "Infill Development: Perspectives and Evidence from Economics and Planning." Pp. 473–502 in *The Oxford Handbook of Urban Economics and Planning,* edited by Nancy Brooks, Kieran Donaghy, and Gerrit-Jan Knaap. New York: Oxford University Press.

McFarlane, Audrey G. 1999. "Race, Space, and Place: The Geography of Economic Development." *San Diego Law Review* 36:295–354.

McLemore, Monica R., Molly R. Altman, Norlissa Cooper, Shanell Williams, Larry Rand, and Linda Franck. 2018. "Health Care Experiences of Pregnant, Birthing and Postnatal Women of Color at Risk for Preterm Birth." *Social Science & Medicine* 201:127–35.

Mesic, Aldina, Lydia Franklin, Alev Cansever, Fiona Potter, Anika Sharma, Anita Knopov, and Michael Siegel. 2018. "The Relationship Between Structural Racism and Black-White Disparities in Fatal Police Shootings at the State Level." *Journal of the National Medical Association* 110(2):106–16.

Metrostudy News. 2016a. "Houston Housing 1Q16: Houston Drops to 2nd Place Texas Market with 10% YoY Decline in Annual New Home Starts; Builders Address Affordability, Ramp up New Home Starts Under $300K." Retrieved March 20, 2019, from https://www.metrostudy.com/38027-2.

Metrostudy News. 2016b. "Houston Housing 4Q15: Rising Affordability Issues Challenge the Top Single-Family Market in the Country." Retrieved April 1, 2019, from https://www.metrostudy.com/houston-housing-4q15-rising-affordability-issues-challenge-the-top-single-family-market-in-the-country.

Miller-Bougdanos, Elizabeth and Robert Bailey. 2013."'Pocket Listings': Legal, Ethnical, MLS and Industry Issues of off-MLS Listings." Presentation given at the NAR Risk Management Forum, San Francisco, CA.

Mora, G. Cristina. 2014. *Making Hispanics: How Activists, Bureaucrats, and Media Constructed a New American.* Chicago: University of Chicago Press.

Moss, Philip and Chris Tilly. 2001. *Stories Employers Tell: Race, Skill, and Hiring in America.* New York: Russell Sage Foundation.

Mueller, Jennifer C. 2017. "Producing Colorblindness: Everyday Mechanisms of White Ignorance." *Social Problems* 64:219–38.

Mueller, Jennifer C. 2018. "Advancing a Sociology of Ignorance in the Study of Racism and Racial Non-Knowing." *Sociology Compass* 12(8):e12600.

National Association of Realtors. 2019. "Summary of July 2019 Existing Home Sales Statistics." Retrieved August 29, 2019, from https://www.nar.realtor/sites/default/files/documents/ehs-07-2019-summary-2019-08-21.pdf.

National Association of Realtors. n.d. (a). "Safety." Retrieved January 20, 2019, from https://www.nar.realtor/safety.

National Association of Realtors. n.d. (b). "Farming & Prospecting." Retrieved January 14, 2019, from https://www.nar.realtor/farming-prospecting.

National Association of Realtors. n.d. (c). "2017 Member Profile." Retrieved January 14, 2019, from https://www.nar.realtor/sites/default/files/reports/2017/2017-member-profile-highlights-05-11-2017.pdf..

National Association of Realtors. n.d. (d). "Highlights from the Profile of Home Buyers and Sellers." Retrieved January 14, 2019, from https://www.nar.realtor/research-and-statistics/research-reports/highlights-from-the-profile-of-home-buyers-and-sellers.

Obstfeld, David, Stephen P. Borgatti, and Jason Davis. 2014. "Brokerage as a Process: Decoupling Third Party Action from Social Network Structure." Pp. 135–59 in Research in the Sociology of Organizations, Vol. 40, edited by D. J. Brass, G. Labianca, A. Mehra, D. S. Halgin, and S. P. Borgatti. Bingley, UK: Emerald Group Publishing.

Oliver, Melvin L. and Thomas M. Shapiro. 2006. Black Wealth, White Wealth: A New Perspective on Racial Inequality. New York: Taylor & Francis.

Pager, Devah and Hana Shepherd. 2008. "The Sociology of Discrimination: Racial Discrimination in Employment, Housing, Credit, and Consumer Markets." Annual Review of Sociology 34(1):181–209.

Pager, Devah, Bruce Western, and Naomi Sugie. 2009. "Sequencing Disadvantage: Barriers to Employment Facing Young Black and White Men with Criminal Records." Annals of the American Academy of Political and Social Science 623(1):195–213.

Pattillo, Mary. 2007. Black on the Block: The Politics of Race and Class in the City. Chicago: University of Chicago Press.

Pattillo, Mary. 2013. "Housing: Commodity versus Right." Annual Review of Sociology 39(1):509–31.

Perrottet, Tony. 2013. "What Makes Houston the Next Great American City?" Smithsonian Magazine. Retrieved October 30, 2018, from https://www.smithsonianmag.com/travel/what-makes-houston-the-next-great-american-city-4870584.

Picca, Leslie Houts and Joe R. Feagin. 2007. Two-Faced Racism: Whites in the Backstage and Frontstage. New York: Routledge.

Pomeroy, C. David, Jr. n.d. "Pasadena, TX." Handbook of Texas. Retrieved April 1, 2019, from http://www.tshaonline.org/handbook/online/articles/hdp02.

Ponton, David, III. 2017. "Criminalizing Space: Ideological and Institutional Productions of Race, Gender, and State-Sanctioned Violence in Houston, 1948–1967." Doctoral Dissertation, Rice University, Houston, TX.

Qian, Zhu. 2010. "Without Zoning: Urban Development and Land Use Controls in Houston." Cities 27(1):31–41.

Rackleff, Neal. 2015. Analysis of Impediments to Fair Housing Choice. Houston: City of Houston Housing and Community Development Department.

Ramirez, Renya K. 2007. Native Hubs: Culture, Community, and Belonging in Silicon Valley and Beyond. Durham, NC: Duke University Press.

Ray, Ranita and Korey Tillman. 2019. "Envisioning a Feminist Urban Ethnography: Structure, Culture, and New Directions in Poverty Studies." Sociology Compass 13(1):e12652.

Ray, Victor. 2019. "A Theory of Racialized Organizations." American Sociological Review 84(1):26–53.

Real Estate New York Group. n.d. "Location, Location, Location: Sub Areas Delineate Locations of Similar Home Values and Neighborhood Characteristics." Retrieved April 3, 2019, from http://reny.net/Albany-County-Sub-Areas.htm.

Reskin, Barbara. 2012. "The Race Discrimination System." *Annual Review of Sociology* 38(1):17–35.

Roberto, Elizabeth. 2018. "The Spatial Proximity and Connectivity Method for Measuring and Analyzing Residential Segregation." *Sociological Methodology* 48(1):182–224.

Rosen, Eva. 2014. "Rigging the Rules of the Game: How Landlords Geographically Sort Low-Income Renters." *City & Community* 13(4):310–40. doi: 10.1111/cico.12087.

Rothacker, Rick and David Ingram. 2012. "Wells Fargo to Pay $175 Million in Race Discrimination Probe." Reuters. Retrieved November 1, 2019, from https://www.reuters.com/article/us-wells-lending-settlement/wells-fargo-to-pay-175-million-in-race-discrimination-probe-idUSBRE86B0V220120712.

Rothstein, Richard. 2017. *The Color of Law: A Forgotten History of How Our Government Segregated America*. New York: Liveright.

Royster, Deirdre A. 2003. *Race and the Invisible Hand: How White Networks Exclude Black Men from Blue-Collar Jobs*. Berkeley, CA: University of California Press.

Rucks-Ahidiana, Zawadi. Forthcoming. "Racial Composition and Trajectories of Gentrification in the United States." *Urban Studies*.

Rugh, Jacob S., Len Albright, and Douglas S. Massey. 2015. "Race, Space, and Cumulative Disadvantage: A Case Study of the Subprime Lending Collapse." *Social Problems* 62(2):186–218.

Sahasranaman, Anand and Henrik Jeldtoft Jensen. 2016. "Dynamics of Transformation from Segregation to Mixed Wealth Cities." *PLoS One* 11(11):e0166960.

San Miguel, Guadalupe, Jr. 2001. *Brown, Not White: School Integration and the Chicano Movement in Houston*. College Station, TX: Texas A&M University Press.

San Miguel, Guadalupe, Jr. 2016. "Huelga Schools in Houston: Community-Based Education in the Struggle for Legal Recognition, 1970." *Journal of Latinos and Education* 15(4):266–74.

Sarnoff, Nancy. 2015. "Housing Market Shows Further Weakening." *Houston Chronicle*. Retrieved October 19, 2015, from https://www.houstonchronicle.com/business/real-estate/article/Housing-market-shows-further-weakening-6494423.php.

Schelenz, Robyn and Nicole Freeling. 2019. "What's in a Name? How the Concepts of Hispanic and Latino Identity Emerged." University of California News Room. Retrieved December 5, 2019, from https://www.universityofcalifornia.edu/news/whats-in-a-name-how-concepts-hispanic-and-latino-identity-emerged.

Schuetz, Rebecca A. 2019. "Practice of Secretive Real Estate Listings Challenged." *Houston Chronicle*. Retrieved November 8, 2019, from https://www.houstonchronicle.com/business/article/Practice-of-secretive-real-estate-listings-14817780.php.

Seamster, Louise. 2015. "The White City: Race and Urban Politics." *Sociology Compass* 9(12):1049–65.

Seamster, Louise and Raphaël Charron-Chénier. 2017. "Predatory Inclusion and Education Debt: Rethinking the Racial Wealth Gap." *Social Currents* 4(3):199–207.

Seamster, Louise and Victor Ray. 2018. "Against Teleology in the Study of Race: Toward the Abolition of the Progress Paradigm." *Sociological Theory* 36(4):315–42.

Shapiro, Thomas M. 2017. *Toxic Inequality: How America's Wealth Gap Destroys Mobility, Deepens the Racial Divide, and Threatens Our Future*. New York: Basic Books.

Sharp, Gregory and Matthew Hall. 2014. "Emerging Forms of Racial Inequality in Homeownership Exit, 1968–2009." *Social Problems* 61(3):427–47.

Shi, Lan and Christina Tapia. 2016. "The Disciplining Effect of Concern for Referrals: Evidence from Real Estate Agents." *Real Estate Economics* 44(2):411–61.

Small, Mario Luis. 2009. "'How Many Cases Do I Need?' On Science and the Logic of Case Selection in Field-Based Research." *Ethnography* 10(1):5–38.

Small, Mario L. 2015. "De-Exoticizing Ghetto Poverty: On the Ethics of Representation in Urban Ethnography." *City & Community* 14(4):352–58.

Smith, Ryan. 2017. "What Do Real Estate Agents Look for in Loan Officers?" *Mortgage Professional America Magazine*. Retrieved September 10, 2019, from https://www.mpamag.com/news/what-do-real-estate-agents-look-for-in-loan-officers-42707.aspx.

Social Explorer. (n.d.). "Home Page." Retrieved May 1, 2020, from http://www.socialexplorer.com.

Sorto, Juan Antonio. 2018. "How Houston's Denver Harbor Used a Land-Use Tool to Curb Gentrification." *Urban Edge*. Retrieved December 3, 2019, from https://kinder.rice.edu/2018/11/20/how-houstons-denver-harbor-used-land-use-tool-curb-gentrification.

Steil, Justin P., Len Albright, Jacob S. Rugh, and Douglas S. Massey. 2018. "The Social Structure of Mortgage Discrimination." *Housing Studies* 33(5):759–76.

Steptoe, Tyina L. 2016. *Houston Bound: Culture and Color in a Jim Crow City*. Berkeley, CA: University of California Press.

Stovel, Katherine and Lynette Shaw. 2012. "Brokerage." *Annual Review of Sociology* 38(1):139–58.

Stuart, Guy. 2003. *Discriminating Risk: The U.S. Mortgage Lending Industry in the Twentieth Century*. Ithaca, NY: Cornell University Press.

Taos County Association of Realtors. n.d. "MLS Areas Map." Retrieved April 4, 2019, from https://taoscountyassociationofrealtors.com/mls-areas-map.s

Tavory, Iddo and Stefan Timmermans. 2013. "A Pragmatist Approach to Causality in Ethnography." *American Journal of Sociology* 119(3):682–714.

Taylor, Keeanga-Yamahtta. 2019. *Race for Profit: How Banks and the Real Estate Industry Undermined Black Homeownership*. Chapel Hill, NC: University of North Carolina Press.

Terrill, William and Michael D. Reisig. 2003. "Neighborhood Context and Police Use of Force." *Journal of Research in Crime and Delinquency* 40(3):291–321.

Texas A&M Real Estate Center. n.d. "Housing Activity for Harris County." Retrieved March 27, 2019, from https://www.recenter.tamu.edu/data/housing-activity/#!/activity/County/Harris_County.

Texas Department of Housing and Community Affairs v. Inclusive Communities Project, Inc., 135 S. Ct. 2507 (2015).

Thomas, Melvin E., Richard Moye, Loren Henderson, and Hayward Derrick Horton. 2018. "Separate and Unequal: The Impact of Socioeconomic Status, Segregation, and the Great Recession on Racial Disparities in Housing Values." *Sociology of Race and Ethnicity* 4(2):229–44.

Timmermans, S. and I. Tavory. 2012. "Theory Construction in Qualitative Research: From Grounded Theory to Abductive Analysis." *Sociological Theory* 30(3):167–86.

Trafficante v. Metropolitan Life Insurance Company, 409 U.S. 205 (1972).

Treitler, Vilna Bashi. 2013. *The Ethnic Project: Transforming Racial Fiction into Ethnic Factions*. Stanford, CA: Stanford University Press.

Turner, Margery Autstin, Rob Santos, Diane K. Levy, Doug Wissocker, Claudia Aranda, Rob Pitingolo, and The Urban Institute. 2013. *Housing Discrimination Against Racial and Ethnic Minorities 2012*. Washington, DC: U.S. Department of Housing and Urban Development.

United States v. American Institute of Real Estate Appraisers of the National Association of Realtors, the Society of Real Estate Appraisers, the United States League of Savings Associations, and the Mortgage Bankers Association, 442 F. Supp. 1072. (1977).

United States v. National Association of Real Estate Boards, et al., 339 U.S. 485 (1950).

Ura, Alexa. 2017a. "Pasadena Drops Appeal, Will Remain Under Federal Oversight of Election Laws." *The Texas Tribune*. Retrieved March 7, 2019, from https://www.texastribune.org/2017/10/03/pasadena-remain-under-federal-oversight-election-laws.

Ura, Alexa. 2017b. "Voting Rights Battle in Pasadena Could Have Texas-Wide Legal Ramifications." *The Texas Tribune*. Retrieved March 7, 2019, from https://www.texastribune.org/2017/07/11/voting-rights-battle-pasadena-could-come-wide-legal-ramifications.

U.S. Census Bureau. 2010. "Equal Employment Opportunity Tabulation." Retrieved January 31, 2019, from http://data.census.gov.

U.S. Census Bureau. 2017. "American Housing Survey (AHS)." Retrieved September 12, 2019, from https://www.census.gov/programs-surveys/ahs/data/interactive/ahstablecreator.html.

U.S. Census Bureau. n.d. "Historical Data: New Residential Construction." Retrieved August 22, 2019, from https://www.census.gov/construction/nrc/historical_data/index.html.

U.S. Department of Housing and Urban Development. 2013. "Implementation of the Fair Housing Act's Discriminatory Effects Standard." *Federal Register* 78(32):11460–82.

U.S. Department of Housing and Urban Development. 2015. "Affirmatively Furthering Fair Housing." *Federal Register* 80(136):42272–371.

U.S. Department of Housing and Urban Development. 2020. "Preserving Community and Neighborhood Choice." *Federal Register* 85(153):47899–912.

U.S. Department of Justice. 2012. "Justice Department Reaches Settlement with Wells Fargo Resulting in More Than $175 Million in Relief for Homeowners to Resolve Fair Lending Claims." *Justice News*, July 12.

U.S. Government Accountability Office. 2010. "Housing and Community Grants: HUD Needs to Strengthen Its Requirements and Oversight of Jurisdictions' Fair Housing Plans." A report to Congressional Requesters. Office of Public Affairs.

U.S. Government Accountability Office. 2012. "Residential Appraisers: Regulators Should Take Actions to Strengthen Oversight." Testimony before the Subcommittee on Insurance, Housing and Community Opportunity, Committee on Financial Services, House of Representatives. Office of Public Affairs.

Vojnovic, Igor. 2003. "Governance in Houston: Growth Theories and Urban Pressures." *Journal of Urban Affairs* 25(5):589–624.

Wang, Qi, Nolan Edward Phillips, Mario L. Small, and Robert J. Sampson. 2018. "Urban Mobility and Neighborhood Isolation in America's 50 Largest Cities." *Proceedings of the National Academy of Sciences of the USA* 115(30):7735–40.

Wells, Amy Stuart. 2018. "The Process of Racial Resegregation in Housing and Schools: The Sociology of Reputation." Pp. 1–14 in *Emerging Trends in the Social and Behavioral Sciences*. Wiley Online Library. Hoboken, NJ: Wiley.

Wells, Amy Stuart, Douglas Ready, Lauren Fox, Miya Warner, Allison Roda, Tameka Spence, Elizabeth Williams, and Allen Wright. 2014. *Divided We Fall: The Story of Separate and Unequal Suburban Schools 60 Years After Brown v. Board of Education.* The Center for Understanding Race and Education. Retrieved February 6, 2019, from https://www.tc.columbia.edu/i/a/document/31307_FinalReport.pdf.

Williams, Richard, Reynold Nesiba, and Eileen Diaz McConnell. 2005. "The Changing Face of Inequality in Home Mortgage Lending." *Social Problems* 52(2):181–208.

Woods, Louis Lee, II. 2012. "The Federal Home Loan Bank Board, Redlining, and the National Proliferation of Racial Lending Discrimination, 1921–1950." *Journal of Urban History* 38(6):1036–59.

Woodward, Comer Vann. 2002 [1955]. *The Strange Career of Jim Crow.* New York: Oxford University Press.

Wortham, Stanton, Katherine Mortimer, and Elaine Allard. 2009. "Mexicans as Model Minorities in the New Latino Diaspora." *Anthropology & Education Quarterly* 40(4):388–404.

Zillow. n.d. "Home Values." Retrieved January 15, 2018, from https://www.zillow.com/research/data.

Index

For the benefit of digital users, indexed terms that span two pages (e.g., 52–53) may, on occasion, appear on only one of those pages.

Tables and figures are indicated by *t* and *f* following the page number